Myth and Metropolis

FOR AUDREY AND PETER

MYTH AND METROPOLIS

Walter Benjamin and the City

Graeme Gilloch

Polity Press

First published in 1996 by Polity Press
in association with Blackwell Publishers Ltd.

First published in paperback 1997.

Editorial office:
Polity Press
65 Bridge Street
Cambridge CB2 1UR, UK

Marketing and production:
Blackwell Publishers Ltd
108 Cowley Road
Oxford OX4 1JF, UK

Published in the USA by
Blackwell Publishers Inc.
350 Main Street
Malden MA 02148, USA

ISBN 0–7456–1125–7
ISBN 0–7456–2010–8 (pbk)

A CIP catalogue record for this book is available from the British Library
and has been applied for from the Library of Congress.

Typeset in Palatino 10.5 on 12 pt by Photoprint, Torquay, Devon
Printed in Great Britain by Hartnolls Ltd, Bodmin, Cornwall

This book is printed on acid-free paper.

Contents

Acknowledgements

I am very grateful to a number of individuals and institutions who contributed to this book since its beginnings as a doctoral thesis at the University of Cambridge. I would especially like to thank John Thompson for his guidance, support and patience throughout. I would also like to thank Barry Sandwell who first introduced me to Benjamin's work. I am grateful to David Frisby, Andrew Bowie, Jon Fletcher, Anthony Giddens, Hans-Joachim Hahn, Thomas Regehly (and the Kolloquium für Kritische Theorie in Frankfurt am Main) and Charles Turner for their thoughtful comments, suggestions and ideas. All errors, omissions and oversights are of course mine.

I wish to express my gratitude to those institutions whose generous financial support made this book possible: the Economic and Social Research Council, the German Academic Exchange Service (DAAD), the University of Wisconsin–Madison, the British Council and especially the Leverhulme Trust.

I am grateful to the Akademie der Kunst in Berlin for access to their archives and to the T. W. Adorno-Archiv (Frankfurt am Main) and Suhrkamp Verlag and Harvard University Press for kindly giving permission to include archival and previously untranslated material from Benjamin's work. (Harvard University Press will publish the first volume of a three-volume collection of selected essays of Walter Benjamin in the Fall of 1996.) I am also grateful to Telos Press Ltd. for permission to include material first published with them. I am grateful to Verso/New Left Books for permission to include material from *One-Way Street and Other Writings*, 1985 and *Charles Baudelaire: A Lyric Poet in the Era of High Capitalism*, 1983, both by Walter Benjamin. Thanks are also due to

Gill Motley and the staff at Polity Press and Blackwells for their patience and help.

I would especially like to thank Bernadette Boyle for all her encouragement and help. Above all, I wish to thank my parents, Audrey and Peter, for all their understanding, patience and support.

Every effort has been made to trace all the copyright holders but if any have been inadvertently overlooked, the publishers will be pleased to make the necessary arrangement at the first opportunity.

List of Abbreviations

Where possible, existing English language translations have been used. Other translations are my own. References to material in the *Passagen-Werk* are given by *Konvolut* number and page (e.g., J67,1, *GS* V, p. 438) or page of translation (e.g., N6,5, Smith ed., 1989, p. 57). The following abbreviations are used in the text:

GS   *Gesammelte Schriften*, vol I–VII, ed. Rolf Tiedemann and Hermann Schweppenhäuser, with the collaboration of Theodor Adorno and Gershom Scholem. Frankfurt am Main: Suhrkamp Verlag, 1974; Taschenbuch Ausgabe, 1991.

AB   *Theodor W. Adorno – Walter Benjamin Briefwechsel 1928–40*, ed. Henri Lonitz. Frankfurt am Main: Suhrkamp Verlag, 1994.

AP   *Aesthetics and Politics: Debates between Bloch, Lukács, Brecht, Benjamin, Adorno*, tr. and ed. Ronald Taylor, with an afterword by Frederic Jameson. London: Verso, 1980.

BK   *Berliner Kindheit um Neunzehnhundert*, with an afterword by Theodor Adorno. Frankfurt am Main: Suhrkamp Verlag, 1950.

BR   *Briefe*, ed. Gershom Scholem and Theodor Adorno. 2 vols. Frankfurt am Main: Suhrkamp Verlag, 1978.

CB   *Charles Baudelaire: A Lyric Poet in the Era of High Capitalism*, tr. Harry Zohn. London: Verso, 1983.

COR   *The Correspondence of Walter Benjamin*, ed. and annotated by Gershom Scholem and Theodor Adorno, tr. Manfred Jacobson and Evelyn Jacobson, with a foreword by Gershom Scholem. Chicago and London: University of Chicago Press, 1994.

CP   'Central Park', tr. Lloyd Spencer, *New German Critique*, 34 (Winter 1985), pp. 28–58.

GER   *The Correspondence of Walter Benjamin and Gershom Scholem 1932– 1940*, ed. Gershom Scholem, tr. Gary Smith and André Lefèvre, with an introduction by Anson Rabinbach. Cambridge, Mass.: Harvard University Press, 1992.

ILL   *Illuminations*, ed. with an introduction by Hannah Arendt, tr. Harry Zohn. London: Fontana, 1973.

MOD   *Moscow Diary*, ed. Gary Smith, tr. Richard Sieburth, with a preface by Gershom Scholem. Cambridge, Mass., and London: Harvard University Press, 1986.

OGTD   *The Origin of German Tragic Drama*, tr. John Osbourne, with an introduction by George Steiner. London: Verso, 1985.

OWS   *One–Way Street and Other Writings*, tr. Edmund Jephcott and Kingsley Shorter, with an introduction by Susan Sontag. London: Verso, 1985.

UB   *Understanding Brecht*, tr. Anna Bostock, with an introduction by Stanley Mitchell. London: Verso, 1983.

Introduction

Benjamin and the city

In *Konvolut* N of his ill-fated study of nineteenth-century Paris, the *Passagenarbeit*, Walter Benjamin writes: 'the pathos of this project . . . I find every city beautiful' (N1,6, Smith ed., 1989, p. 44). What is remarkable about this candid statement is its location in a vast study dedicated to the critical revelation of the modern metropolis as the phantasmagoric site of mythic domination, to the representation of the city as the essential locus of modern capitalism and its attendant evils of exploitation, injustice, alienation and the diminution of human experience. It is both characteristic and informative that Benjamin should choose to situate such an affirmation of the urban complex in a study specifically concerned with the grotesque character of the city and the dehumanizing tendencies of metropolitan daily life. For Benjamin, the great cities of modern European culture were both beautiful and bestial, a source of exhilaration and hope on the one hand and of revulsion and despair on the other.[1]

The city for Benjamin was magnetic: it attracted and repelled him in the same moment. He was an urbanite, a metropolitan whose life was split between two cities: Berlin, where he was born, and Paris, to which he fled in 1933. Gershom Scholem notes that 'Benjamin had a deep love for Berlin' (1976, p. 176). Benjamin himself recognized that Berlin was a vital backdrop to, and component of, his work. In a letter to Scholem of 17 April 1931, he remarks: 'the most sophisticated civilisation and the most "modern" culture are not only part of my private comfort; some of them are the very means of my production' (Scholem, 1982, p. 232). Berlin was, as Bertolt Brecht notes, 'impossible to live in, impossible to leave',[2] and it was indeed only under the most desperate and compelling of circumstances that Benjamin did leave his native city eventually. By early 1933, the rise of the National Socialists in Germany had finally made continuing residence in Berlin too hazardous. Benjamin left Berlin for the last time in March and travelled to Paris, a city which he had visited on numerous occasions and for which he had frequently expressed a predilection. Scholem recalls a conversation with Benjamin in Paris in 1927 in which 'Benjamin said that he would like best to settle in Paris because he found the city's atmosphere so much to his liking' (1982, p. 130). Indeed, Benjamin resisted leaving the city that had adopted him even when France was invaded in 1940. Despite numerous entreaties and warnings from friends and colleagues at the Institute for Social Research, most notably Theodor Adorno and Max Horkheimer, who were themselves safely ensconced in exile in New York, Benjamin refused to leave his adored Paris until it was too late. His eventual attempt to escape to Spain was thwarted at the last moment, and, tragically, he committed suicide on the border in September 1940.

Although the city was beautiful, beloved, congenial, and vital for his literary production, Benjamin was perhaps never fully convinced that the urban complex could be the site of lasting contentment. Indeed, his writings on the city are concerned with critically unmasking the delusions, pretensions and barbarism of precisely that urban environment and social milieu which he found so indispensable, so much a part of his 'private comfort'. Hoffman notes that 'urban life was essential to Benjamin, yet also barely tolerable' (1983, p. 150). He both loved and loathed the city. It is this paradox, this unresolved tension, that lies at the heart of Benjamin's fascination with the modern metropolis.

The modern city, its architecture, spaces, street life, inhabitants and daily routines are a recurring set of themes in Benjamin's *oeuvre*. Benjamin produced a plethora of texts focusing on the character of urban experience and, in particular, a number of sketches of the cities that he visited during the mid- to late 1920s.[3] *Denkbilder* ('thought-images') was the general designation for a variety of texts that included a series of short cityscapes beginning with an impressionistic essay on Naples written around September/October 1924. A second such city portrait, 'Moscow' (1927), appeared as a result of Benjamin's visit to the Soviet capital during the winter of 1926–7. More of these urban pen-pictures were to follow: 'Weimar' (June 1928), 'Marseilles' (October 1928 – January 1929), an essay entitled 'Paris, the City in the Mirror' (January 1929), 'San Gimignano' (published 30 August 1929), and 'North Sea' (a sketch of the city of Bergen in Norway, completed on 15 August 1930).

In addition to these miniatures, Benjamin was engaged in the production of more extensive texts concerned with the description and analysis of the urban setting. In 1927 he embarked on an ever-expanding analysis of the Parisian arcades of the nineteenth century (the so-called *Passagenarbeit* or 'Arcades Project'), an enterprise that from modest beginnings was to come to dominate all his intellectual endeavours. The project was to yield an *exposé* ('Paris, Capital of the Nineteenth Century') and nearly a thousand pages of notes, drafts and quotations. The longest section of this assemblage, *Konvolut* J, was concerned with the writings of Charles Baudelaire, and by 1937 Benjamin was planning to compose a separate, though intimately related, study of the poet. Intended as a model of the larger 'Arcades Project', Benjamin drafted and then rewrote the central section of this study under the titles 'Paris of the Second Empire in Baudelaire' and 'On Some Motifs in Baudelaire'. In addition to these Paris writings, Benjamin composed a lengthy essay recording his childhood impressions of the city of Berlin. Written in 1932, shortly before his exile, the 'Berlin Chronicle' was later to be rewritten for publication under the title 'A Berlin Childhood around 1900'. These two texts stood in the closest relation to the Paris materials he had assembled, and indeed constituted methodological and historiographic experiments for the ongoing 'Arcades Project'.

These were not Benjamin's only texts on the theme of the city. Between 1927 and 1933 he was involved in the production of some eighty-four radio broadcasts (for Berliner Rundfunk and Südwestdeutscher Rundfunk in Frankfurt am Main). A number of these took facets of everyday life in Berlin as their subject-matter: for example, 'Berlin Dialect', 'Street-Trade and the Market in Old and New Berlin', 'A Berlin Street Boy' and 'Tenement Building'.[4] Furthermore, in his capacity as a literary reviewer, Benjamin wrote on several contemporary books dealing with city life, urban architecture and metropolitan experience, the most important of which were concerned with the writings of his friend and colleague on the 'Arcades Project', Franz Hessel.[5] The *Denkbilder*, then, may be seen as the point of departure for an enduring preoccupation with the city.

There has been a tremendous upsurge of interest in Benjamin's work since the publication of the *Gesammelte Schriften* began in 1974 under the editorship of Rolf Tiedemann and Hermann Schweppenhäuser. This has been given added impetus recently by a number of exhibitions and international conferences staged to mark the fiftieth anniversary (1990) of Benjamin's death and the centenary (1992) of his birth. Benjamin has been catapulted from relative obscurity to being regarded, particularly in Germany and France, but increasingly in Anglo-American circles as well, as one of the foremost intellectual figures of his generation.[6] Although Benjamin's fascination with the city is frequently mentioned by commentators, this theme has not proved a principal focus of sustained attention. His essays 'Naples' and 'Moscow' (and the 'Moscow Diary') have attracted little scholarly interest.[7] They have been deemed, and largely dismissed as, 'travel pieces' (Smith ed., 1988, p. 18) and Sunday newspaper material (Buck-Morss, 1989, p. 27). More surprisingly, the Berlin studies have fared only moderately better. While it is true that a number of short articles have concerned themselves with these writings,[8] there has been relatively little sustained analysis of Benjamin's reflections on his native city, with the notable exception of Anna Stüssi's thorough (but as yet untranslated) examination of 'Berlin Childhood'. The Paris writings have fortunately attracted more systematic consideration. The publication of the (still untranslated) *Passagenarbeit* as the fifth volume of the *Gesammelte Schriften* in 1982 produced a spate of 'special editions',[9] features and even a conference in Paris in 1985. Apart from Frisby's stimulating analysis of Benjamin's Paris writings as part of his *Fragments of Modernity*, it was not until 1989 that the first book-length examination in English of the 'Arcades' material was published (Buck-Morss's *The Dialectics of Seeing*). More recently, the Paris writings have been discussed with reference to Benjamin's critique of tradition (McCole, 1993), his Surrealist interests and motifs (Cohen, 1993), and with respect to the themes of melancholy and allegory (Pensky, 1993). It is strange that despite this recent proliferation of material, the significance of the earlier city writings for the Paris studies has not been explored in depth. With the exception of Buck-Morss's study (1989),[10] there has been little attempt to explore the relationships, interconnections, thematic continuities and contradictions in the various city writings taken as a whole.

This study provides a detailed reading and examination of Benjamin's city writings with a view to uncovering such relationships. My aim is to identify and explore Benjamin's critical insights into the character and experience of the metropolis, and thereby to indicate the methodological and thematic significance of his work for social theory. Benjamin's texts seek to devise an innovative, appropriate mode of representation for the city. They examine and articulate the complex relationships between the organization of time, space and human activity in the urban environment. His writings attempt to give voice to the character and political significance of particular individual and collective experiences within the urban setting. His work resists both the one-dimensional negation and the blind affirmation of modern social forms, and instead presents an appreciative, critical theory of metropolitan life. Benjamin's ambivalent vision of the city results in a sensitive and sophisticated reading of modern culture.

Benjamin's enterprise is not free of difficulties, however. His texts present paradoxical or at best incomplete formulations. Far from in any sense solving the aporias of Critical Theory, he succeeds only in generating an equally elusive, enigmatic set of concepts. But within these paradoxes, and in his integration of a diverse assortment of elements from Marxism, Judaic mysticism, German Romanticism and *avant-garde* modernist approaches, Benjamin seeks to develop a set of highly original and illuminating textual practices which challenge accepted forms of social-theoretical discourse. His critical, redemptive reading of the city-as-text is complemented by his innovative, immanent writing of the text-as-city. My goal in this book is to explore these configurations of reading and writing, of ruination and redemption, of myth and the metropolis.

In the remainder of this introduction I will be concerned with an initial delineation of the principal themes and recurrent motifs of Benjamin's city writings. Benjamin's cityscapes appear to be underpinned by a number of intricately interconnected yet distinctive concerns which may be considered under the following rubrics: physiognomy, phenomenology, mythology, history, politics and text. These form a set of directions or co-ordinates to aid the navigation and mapping of his cityscapes.

Physiognomy

For Benjamin, the urban complex is the quintessential site of modernity. The social totality is crystallized in miniature in the metropolis. The city constitutes a monad: it is an entity that encapsulates the characteristic features of modern social and economic structures, and is thus the site for their most precise and unambiguous interpretation.[11] In the spaces and structures of the modern metropolis, contemporary culture presents itself most readily and acutely for decipherment. It is thus through the critical reading of the structuring principles and practical modes of metropolitan life that Benjamin endeavours to construct a fragmentary but insightful critique of modern capitalist society and elaborate a set of imperatives for Critical Theory and revolutionary practice.

The notion of physiognomical reading is interwoven with Benjamin's monadological approach.[12] In his radio broadcast 'Das dämonische Berlin' Benjamin gives the following description of the writer Heinrich Heine von Hoffman as physiognomist:

> he perceived the extraordinary . . . in specific people, things, houses, objects, streets etc. As you have perhaps heard, one calls people who are able to discern from people's faces, from their gait, from their hands or from their head-shape, their character, occupation, or even their fate, 'physiognomists'. Hoffman was less an observer [*Seher*] than a scrutinizer [*Anseher*]. That is the best German translation of 'physiognomist'. A major concern of his scrutiny was Berlin, both the city and its inhabitants. (*GS* VII, p. 89)

In his cityscapes Walter Benjamin seeks to present urban 'physiognomies', readings or decipherments of the metropolitan environment in which the key to understanding social life is, on one level, located in the physical structure of the cities themselves. For Benjamin, the buildings, spaces, monuments and objects that compose the urban environment both are a response to, and reflexively structure, patterns of human social activity. Architecture and action shape each other; they interpenetrate. The metropolis constitutes a frame or theatre for activity. The buildings of the city, and its interior setting in particular, form casings for action in which, or on which, human subjects leave 'traces', signs of their passing, markers or clues to their mode of existence.[13] Benjamin states that 'living means leaving traces' (*CB*, p. 169), and these traces left behind by the modern city dweller must be carefully preserved by the urban physiognomist, and their meaning deciphered. For Benjamin, the urban physiognomist is part archaeologist, part collector and part detective.[14]

The 'character' of a city may be read from its numerous faces. The city as a monad in turn contains within itself monadological fragments. Benjamin notes: 'in thousands of eyes, in thousands of objects, the city is reflected' (*GS* IV, p. 358). Whether it is the inconspicuous churches in Naples, the wooden hut nestling next to the tenement block in Revolutionary Moscow, the towering monuments to imperial glory in Berlin, or the various dream-houses (arcade, railway station, museum) in Paris, the city's architecture forms a secret, unwritten 'text' to be 'read' by the urban physiognomist. Physiognomic reading is for Benjamin a critical enterprise, one which, though preoccupied with the external, superficial manifestations of the metropolis, none the less penetrates beneath the façades of things to reveal their true character.

Phenomenology

Benjamin is concerned with the physical structure of the city and the material objects found therein as a setting for, and as indices of, social activity. He seeks to identify and examine the mundane experiences of the urban population. He offers nothing less than a 'micro-sociology of everyday life and of the city' (Tacussel, 1986, p. 48). Benjamin is particularly interested in the minutiae and marginalia of the urban setting. His description of the French photographer Eugène Atget is almost a self-portrait in this respect:

> Atget always passed by the 'great sights' and so-called 'landmarks'; what he did not pass by was a long row of boot lasts; or the Paris courtyards, where from night to morning the hand-carts stand in serried ranks; or the tables after people have finished eating and left, the dishes not yet cleared away – as they exist in their hundreds of thousands at the same hour; or the brothel at Rue . . . No. 5, whose street number appears, gigantic, at four different places on the building's façade. (*OWS*, pp. 250–1)

Benjamin himself 'passed by' the landmarks of the city, and instead was preoccupied with, and stressed the significance of, apparently banal and trivial features of the metropolis. His cityscapes seek to develop 'a dialectical optic that perceives the everyday as the impenetrable and the impenetrable as the everyday' (*OWS*, p. 237). They draw upon the most diverse elements: a disfigured beggar in Naples, a streetcar ride in Moscow, a small meeting-house in Berlin, the site of a double suicide, and the dilapidated Parisian shopping arcades on the brink of demolition and the often eccentric clientele that frequented them in their heyday.

The main themes of this phenomenology of the city are the fragmentation, commodification, interiorization and marginalization of experience. Benjamin is engaged in the representation of the city as 'a landscape of noisy life' (f°3, *GS* V, p. 1056). His cityscapes are concerned with changing patterns of street life and, in particular, the impact of the crowd upon the individual psyche. The hallmark of modern experience is 'shock'. This in turn engenders forgetfulness and a distinctive form of memory, the *mémoire involontaire*. In addition, the accelerated tempo and new, machine-based rhythms of metropolitan life lead to a distinctively modern temporal sensibility rooted in the commodification of time (equation of time and money) and repetition (fetishism and fashion).

The character of economic practices and patterns of exchange assume an important place in Benjamin's analysis. From the chaos of the Neapolitan street markets to the careful displays of artefacts in the arcades and department stores of Berlin and Paris, Benjamin is preoccupied with the city as the site of the commodity. He moves away from the traditional Marxist emphasis on forms of production, however, to explore modes of commodity display, advertising and consumption. It is not so much the experience of the alienated worker but that of the fetishizing customer which takes centre stage in these analyses. Benjamin draws upon and modifies Georg Lukács's account of commodity culture as the reification of human consciousness and develops Georg Simmel's account of the origins and consequences of fashion.

Benjamin focuses on the shifting relationship between interior and exterior spaces, public and private life. In 'Naples' he emphasizes the communal character of everyday life. A principal concern of the essay on Moscow is the abolition of the private domain through collectivization. By contrast, in his analyses of Berlin and Paris, he stresses the interiorization of social life and the erotic by the bourgeois private citizen. The bourgeois domicile is revealed as a gloomy, ramshackle site of imprisonment. The arcade itself is nothing other than a street transformed into an interior setting. Interiorization is bound up with the compartmentalization of space and the removal of disruptive and disturbing figures from everyday life. The poor and the dispossessed vanish as modern 'hygiene' demands the institutionalization and confinement of the dead, the sick, the insane and the disabled.

Ernst Bloch gives the following description of Benjamin's approach:

A sense for the peripheral: Benjamin had what Lukács so drastically lacked: a unique gaze for the significant detail, for what lies alongside, for those fresh elements which, in thinking and in the world, arise from here, for the individual things which intrude in an unaccustomed and non-schematic way, things which do not fit in with the usual lot and therefore deserve particular, incisive attention. Benjamin had an incomparable micro-philological sense for this sort of detail, for this sort of significant periphera, for this sort of meaningful incidental sign. (Smith ed., 1988, p. 340)

One of Benjamin's principal goals is to give voice to the 'periphera', the experiences of those whom modern forms of order strive to render silent and invisible. Objects that are obsolete, outdated and ridiculous are salvaged and made to tell their tale. The sauntering *flâneur*, the self-conscious dandy, the loud-mouthed beggar, the suffering prostitute, the wretched rag-picker: marginal, disregarded figures inhabit Benjamin's pages on the city. The 'invisible' are made visible; the mute are given a voice. Benjamin's 'phenomenology' of the city is an attempt to comprehend the experience of modernity via the examination of some of its most eccentric and despised representatives.[15]

Mythology

A key feature of Benjamin's writings on the metropolitan environment is his identification and critical analysis of the mythic. His decipherment of the city from the objects and architecture of the urban complex and his consideration of the forms of experience encountered therein fundamentally combine to unmask the modern metropolis as the site of the phantasma-goric and the mythic. It is important to recognize that although Benjamin uses the term 'myth' in a number of contrasting ways, these different meanings are seldom explicitly formulated or clarified.[16] 'Myth' appears to have at least a fourfold significance for him: as fallacious thought, as compulsion, as tyranny, and as a metaphorical device.

First, Benjamin uses the term to refer to erroneous thought and misrecognition. According to this view, which is clearly derived from the Enlightenment tradition, 'myth' refers to archaic forms of perception and experience. Myths are stories which served to explain and account for natural occurrences, catastrophes and other phenomena with reference to superhuman beings, spirits, demons and magic. Myth is rooted in superstition, ignorance and fear. The destructive forces of irrationality, obsession and intoxica-tion hold sway in mythic consciousness. Myths are fallacious ideas, illusions and fantasies. Benjamin describes the domain of

myth as 'a primeval forest where words swing like chattering apes
from bombast to bombast, avoiding at all costs the ground which
would disclose their inability to stand – for this is the Logos where
they should stand and give an account of themselves'. (*GS* I,
p. 163, cited by Menninghaus in Smith ed., 1988, p. 298). Myth
stands in opposition to true knowledge, both the revelations of
religious thought and the rational understanding of the world
provided by modern science.

The second sense in which Benjamin uses the term is with
reference to creaturely compulsion. Myth is the antithesis of truth
and human freedom. Nature is not only incomprehensible but
also omnipotent. Myth involves human powerlessness in the face
of unalterable natural laws and the subordination of reason before
the blind, uncontrollable forces of the natural environment.
Human actions are dominated by the necessities of instinctual
drives and desires. In myth, human life is not self-determined or
self-governed, but rather is subject to fate and the whim of the
gods. This human impotence has an important temporal dimension. The rhythms of nature hold sway over mythic consciousness, which, as a result, has a cyclical character. Renewal is
followed by decay and then by renewal once more. Benjamin
notes: 'the essence of mythic events is recurrence' (D10a,4, *GS* V,
p. 178). Human beings, like nature, are doomed to the continual
repetition of what has gone before. Myth is the unchanging, a
state of apparent 'timelessness'.

Third, Benjamin uses the term 'myth' to denote the reversal or
inversion of this human submission to nature in the modern
period. Modernity presents itself as the end of myth. On the one
hand, it is the epoch of rational thought and understanding, and
on the other, the scientific and technological accomplishments
born from this knowledge bring ever greater liberation from the
compulsions of necessity. For Benjamin, the modern epoch has
brought neither the furtherance of enlightened thought nor the
realization of reason; instead, modernity is characterized by a
reversion to, or the continuing domination of, mythic forms. The
destructive energies of myth proliferate in the modern world in
new guises. For Benjamin, prefiguring the critique of the
Enlightenment and its consequences that Theodor Adorno and
Max Horkheimer were to develop in their 1947 study *Dialectic of
Enlightenment*, enslavement by natural forces has been transformed into the enslavement of nature. Technology and instrumentalism are not indicative of liberation, but are manifestations
of a new epoch of illusion, ignorance and barbarism. Myth

becomes human tyranny.[17] The natural world has become 'disenchanted' only for the purposes of avaricious exploitation. According to Horkheimer and Adorno, 'what men want to learn from nature is how to use it in order to wholly dominate it and other men' (1986, p. 4). Human beings come to worship their own products in commodity fetishism. The modern individual is governed by the unchanging rhythms of the machinery he or she must serve. The industrial production line is the modern manifestation of repetition. The endless stream of identical artefacts and the cyclical character of fashion are the contemporary, phantasmagoric manifestations of recurrence. Modern capitalism is to be understood as a reconfiguration of the archaic and an intensification of myth. Modernity has not progressed beyond 'prehistory', but instead constitutes 'a perpetual relapse into the always-the-same of myth' (Wolin, 1986, p. 211). Benjamin notes: 'as long as there is still a beggar, there is still myth' (K6,4, GS V, p. 505).

The metropolis is the principal site of the phantasmagoria of modernity, the new manifestation of myth. Frisby writes: 'the world of myth permeates the modern world of newness in such a way that, along with the Surrealists, one can speak of the creation of modern myths of urban life' (1988, p. 208). The city proclaims itself as the triumph of culture and civilization over the natural, as a fortress built against mythic forces. Benjamin writes with irony:

> Great cities – whose incomparable sustaining and reassuring power encloses those at work within them in the peace of a fortress and lifts from them, with the view of the horizon, awareness of the ever-vigilant elemental forces – are seen to be breached at all points by the invading countryside. Not only by the landscape, but by what in untrammelled nature is most bitter: ploughed land, highways, night sky that the veil of vibrant redness no longer conceals. The insecurity of even the busiest areas puts the city dweller in the opaque and truly dreadful situation in which he must assimilate, along with isolated monstrosities from the open country, the abortions of urban techtronics. (*OWS*, p. 59; see also I1a,8, *GS* V, p. 284)[18]

The metropolis is a monument to the conquest and subjugation of nature by humankind, and constitutes the principal site of human progress, of the wonders and marvels of technological innovation. Through its tireless parades of novelties and its bombastic monuments, exhibitions and museums, the modern metropolis presents a deceptive vision of past and present. The promises of

continual progress and endless improvement are among the
mystifications of capitalism. The city is home not to critical
thought, but to the false consciousness engendered by bourgeois
ideology, to the myths of the modern.

The fourth sense in which Benjamin uses the term 'myth' is as a
trope or metaphor. Just as the city is imbued with the mythic, so
too are Benjamin's cityscapes. His writings make extensive and
repeated reference to mythological figures to both comic and
critical effect.[19] The metropolitan labyrinth is home to Theseus
and Ariadne. One encounters Orpheus and Euridice saying their
farewells in the railway station and, on another occasion, at the
threshold of the modern underworld, the Paris Métro. This
amusing and playful use of mythic figures serves to parody
modern bourgeois neoclassicism and the pretensions accompany-
ing the so-called heroism of modern life, a notion explored in
Benjamin's writings on Baudelaire. These mythological figures
have a more serious purpose as well, however; for they offer clues
to those who seek to defeat monstrous powers and facilitate the
overcoming of myth. The Critical Theorist must also employ
cunning if what is precious is to be saved from the deceitful forces
of myth.

For Benjamin, myth is not simply to be equated with delusion
and misrecognition. Myth contains within it positive elements and
potentialities which must be preserved and utilized. In his
writings on Paris, for example, Benjamin characterizes the
commodity culture of the nineteenth century as a dream-world,
the materialization, albeit in distorted form, of genuine desire and
aspirations. Furthermore, certain forms of mythic experience may
be valuable. Benjamin emphasizes the positive and utopian
moments that may be contained within mimesis, play, intoxication and intuition.[20] Benjamin's dialectical vision of myth is
perceptively identified by Lindner, who views it with some
disquiet:

> Either it should – against civilising rationality – gain access to a
> reconstituted mythology and make a claim for myth in the sense of a
> liberated sensuality, polyvalence, fantasy and play, or it should
> denounce modern rationality itself as the exacerbation of myth in the
> sense of fate, spell, compulsive repetition, and fetishism . . .
> [Benjamin] evades exactly such alternatives. (1986, p. 39)

Benjamin's evasion is more illuminating than infuriating, however. He does not advocate the one-dimensional negation of

mythic forms, but demands critical redemption. Menninghaus astutely observes that Benjamin's work is concerned with the 'dialectic of breaking apart *and* rescuing myth' (Smith ed., 1988, p. 323). Benjamin's dialectical understanding of myth, his shifting and ambivalent understanding of its positive and negative moments, is intimately related to his fluctuating response to the metropolis, the home of myth.

History

A vital theme in Benjamin's cityscapes is his critique of the city as the locus of an illusory and deceptive vision of the past. False history, myth, is to be liquidated through the revelation and representation of a different, hidden past. This in turn is to be achieved by adherence to a particular set of critical and redemptive historiographic principles. Benjamin articulates a number of models for the development of a demythologizing critical theory of society:

1 Archaeological: an approach concerned with the salvation and preservation of the objects and traces of the past that modern society threatens to destroy.
2 Memorial: Benjamin exhorts the Critical Theorist to oppose the modern propensity for amnesia, to remember those whose struggles and sufferings in the past would otherwise be forgotten.
3 Dialectical: Benjamin develops his conception of the dialectical image, the momentary mutual recognition and illumination of past and present.

In his methodological and historiographic writings for his study of Paris in particular,[21] Benjamin claims that the modern is not to be understood as the end-point of a continuous, linear, developmental process or as the culmination of human endeavour and achievement. Modernity does not constitute the height of civilization but rather only a refinement or fine tuning of barbarism. He denounces the smug complacency inherent in the concept of 'progress'. For Benjamin, 'that epoch which understood itself as the embodiment of modernity, of technical and scientific progress, and of universal history in a historicist sense, is to be represented in the final analysis as the catastrophic scene of failed emancipation' (Lindner, 1986, p. 37). Benjamin regards history as permanent catastrophe and ceaseless ruination. For him, 'progress' is merely the nothing-new that struts boastfully around the city streets in the borrowed garb of the latest fashions. It is the always-the-same dressed up as the ever-new. On the one hand, Benjamin attempts to reveal novelty, fashion and innovation as the unchanging, and on the other, to unmask the superficially enduring (class society and the hegemony of the bourgeoisie) as the temporary and transitory. His task then is to reveal the complex interrelations between the old and the new, the most ancient and the most recent, to articulate the prehistory of modernity.

The modern reveals itself as ruin. This notion of ruination is rooted in a recognition of the importance of an object's 'afterlife'. For Benjamin, the truth of an object or event is only discernible when it is on the point of oblivion. This is more than a simple appreciation of the wisdom of hindsight, however. The origins of such a conception of ruin and afterlife are to be found in Benjamin's understanding of the task of criticism derived from early Romanticism and his preoccupation with the allegorical gaze underpinning the German Baroque. For Benjamin, the truth content of a thing is released only when the context in which it originally existed has disappeared, when the surfaces of the object have crumbled away and it lingers precariously on the brink of extinction. This destruction of deceptive appearance facilitates a process of reconstruction. Benjamin is fundamentally concerned with the rescue and preservation of the artefacts, images and ideas liberated through this process, and with their subsequent reuse or refunctioning in the pressing political struggles of the moment. History itself is a construction of the present age and must always be read backwards from the ruins which persist in the here and now. It is to be conceived as both a destructive and fundamentally redemptive enterprise.

Politics

Benjamin's writings constitute an account of history-as-catastrophe, a vision which is concerned with the representation of the city as a locus of perpetual suffering and enduring conflict. In his consideration of Bertolt Brecht's series of poems *Handbook for City-Dwellers*, Benjamin writes: 'in this handbook the city is seen as the arena of the struggle for existence and of the class struggle. . . . Cities are battlefields' (*UB*, pp. 60–1). Such battles not only determine the shape of contemporary society but also, because history is generated by the fusion of past and present, fundamentally give form to the whole course of human history. Benjamin's advocacy of alternative and subversive historical practices, of what might be termed a 'counter-history', not only aims to unmask the modern city as the pre-eminent site of bourgeois hegemony and myth, but also seeks to empower the marginal and the oppressed.

To this end, the cityscapes offer a phenomenology of the marginal figures of the metropolitan environment. They relate the experiences of the child, the prostitute, the beggar, the rag-picker and others. Indeed, for Benjamin, it would seem that the dispossessed and despised occupy a privileged position within the domain of knowledge. They have access to a vision of society that is dereifying and critically negating. In 'Berlin Chronicle' Benjamin writes: 'only those for whom poverty or vice turn the city into a landscape in which they stray from dark till sunrise know it in a way denied to me' (OWS, p. 316). Those who inhabit the fringes of the urban complex become a source of revolutionary insight and illumination. A word of caution is needed here. While Wohlfarth notes that for Benjamin 'only the deformed can rectify the world's deformity' (Wohlfarth, 1986a, p. 147), it is important to recognize that Benjamin is not engaged in some crude elevation of the *Lumpenproletariat* to the central position in modern class struggle. Indeed, there is reason for treating Wohlfarth's characterization with caution. It is important to realize that the rag-picker, the prostitute and the beggar are principally metaphorical figures for Benjamin, constituting emblems or models of and for redemptive practice. They are not alone in this respect. Benjamin also draws upon a host of bourgeois social types in his city writings: the middle-class child, the poet, the *flâneur*, the dandy and the gambler. These figures too are important sources of illumination within the metropolitan environment. His concern is thus not so much with the 'deformed' as with outsiders irrespective of class position. Furthermore, such bourgeois types are, on occasion, compared in a somewhat naïve manner with the poor and destitute. The relationships and correspondences posited by Benjamin between the *flâneur* and the sandwichman, the gambler and the assembly-line worker, the poet and the prostitute, sometimes reveal a perplexing and unfortunate lack of discrimination. Indeed, his attitude towards such figures is frequently myopic, unsympathetic and occasionally even crass.

Benjamin's fascination with such figures is bound up with his wish to explore and identify the relationship between the intellectual and the metropolitan population. The role of the intellectual as historian and writer in the revolutionary struggle is a theme of great importance in Benjamin's city and other writings. Does the intellectual place him or herself at the service of the urban masses as their instrument or their leader? Alternatively, should he or she seek to preserve his or her independence from the urban population because of the depersonalizing, dehumanizing tendencies of modern mass society? Such questions animate his essay on Moscow and related texts, and also resurface in the *Passagenarbeit*, where his political disillusionment gradually unfolds. The affirmation of the radical potential of the so-called dreaming collectivity that informed this work, perhaps as late as 1935, gave way to an increasingly pessimistic rejection of the dehumanized metropolitan masses. Crudely put, while in the initial phases of the 'Arcades Project' the urban populace benignly prefigures the socialist revolution, in the later stages it ominously foreshadows the Nazi *Volksgemeinschaft*. At different moments, then, the metropolitan population, like the city itself, embodies the promise of Heaven or the terror of Hell.

My overall concern is twofold. First, I wish to suggest that in his loving and loathing of the modern city, Benjamin's delineation of features vital to a critical theory of modern social forms is both highly idiosyncratic and peculiarly ambivalent. His work defies simple categorization, and subverts orthodox versions of historical materialist doctrine. As a result, attempts to locate Benjamin firmly within the historical materialist tradition have not always illuminated his elusive concepts with the precision and subtlety they deserve; nor have they helped to interpret and clarify Benjamin's sometimes vague, continually shifting convictions. Benjamin's city writings contain some important insights into his political views, for they crucially incorporate his uncertain and hesitant responses to the socio-political upheavals, tendencies and imperatives of his time. On one level, the cityscapes are perhaps best seen as evidence of his ambivalence towards mass political movements and his consequent reluctance to make firm political commitments. His visit to Moscow in 1926–7 provided him with an opportunity to examine at close quarters the impact of the Soviet system on social and cultural life. 'Moscow' and 'Moscow Diary' may be seen as constituting indices of Benjamin's political naïvety, unease and, eventually, his growing disenchantment with the Communist regime he encountered in post-Revolutionary Russia. While Benjamin's Berlin writings are fundamentally underpinned by his horror at the rise of Nazism and the experience of forced emigration, they do not appeal directly to proletarian resistance and struggle; in their depiction of a bourgeois childhood, they instead recall a period of impotence before the city. While there is, as will be seen, a distinctive political dimension to the Berlin texts, it is hard to reconcile any straightforward vision of Benjamin-as-Marxist with his concern with the magic and misery of childhood, with the character of personal memory and the fate of long-dead school friends and relatives. The Paris writings emphasize Benjamin's paradoxical attempt to contribute to the historical materialist tradition, not so much via a consideration of Marx, proletarian movements or the Paris Commune as through the analysis of Baudelaire, bourgeois consumer fantasies and the World Exhibition. Scholem, a not disinterested observer in these matters, writes: 'to be sure, he regarded the bourgeois world with considerable cynicism, but even this did not come easily to him' (1982, p. 54).

My second concern is to show that, although Benjamin does not always observe his own literary prescriptions and can be said to occupy at best a somewhat marginal position within the discourse of historical materialism, this does not mean that he has little to offer modern Critical Theory. Paradoxically, and hence for Benjamin most appropriately, it is precisely in the points where he diverges from the imperatives of more orthodox Marxist thinking that his enduring significance is located: in his critique of the notion of progress and the increasing technological control of nature by humankind as mythic domination; in his concern with the redemption of the forgotten sufferings and the retrieval of the lost utopian aspirations of past generations; in his insistence upon the critical vision and political role of the marginal figures in modern society; and in his articulation of 'autobiography' as subversive historical practice. It is not so much, then, in his tortuous Marxism that Benjamin's most precious insights are situated, but in his equally problematic admixture of Messianism and Modernism. Benjamin offers an intermittent, non-systematic, but stimulating engagement with, and critique of, the Marxist tradition.

Text

How is the writer to capture the momentary and fleeting? How is he or she to express the ineffable, to represent the contingent? To give form to the modern – this task, Herculean in character, was for Baudelaire that of the poet of modernity. Benjamin is also concerned in his city writings with the problem of representation.

In his essay 'San Gimignano' he writes: 'to find words for that which one has before one's eyes – how difficult that can be' (*GS* IV, p. 364). His readings of the metropolitan landscape involve an attempt to overcome this problem through the development of an innovative and experimental literary style.[22] A number of vital, interconnected textual imperatives run through Benjamin's representation and critique of the modern metropolis: an imagistic approach; a concern with perspective, a demand for immediacy and for immanence.

In his writings Benjamin is preoccupied with the visual and imagistic. The early cityscapes are *Denkbilder*, 'thought-images', which seek to portray the city, be it Naples, Moscow or Marseilles, through a kind of journalistic reportage. The Berlin texts are primarily composed of constellations of remembered images (autobiography and personal narrative are attempts to recapture the 'at first sight' of the city), and in the *Passagenarbeit* Benjamin stresses the visual character of history and the methodological imperative of the dialectical image. The cityscapes are attempts, therefore, to translate the seen into the written, the picture into the word, to articulate what Buck-Morss refers to in the title of her 1989 study as 'the dialectics of seeing'.

Photography and motion pictures provide models for the depiction of the urban complex. Benjamin exhorts writers to 'start taking photographs' (*UB*, p. 95) and to deploy themselves 'at important points in the sphere of imagery' (*OWS*, p. 238).[23] It is film, however, which is most important for Benjamin in this visualization of the urban environment. He notes that 'only film commands optical approaches to the essence of the city' (*OWS*, p. 298); this is because it is able to capture the flux and movement of the urban environment, to record the spontaneous and the ephemeral.[24] The shifting vantage-point of the film camera is also important. Benjamin's concern with the depiction of the urban is interwoven with a conscious refusal of or resistance to the presentation of an overarching, integrated, coherent view of the city as a whole. The imagistic approach highlights the fleeting, fluid character of modern metropolitan existence. It denies a systematic, stable perspective. The representation of the city demands a discontinuous, fragmented literary form and style.[25] Benjamin is engaged in an archaeological excavation of the city to salvage its fragments so that they can be refunctioned. Each element recovered is monadological, containing within it the totality whence it came, and is also illuminating as part of the new montage in which it is assembled.

The imperatives of an imagistic and fragmentary literary form result in Benjamin's rejection of conventional narrative structures and his insistence upon more direct, immediate textual practices. He states bluntly:

> Significant literary work can only come into being in a strict alteration between action and writing; it must nurture the inconspicuous forms that better fit its influence in active communities than does the pretentious universal gesture of the book – in leaflets, brochures, articles and placards. Only this prompt language shows itself equal to the moment. (*OWS*, p. 45)

Benjamin's search for a 'prompt language' involves engagement with the quotation and with the principle of montage. Diverse, incongruent elements are rudely dragged from their intellectual moorings to be reassembled in radical and illuminating configurations. The 'shock-like' character of modern social life finds its expression in this montage of heterogeneous fragments.[26]

Benjamin is engaged in the bold, if flawed, venture of making historical materialist discourse 'Surrealistic'.[27] He asserts the affinity of a radical and thoroughgoing political critique and formal literary innovation. In 'The Author as Producer', he interweaves formal textual concerns and political orientation: progressive (modernist) literary techniques go hand in hand with progressive political (historical materialist) commitments. Benjamin argues:

> I should like to demonstrate to you that the tendency of a work of literature can be politically correct only if it is also correct in the literary sense. . . . [T]he correct political tendency of a work extends also to its literary quality: because a political tendency which is correct comprises a literary tendency which is correct. (*UB*, p. 86)

Benjamin seeks to produce texts which not only give an account of the city, but have metropolitan experiences fundamentally embedded within them: form and content coalesce. The dominance of the visual, the predilection for the fragmented and the concern with the immediate and with 'shock' are both definitive characteristics of modern urban life and central formal properties of Benjamin's texts. As a modernist, Benjamin regards the city as a space of intoxication, of excitement and distraction. As a historical materialist, he rejects it as the site of bourgeois domination. Fluctuating between these positions, his texts both embody and resist those tendencies he considered central to, and characteristic of, modern capitalist society. In his loving and loathing of the urban complex, Benjamin may be seen as deeply enmeshed in those paradoxes that constitute the 'heroism of modern life'.[28]

In this study I trace and analyse the complex unfolding of these themes from their initial announcement (Benjamin's 'noteworthy and important observations') and incipient formulation in the essays on Naples and Moscow (the earliest, most detailed and arguably most important of the city *Denkbilder*) to their fuller articulation and more detailed exposition in the Berlin and Paris writings. In stressing this thematic continuity, however, it is important to remember that even in their most expansive formulation in the *Passagenarbeit*, Benjamin's city writings remain fragmentary, broken and disconnected. His cityscapes do not form a neat, linear, sequential series. They do not culminate in the postulation of a definitive account of the experience of modernity. His archaeology of the metropolis leads ever deeper into the underworld of modern experience, delving ever further into the rich complexities of urban social life. But his writings are 'rhapsodic' and repetitive, rather than systematic and cumulative. There is elaboration rather than development. The cityscapes involve a circling, a continual return to the same loci, the same figures, the same objects, but each time from a different direction, from a shifted vantage-point. In Benjamin's text-as-city, just as in the labyrinth of the modern metropolis, there is continual movement but no progress.[29]

1

Urban Images: From Ruins to Revolutions

Naples

Introduction

My concern in this chapter is to examine Benjamin's initial attempts to represent the urban environment and its population, to give voice to his fascination with the city. Although not the only such cityscapes written by Benjamin in the early to mid-1920s, his essays on Naples and Moscow constitute the most thematically developed and methodologically explicit of these texts. A detailed critical reading of them illuminates the significance and the limitations of the *Denkbild* as a form of critical social analysis. It is my contention that these two formative texts introduce motifs and techniques whose elaboration and refinement became key aspects of Benjamin's subsequent writing.

The year 1924 was a watershed in Walter Benjamin's intellectual and personal life. He travelled to the island of Capri around the end of April to join a party of friends, among them Ernst Bloch and Erich and Lucie Gutkind. His stay, broken by a few excursions to the Italian mainland, lasted some six months. A number of factors prompted the trip. His principal goal was to find a place in which he could work undisturbed on his *Habilitationsschrift* (his now famous study of Baroque drama entitled *Ursprung des deutschen Trauerspiels*[1]) for the Johann Wolfgang Goethe University in Frankfurt am Main. But Scholem points out that Benjamin had other important reasons for wanting to escape his native city at this particular time. On the one hand, Capri offered itself as a place of much-needed refreshment, a sanctuary from pressing family anxieties and marital discord;[2] on the other, it was at that time an inexpensive place to live, an important consideration for Benjamin, whose financial situation was always precarious and frequently disastrous.

While on Capri, Bloch introduced Benjamin to Georg Lukács's recently published *History and Class Consciousness*. Benjamin's avid reading of this seminal text was his first serious engagement with historical materialist thought, with which he was to have an uneasy relationship for the rest of his life. Benjamin's new-found enthusiasm for Marxist ideas, kindled by the writings of Lukács, was fuelled by someone else he encountered on Capri: the Bolshevik actress and theatre director from Riga, Asja Lacis. She was to prove a decisive influence upon the rest of Benjamin's life and work.[3]

In his letter to Scholem of 16 September 1924, Benjamin mentions a visit to Naples and notes: 'I have collected a lot of material on Naples, noteworthy and important observations that I may be able to develop into something' (*COR*, p. 250). This 'something' was to be a short essay, written in conjunction with Lacis during the ensuing weeks in Italy, simply entitled 'Naples'. It was eventually published in the *Frankfurter Zeitung* of 19 August 1925.[4] It is perhaps not surprising, given the constellation of pressing personal and intellectual concerns outlined above, that critics and commentators have focused on the progress of the *Habilitationsschrift* and/or Benjamin's romantic entanglements during this period. But as a consequence, his essay on Naples has received scant attention (with a few notable exceptions). It is precisely the plethora of Benjamin's other pressing preoccupations, however, that makes this essay so intriguing. Given his emotional and intellectual concerns and crises in the summer of 1924, why did Benjamin choose to write about Naples?

The first part of this chapter consists of a detailed exploration of Benjamin's essay in an attempt to answer this question. 'Naples' contains within it the genesis and tentative initial articulation of a number of vital methodological and thematic considerations. Susan Buck-Morss astutely notes that in the Naples essay, 'hardly noticeable to the reader, an experiment is underway, how images, gathered by a person walking the streets of a city, can be interpreted against the grain of idealist literary style' (1989, p. 27). This experiment in the representation of the city was to culminate in the *Passagenarbeit*, Benjamin's unfinished analysis of nineteenth-century Paris, regarding which Buck-Morss writes: 'the moment [of origin] is arguably the summer of 1924, and the place is not Paris, but Italy' (1989, p. 8). If Buck-Morss is correct – and certainly I agree with her analysis on this point – what Benjamin found 'noteworthy and important' during that summer day in Naples in 1924 was a series of insights and issues that were to come to dominate all his intellectual activities.

Buck-Morss perceptively identifies the essay as the starting-point for Benjamin's enduring concern with the urban setting, and correctly notes that the essay on Naples has 'central methodological import for the *Passagen-Werk*' (1989, p. 27). She then writes somewhat dismissively, however, that 'it is to be compared with those articles that still comprise the "travel" section of Sunday newspapers. There is no lack of humour or entertainment. There is no explicit political message' (ibid.).[5] Yet for Benjamin, the development of a 'journalistic' style, of an original, immediate literary form, is importantly interlaced with his political concerns. He states that 'the newspaper is, technically speaking, the writer's most important strategic position' (*UB*, p. 91).[6] Indeed, if one were to disregard 'journalistic' writings as politically inconsequential, then Benjamin's *oeuvre* would shrink considerably. A recurrent theme of Benjamin's texts on the city is the attempt to devise a mode or style of writing that in some way incorporates or embodies within it urban experience. As Buck-Morss herself recognizes, 'the effect of technology on both work and leisure in the modern metropolis had been to shatter experience into fragments, and journalistic style reflected that fragmentation' (1989, p. 23). 'Naples' is more than just a Sunday newspaper article or colour supplement feature. It is an attempt to capture the fleeting, momentary character of social life in a set of images. The *Denkbilder* are a form of literary 'snapshot', in which the ephemeral is frozen and preserved. The fragmentary style pursued by Benjamin in his writings on the city is in keeping with his understanding of the modern urban complex as the locus of the disintegration of experience and with his recognition of the need to salvage the disregarded debris of contemporary society. The city is a vast ruin demanding careful excavation and rescue. 'Naples' is an early example of Benjamin's attempt to develop a redemptive critical practice. As will become evident, the *Denkbild* fundamentally prefigures the dialectical image, a notion which constitutes the crucial historiographic category in Benjamin's analysis of Paris.

It is not so much this methodological import but a thematic schema which Buck-Morss emphasizes. She stresses the connection between 'Naples' and Benjamin's subsequent writings on the city thus:

> To the West is Paris, the origin of bourgeois society in the political-revolutionary sense; to the East, Moscow in the same sense marks its end. To the South, Naples locates the Mediterranean origins, the myth-enshrouded childhood of Western civilisation; to the North, Berlin locates the myth-enshrouded childhood of the author himself. (1989, p. 25)

While the interwoven character of the mythic and the urban is a central theme of this study, I regard the above conceptualization as rather grandiose. If 'Naples' is, as Buck-Morss states, concerned with the depiction of 'the myth-enshrouded childhood of Western civilisation', it is rather puzzling that Benjamin should write about everyday Neapolitan life and not, for example, about the nearby ruins at Pompeii. In my view, Benjamin's essay is far more modest in its intentions. It is about contemporary rather than classical forms of life. It contains brief but vivid descriptions of the city's buildings and streets, markets and festivities, beggars and children. The ruins of classical civilization are mentioned only in regard to their utility in the present: namely, the swindles perpetrated on hapless tourists who come to visit them. Buck-Morss's scheme may be a neat one, but it does not withstand serious examination. It misses the actual significance of the essay: Benjamin's interest, not in Naples as the cradle of Western civilization, but in the particular forms of mundane life found within the urban environment. He explores a set of fundamental relationships: between architecture and urban experience, public and private spheres, sacred and profane, ritual and improvisation, individual and collectivity. To capture immediately the complexity and fluidity of the everyday within a literary form that mimics the rhythm and tempo of metropolitan life – this is the key purpose of the 'thought-image', not some comprehensive mapping of the developmental stages of Western civilization. Hence Buck-Morss both over-elaborates and underestimates 'Naples'. While recognizing the formal significance of the *Denkbild*, she underplays it, and fails to notice the incipient political features which inform it. At the same time, she locates its thematic content within an inappropriately grand framework which misses its actual import.

Naples and Porosity

The key concept in Benjamin's experiment in urban representation is that of 'porosity'.[7] By this term, Benjamin seeks to describe what he perceives as the particular and characteristic form of social, spatial and temporal organization in Naples.[8] Porosity refers to a lack of clear boundaries between phenomena, a permeation of one thing by another, a merger of, for example, old and new, public and private, sacred and profane. The city is characterized by 'spatial anarchy, social intermingling, and, above all, imper- manence' (Buck-Morss, 1989, p. 26). In centring the notion of porosity, Benjamin directs attention to a number of motifs. With respect to the physical structure of the city, it highlights the notions of dislocation and disorientation within the urban environment. It further suggests the transience and instability of architectural and social forms, the interpenetration of modern and archaic, interior and exterior. Porosity points to the significance of what is hidden; what is concealed is the key to the interpretation of the urban setting. In the case of Naples, it is the permeation of the city by Catholic ritual which is crucial to deciphering its character. Lastly, porosity points to the relationship between architecture and action, and in particular the indeterminate, improvised character of everyday life as dramatic performance.

Porosity and cityscape Porosity refers to an absence of spatial boundaries and divisions. For Benjamin, Naples is a city that lacks distinct spatial arrangement and clear demarcation. It is an unplanned, chaotic entity which constitutes what one might describe as an 'organic' totality. Spaces and buildings interpen- etrate and merge. This lack of clear geographical and architectural boundaries makes navigation in the urban complex difficult. The undifferentiated character of the Neapolitan cityscape gives it a particularly labyrinthine quality. It is 'anarchical, embroiled, village-like in the centre, into which large networks of streets were hacked only forty years ago' (*OWS*, p. 170). There is a dearth of landmarks. Benjamin writes: 'no-one orients himself by house numbers. Shops, wells and churches are the main reference points – and not always simple ones' (ibid.). Porosity is particularly conducive to losing oneself. Finding one's way around Naples is a haphazard adventure. Guidebooks and maps are of no use. Benjamin notes that 'even Baedeker cannot propitiate' (*OWS*, p. 168) the straying tourist. Navigation in the labyrinth is not a matter of the intellect and calculation, but instead is dependent upon chance and the use of one's senses. One can locate oneself only through the sight, sound and smell of one's immediate surroundings, not through the careful study of a map. The city is a landscape[9] which the observant traveller must learn to identify and read. To wander the streets of the city, deciphering its spaces and structures as one walks, is the joy of the *flâneur* and the physiognomist.[10] The concept of the urban complex as a maze and the desire to lose oneself within it are the most important motifs in Benjamin's writings on the city, and they find their initial articulation here, in the porous urban landscape of Naples.

Porosity has an important temporal dimension. Transience and impermanence are fundamental features of the Neapolitan urban environment. In Naples 'the stamp of the definite is avoided. No situation appears intended for ever, no figure asserts it's "thus and not otherwise" ' (*OWS*, pp. 169–70). The merging or fusing of differing forms into an amorphous agglomeration applies to old and new architectural structures in the city. Benjamin notes: 'one can scarcely discern where building is still in progress and where dilapidation has already set in' (*OWS*, p. 170). The appearance of the cityscape remains fundamentally unaltered. The modern and the ancient are indivisible. The new, in so far as it cannot be distinguished from pre-existing entities that are already ruins, is immediately recognizable as the always-the-same. In 'Naples', Benjamin aims to reveal the process of construction as the production of instant ruins. Naples is the perpetual ruin, the home of the nothing-new. In the ruin, the cultural merges into the natural landscape, becoming indistinguishable from it. The notion of the ruin is thus fundamentally linked to the figure of the labyrinth. Benjamin notes, regarding the ruined city of Pompeii, that 'one could make good use of one of Ariadne's threads when visiting Pompeii today. It is the greatest labyrinth, the greatest maze in the world' (*GS* VII, p. 214). These notions of the interpenetration of the archaic and the modern, the relationship between the enduring and the fleeting, and the city as a space of disintegration and ruination are recurrent in Benjamin's cityscapes.

The clearest example of spatial/architectural porosity in Naples is the mingling of public and private spaces. Transience is marked by the instability of boundaries, the reversal of interior and exterior. The relationship between public and private domains is a key theme in all Benjamin's cityscapes. His writings on Berlin and Paris explore the character of the bourgeois domestic setting, and identify the interiorization of social activity as a distinctive feature of modern capitalist society. In Naples such a transformation occurs in reverse. Benjamin notes: 'What distinguishes Naples from other large cities is something it has in common with the African *kraal*; each private act is permeated by streams of communal life. To exist, for the North European the most private of affairs, is here, as in the *kraal*, a collective matter' (*OWS*, p. 174). On the one hand, the private bursts out of its confines and erupts into public gaze on the streets of the city. On the other, the public invades and pervades interior settings. The domestic setting is perhaps the best example. In his essay on the city of Bergen ('North Sea'), Benjamin notes that 'the house still has strong boundaries' (*GS* IV, p. 383). The 'gloomy box' (*OWS*, p. 171) of the northern European home is a clearly delineated private spatial entity. By contrast, it is only in certain districts of Naples that 'the house, in the Nordic sense, [forms] the cell of the city's architecture' (*OWS*, p. 170). The Neapolitan dwelling is not, like the interiors in Berlin and Paris, a sanctuary or haven from public life, the site of private fantasy. Instead, 'the house is far less the refuge into which people retreat than the inexhaustible reservoir from which they flood out' (*OWS*, p. 174). Benjamin notes that the Neapolitans often move their furniture and household items into the street, thereby reassembling the domestic in visible, public space.[11] The interior is thus fractured and opened to the gaze of neighbours and strangers.

At the same time, the communal invades and pervades the domicile. Benjamin writes:

> Just as the living room reappears on the street, with chairs, hearth and altar, so, only much more loudly, the street migrates into the living room. Even the poorest one is as full of wax candles, biscuit saints, sheaves of photos on the wall, and iron bedsteads, as the street is of carts, people and lights. Poverty has brought about a stretching of frontiers that mirrors the most radiant freedom of thought. There is no hour, often no space, for sleeping and eating. (*OWS*, pp. 174–5)

The spatial anarchy of the city is illustrated in miniature by the Neapolitan 'bedroom'. Benjamin states:

> How could anyone sleep in such rooms? To be sure, there are beds, as many as the room will hold. But even if there are six or seven, there are often twice as many occupants. For this reason one sees children late at night – at twelve, even at two – still in the streets. At midday they then lie sleeping behind a shop counter or on a

stairway. This sleep, which both men and women also snatch in shady corners, is therefore not the protected Northern sleep. Here, too, there is interpenetration of day and night, noise and peace, outer light and inner darkness, street and home. (*OWS*, p. 175)

Time and space are not compartmentalized and allotted for the performance of specific activities. They are frames for possibilities and potentialities.

Benjamin's reference to the children of Naples is important, for it announces a theme that will feature in all his writings on the urban complex: the experience of the child in the city. Childhood, play, games and toys are recurrent motifs in the cityscapes. In Naples, the child, like the adult, experiences an absence of formal structures and boundaries. Indeed, children even move in and out of the family group according to changing circumstances. Benjamin writes: 'if their increase becomes devastating, if the father of a family dies or the mother wastes away, close or distant relatives are not needed. A neighbour takes a child to her table for a shorter or longer period, and thus families interpenetrate in relationships that can resemble adoption' (*OWS*, p. 176). Hence, the composition of the family itself is unstable and shifting. Families intermingle, interpenetrate and coalesce as orphans and others are temporarily incorporated and absorbed. The Neapolitan family is a flexible, open agglomeration of kith and kin. These processes of familial incorporation only 'resemble adoption', for they occur through informal networks rather than state agencies and institutions. Like the architecture of the city, Neapolitan family and social life are 'dispersed, porous and commingled' (*OWS*, p. 174).[12]

Porosity and ritual   Ruination and the reversal of interior/exterior space combine to fracture the superficial appearance of things, thereby permitting illumination of what is hidden. Porosity fundamentally involves the discovery of what lies concealed, and in 'Naples', this refers above all to the sacred within the profane.[13] An architectural observation is the starting-point for this insight. Benjamin observes: 'the typical Neapolitan church does not ostentatiously occupy a vast square, visible from afar, with transepts, gallery and dome. It is hidden, built-in' (*OWS*, p. 170). He adds that, as a result, it is 'impossible to distinguish the mass of the church from that of neighbouring secular buildings' (ibid.). The threshold between the prosaic and the holy is easily traversed. Benjamin writes of the visitor thus: 'a single step takes him from the jumble of dirty courtyards into the pure solitude of a tall, whitewashed church interior' (ibid.). The sacred is inseparable from, because hidden within, the profane. This is given temporal as well as spatial form.[14] In 'Naples', Benjamin notes that 'a grain of Sunday is hidden in each weekday, and how much weekday in this Sunday!' (*OWS*, p. 172). The ritual life of religion and the mundane, day-to-day activities of the ordinary people interpenetrate and merge to form a single totality. Benjamin notes that 'irresistibly the festival penetrates each and every working day' (*OWS*, p. 171).[15] Naples is 'crammed full of festal motifs nestling in the most inconspicuous places' (*OWS*, p. 172).

Roman Catholicism permeates and saturates every aspect of Neapolitan life. The city is 'held together at the corners, as if by iron clamps, by the murals of the Madonna' (*OWS*, p. 170). Part of this fusion of sacred and profane is the tolerant attitude taken by the Catholic Church towards the vices and misdeeds of its congregation. Benjamin notes:

> Nowhere can this people live out its rich barbarism, which has its roots in the city itself, more securely than in the lap of the Church. It needs Catholicism, for even its excesses are then legalised by a legend, the feast day of a martyr. Here Alfonso de Ligour was born, the saint who made the practice of the Catholic Church supple enough to accommodate the trade of the swindler and the whore. (*OWS*, p. 167)

It is not just these whom the Church condones, however. The priesthood is a fundamental part of the network of informal social control in Naples, acting as mediator in dealings between injured and guilty parties and the local criminal organization, the *camorristas*.[16] Toleration of indiscretions is reciprocal. Benjamin begins his essay on Naples with the description of the following rather extraordinary incident: 'Some years ago a priest was drawn through the streets of Naples for indecent offences. He was followed by a crowd hurling maledictions. At a corner a wedding procession appeared. The priest stands up and makes the sign of the cross and the cart's pursuers fall on their knees' (ibid.).[17]

This spectacle, which opens Benjamin's essay, may seem a rather trivial incident, but it has both thematic and methodological significance. First, it reflects a number of substantive themes in his essay: the continual inversion of sacred and profane, the power of

Catholicism,[18] and the public and carnivalistic form of Neapolitan life. Most important, though, it is suggestive of Benjamin's technique in the 'thought-images', for it is precisely in such marginal events that Benjamin seeks his most precious insights. His concern is not just with the physiognomic reading of the city's architecture, but with the manner in which social forms and patterns may be condensed in particular incidents and concisely represented in specific images. Whether it is the chastisement of a miscreant clergyman, a streetcar ride ('Moscow'), the forlorn search for peacock's feathers ('Berlin Chronicle' and 'Childhood') or the precautions taken by a pedestrian crossing the street (Paris),[19] Benjamin regards the marginalia of the city as the most important clues for its decipherment.

Porosity and improvisation   The notion of public spectacle is particularly important in Naples. The concept of porosity embraces improvisation[20] and performance. The city is transformed into a theatre. Benjamin writes: 'porosity results not only from the indolence of the Southern artisan, but also, above all, from the passion for improvisation, which demands that space and opportunity be at any price preserved. Buildings are used as a popular stage' (*OWS*, p. 170). This representation of the urban setting as theatre and of social life as drama and performance are recurrent though always underdeveloped facets of Benjamin's city writings.[21] The metaphor is above all an attempt to establish a relationship between the physical structure of the city and the activities of its inhabitants, to conceptualize the physiognomical. Benjamin writes: 'buildings and action interpenetrate in the courtyards, arcades and stairways. In everything they preserve the scope to become a theatre of new, unforeseen constellations' (*OWS*, pp. 169–70). Neapolitan life is a fluid, unpredictable drama in which the city becomes a theatre for a host of improvised activities and ostentatious performances. Benjamin relates the manner in which the opening of the underground system in the city was transformed into a carnivalistic celebration. He writes: 'how could I forget the opening of the underground railway, which one was unable to use for days because all the ticket offices were besieged by street children, whose clamour drowned out the drone of the arriving train and whose ear-splitting screams filled the tunnels during the journey' (*GS* III, p. 135).[22]

It is with respect to the economic life of the city that the theatrical character of Naples is principally described, however. Benjamin identifies a number of *ad hoc*, fluid configurations based upon gambling and idleness, swindling and begging, and the bazaar and the auction. Gambling provides the essential model for economic activity in the city. Benjamin writes:

> Lotto, alluring and consuming as nowhere else in Italy, remains the archetype of business life. Every Saturday at four o'clock, crowds form in front of the house where the numbers are drawn. Naples is one of the few cities with its own draw. With the pawnshop and lotto the state holds the proletariat in a vice: what it advances to them in one hand it takes back in the other. The more discreet and liberal intoxication of Hazard, in which the whole family takes part, replaces that of alcohol. And business life is assimilated to it. (*OWS*, p. 173)

Gain depends not so much upon rational calculation and sustained industry as upon speculation and idleness. Prosperity is awarded or withheld by fate rather than by individual activity. Gambling is an aspect of what Benjamin terms 'the phantasmagoria of modernity'. In the *Passagenarbeit* he notes that in gambling the link between (labour-) time and money is severed. Its corollary is thus indolence.[23] This equation is prefigured in 'Naples', where Benjamin writes: 'Trade, deeply rooted in Naples, borders on a game of chance and adheres closely to the holiday. The well-known list of the seven deadly sins located pride in Genoa, avarice in Florence, voluptuousness in Venice, anger in Bologna, greed in Milan, envy in Rome, and indolence in Naples' (ibid.). Commercial enterprise corresponds to the dictates of chance. The Neapolitan is above all an economic opportunist, ever ready to turn an accident or event into a source of pecuniary gain. Benjamin relates the following anecdote as symptomatic:

> There are delightful stories of the Neapolitan's playful love of trade. In a busy piazza a fat lady drops her fan. She looks around helplessly; she is too unshapely to pick it up herself. A cavalier appears and is prepared to perform his service for fifty *lire*. They negotiate and the lady receives her fan for ten. (*OWS*, pp. 173–4).

One may wonder if this is such a 'delightful' story for the humiliated, impoverished fat lady, but this does not seem to worry Benjamin unduly. The important point is that, for Benjamin, Naples is the site of the swindle. It is where cunning and quick-wittedness are paramount attributes. Performance and theatre are essential components of this. The making of money involves 'the virtuosity of the variety show' (*OWS*, p. 171).[24] The

nearby ruins of Pompeii provide a host of opportunities for
financial acquisition. Benjamin notes that 'everything that the
foreigner desires, admires and pays for is "Pompeii" ' (*OWS*,
p. 169). It is in Pompeii that 'swindling and wretchedness finally
come home' (ibid.). The ruins have a very different significance for
the tourist and the local inhabitant. Whereas for the former they
are an object of contemplation, for the latter they have an
immediate, practical utility as a source of income. For the
Neapolitan, the ruins are not 'dead', but are rather a means of
earning a living. Depending on prevailing interests, the present
enters into distinctive relationships and forms particular configurations with objects from the past. The old is refunctioned in the
context of the present. As will become clear, this is an important
insight for Benjamin in his development of a critical historical
method.

Buck-Morss states that ' "Naples" speaks of the routinisation of
swindle and the professionalisation of begging' (1989, p. 26).
Elsewhere a marginal figure,[25] the beggar is centre stage in
Naples. Benjamin writes: 'Even the most wretched pauper is
sovereign in the dim, dual awareness of participating, in all his
destitution, in one of the pictures of Neapolitan street life that will
never return, and of enjoying in all his poverty the leisure to
follow the great panorama' (*OWS*, p. 170). In Naples poverty and
misery are on display throughout the city; the normal and the
abnormal coexist. In his later writings, Benjamin draws attention
to the confinement and seclusion of forms of abnormality in the
modern city, and, in particular, stresses the significance of the
removal of polluting or disturbing figures from view. The sick, the
dying, the deformed and the insane are institutionalized and
thereby rendered 'invisible'. The Neapolitan beggar, by contrast,
is highly visible. Benjamin writes: 'a beggar lies in the road
propped up against the sidewalk, waving his empty hat like a
leave-taker at a station' (*OWS*, p. 168). The monstrous and the
cruel are not concealed behind the thin façades of modern
civilization, but are shockingly displayed. Naples relishes its own
'rich barbarism'. Indeed, as Benjamin observes in a rather
grotesque image, 'cripples put their deformities on show and the
shock given to day-dreaming passers-by is their joy' (ibid.).
Benjamin's emphasis upon the visibility of destitution in Naples is
not matched, however, by any incisive critique of the conditions
which produce it. In 'One-Way Street' he presents the following
rather contrived analogy: 'we deplore the beggars in the south
forgetting that their persistence in front of our noses is as justified

as a scholar's before a difficult text' (*OWS*, pp. 102–3). This is an obscure, uninformative characterization. The beggar and other figures of urban poverty and destitution, notably the rag-picker and the prostitute in the *Passagenarbeit*, are important elements in Benjamin's cityscapes, but his treatment of them is not always particularly sensitive or insightful. He never adequately grasped, perhaps, the hardships and miseries endured by the marginal figures of the city.

Begging, gambling (the *lotto*) and chicanery are all fundamentally public forms of activity, part of the theatricality of Neapolitan social life. Street-trading is the dominant form of exchange. In the streets of the city, a hotchpotch of assorted goods are unpacked and spread out in a random manner, and 'insolently, crudely, seductively displayed' (*OWS*, p. 174). This activity also has a dramatic dimension. Benjamin writes: 'on another occasion when I got up early, I saw a street-trader arrive who unpacked his wares. The way he did it, though, was a real theatrical performance' (*GS* VII, p. 210). The activities of buying and selling are not confined to specific, purpose-built, interior settings in Naples, but are improvised forms that occur at random in the bustling street. Patterns of modern capitalist production and consumption are poorly developed in Naples. There are no packaged commodities advertised and arranged in formal displays. Features characteristic of modern metropolitan centres, which for Benjamin come to define and generate particular forms of urban experience, are crucially absent or marginal in this city. He notes: 'there is a department store, in other cities the rich magnetic centre of purchasing. Here it is devoid of charm, outdone by the tightly packed multiplicity' (*OWS*, p. 174).

The bazaar, with its bargaining and haggling, its on-the-spot negotiation, is the principal site of commerce in Naples. Porosity and indeterminacy are once again the prevailing features. The possible, the new, merges, however, into the predictable, the old, the unchanging. An essential component of the theatrical character of social life in the city is the Neapolitan love of gesture.[26] Benjamin notes:

> The language of gesture goes further here than anywhere else in Italy. The conversation is impenetrable to anyone from outside. Ears, nose, eyes, breast and shoulders are signalling stations activated by the fingers. These configurations return in their fastidiously specialised eroticism. Helping gestures and impatient touches attract the stranger's attention through a regularity that excludes chance. (*OWS*, p. 176)

Communication in Naples is elaborately choreographed. The spontaneity of the opportunist swindler is matched by the ritualistic performance of the street-vendor, the chaos of the bazaar by the rehearsed drama of the auction. This is the basis of Neapolitan 'business manners' (*OWS*, p. 173). Benjamin describes the activity of the street-vendor thus:

> when, growing heated, he asks fantastic prices, and, while serenely folding up the large cloth that he has spread out for five hundred *lire*, drops the price at every fold, and finally, when it lies diminished on his arm, is ready to part with it for fifty, he has been true to the most ancient fairground practices. (ibid.)

Performance and improvisation combine and coalesce with the repetition of traditional, ritualized forms. The intimate connection between economic exchange and the holiday is illuminating in this respect: the holiday is not only a day of inactivity and rest, but also of festival. The festival 'penetrates each and every working day', transforming the mundane into the extraordinary, street-trade into improvised street-theatre, the city into the locus of carnival.

Naples is a peculiar city. It lacks the spatial and temporal structuring principles characteristic and constitutive of metropolitan life. Modern patterns of socio-economic and political organization exist only in the most incipient and rudimentary state. Thus, Naples may be understood as the site of experiences that may be designated 'traditional', 'communal' or 'premodern' in form. As a consequence of its underdevelopment, it is the locus of the antiquated and the outdated. Buck-Morss points out that 'one sees neither an ancient society nor a modern one, but an improvisatory culture released, and even nourished by the city's rapid decay' (1989, p. 27). It is a lingering, distorted remnant of the archaic in the modern epoch. In his encounter with it, Benjamin seeks to give voice to the anachronistic status of Naples, to express the confrontation between a modern sensibility and a premodern environment, to articulate what may be termed the 'shock of the old'. Porosity, the term he introduces to give voice to such an experience, is interwoven with three different visions of the city, which come to constitute a set of recurring motifs in Benjamin's city writings. The metropolis appears as a place of losing oneself and disorientation (labyrinth), as a site of decay and transience (ruin), and as a place of spontaneity and performance (theatre).

Benjamin claims that in Naples 'nothing is enjoyable, except the famous drinking water' (*OWS*, p. 168). Despite this, he seems to be favourably impressed by it. He sees the activities of the swindler as providing 'delightful stories'. He is appreciative of the city's 'rich barbarism', its robust physicality and ritual theatricality. According to Benjamin, the impermanence and fluidity of spatial and temporal boundaries facilitate spontaneous activity and mirror 'the most radiant freedom of thought'. Naples exists, it seems, in a perpetual state of 'blissful confusion' (*OWS*, p. 174). This reflects a somewhat superficial analysis, however. The chaos and disorder of the city, on the one hand, and the dubious economic practices engaged in by its inhabitants, on the other, are the result not so much of any conscious rejection of systems of modern capitalist order, but of economic underdevelopment, poverty, overcrowding and squalor. Although Benjamin states that in Naples 'poverty and misery seem as contagious as they are pictured to be to children' (*OWS*, p. 168), an incisive, sustained critical engagement with the socio-economic and political forces at work is conspicuously lacking. Benjamin's analysis severs the city from its wider context. Naples appears as an island, a separate, disconnected entity. At the time of Benjamin's visit, Mussolini was in power in Italy, and the Fascist state was in the process of construction; yet these factors are completely overlooked.

Such limitations result from the formal character of the *Denkbilder*. Benjamin advocates the utilization of images of urban life largely shorn of theoretical underpinning and development. He seeks to abstain from abstraction and engage instead in what Adorno was later to condemn as the 'wide-eyed presentation of mere facts' (*AP*, p. 129). The *Denkbilder* are literary 'snapshots', intended to freeze and capture the momentary, fragmentary minutiae of mundane urban existence. They are initial attempts at a mode of representation which will capture the fleeting and transient as the definitive experiences of the city. Their shortcomings stem from an unthematized facticity and an unhelpful ahistoricity. Benjamin's later cityscapes sought to reconcile this fascination for the ephemeral and marginal with the possibility of a sophisticated critical historical analysis through the notions of the 'monad' (in which the universal is discernible within the particular) and the 'dialectical image' (in which the historical object comes into being in the momentary intersection of past and present).

Although 'nothing is enjoyable', Benjamin clearly finds the loud, joyful, boisterous character of Neapolitan social life appealing. In Naples the carnivalesque and the grotesque combine. It is perhaps here that the experimental character of the essay is most evident. For one may discern a characteristic fluctuation between an appreciation of the excitement and stimulation found in the metropolitan environment and a rejection of the city as a locus of barbarism. The city is the space simultaneously of intoxication and of inhumanity. *This* incongruity, however, is not one that Benjamin will resolve in his subsequent writings on the city. It is, rather, precisely the paradox that animates and pervades all his cityscapes. Naples is both beautiful and bestial, Heaven and Hell. Perhaps the most significant feature of 'Naples' is not the porosity of the city, but the indeterminacy of Benjamin's response to it. As Brodersen points out, 'an entire philosophical programme and mode of perception is concealed by the concepts of "porosity" and "interpenetration" respectively' (1990, p. 159). Porosity as ambivalence, as hesitation, as paradox: these are the principal legacies of Benjamin's essay.

Moscow

Introduction

Benjamin's essay on Moscow is the second of the city portraits I wish to consider. In this and related texts one finds a more elaborate, more explicit articulation of many of the themes and problems encountered in his earlier *Denkbild* on Naples. Benjamin's visit to Moscow lasted from 6 December 1926 until 1 February 1927. He arrived in the new Soviet capital from Berlin with hopes of a fruitful and perhaps lengthy stay in the city, but his expectations were not to be fulfilled. A number of personal, political and pecuniary factors – or, more accurately, dilemmas – prompted his trip. In the first instance, Benjamin travelled to Moscow to visit Asja Lacis. Her poor health – she was staying at a sanatorium while recuperating from an illness – meant that she was seldom able to venture out. As a result, Benjamin spent much of his time in the city either alone, struggling to understand and make himself understood in a language in which he made little progress, or in the company of Lacis's friend Bernhard Reich who, although he was Benjamin's only link with the Soviet literary and cultural milieu, was to prove a source of continual irritation.

But Benjamin also had political motives for his journey. Toying with, albeit subsequently rejecting, the idea of joining the German Communist Party, the KPD, he wanted to examine for himself the prevailing system and mode of life in post-Revolutionary Russia. He wished to experience directly the great Communist experiment and assess its socio-cultural impact and prospects.[27] He was especially interested in cultural and artistic developments in the new Soviet state: the situation and tendencies of the Russian *avant-garde*, innovations in drama and theatre, and the conditions and productions of the Soviet film industry. He went primarily with questions, but soon discovered that 'the only real guarantee of a correct political understanding is to have chosen your position before you came. In Russia above all, you can only see if you have already decided' (*OWS*, p. 177). Consequently, his stay served only to perpetuate and exacerbate his political uncertainty and indecision. Benjamin visited Moscow believing that 'it obliges everyone to choose his stand-point' (ibid.), and was to return having evaded precisely any such decision. The fluctuating fortunes of his tense relationship with Lacis and his ambivalent response to Soviet society (the two being interwoven) hence underpin his writings about the city.

Practical and financial considerations were also at the root of the Moscow trip. Benjamin was, initially at least, considering the possibility of moving to Moscow on a more permanent basis. During his stay, therefore, he sought to establish some preliminary official connections through Reich with representatives of the Russian *avant-garde* and the Soviet Prolecult (the official organization for the development of proletarian cultural life). In this he was also unsuccessful. Hoping for much-needed funds, he wrote an article on Goethe for inclusion in the new Soviet encyclopedia, only to have it bluntly rejected by the compilers. He thus had to rely on other sources of income. The trip was partially paid for by an advance from Martin Buber, who had commissioned Benjamin to write an account of his impressions of Moscow and the Soviet Union for his journal *Die Kreatur*. In total, some four articles stemming from the visit appeared in the journal in the course of 1927, including the essay 'Moscow'.[28] It is the themes contained within this text, combined with those found in Benjamin's highly personal, illuminating and often touching *Moscow Diary* (from which the essay was principally composed), that I wish to examine in this section.

The experiment begun in 'Naples', that of giving literary form to the experience of the urban environment, is continued and developed in 'Moscow'. In particular, the methodological prescriptions that were pioneered in the earlier essay are explicitly formulated in Benjamin's letters following the Moscow visit. The fundamental principles of the *Denkbilder* are given formal expression in the following two extracts. In a letter of 23 February 1927 to

Siegfried Kracauer, Benjamin writes of his proposed essay thus: 'I am planning to write something "comprehensive" about Moscow. But as is so often the case with me, this will probably divide itself up into particularly small and disparate notes and for the most part, the reader will be left to his own devices' (*MOD*, p. 129). On the same day he wrote to Buber, informing him that

> My presentation will be devoid of all theory. In this fashion I hope to succeed in allowing the creatural to speak for itself: inasmuch as I have succeeded in seizing and rendering this very new and disorienting language that echoes loudly through the resounding mask of an environment that has been totally transformed. I want to write a description of Moscow at the present moment in which 'all factuality is already theory' and which would thereby refrain from any deductive abstraction, from any prognostication, and even within certain limits from any judgement. (*MOD*, p. 6)

Benjamin's desire to produce an essay that is 'devoid of all theory' is illuminating in two respects. First, the purpose of the *Denkbilder* becomes evident. They are intended as 'snapshots' of urban life. Their theoretical underpinning is paradoxically the elimination or absence of any theory as such. In these textual fragments Benjamin is concerned not with the development of some grand, overarching theoretical framework, but with rendering the fleeting moments and minute details of urban existence through 'small and disparate notes'. His interest is in the immediate, concrete representation (or self-representation) of the material. The 'creatural', an obvious reference to the name of Buber's journal, is to be unfolded from within. The *Denkbilder* are to be 'transparent', so as to allow the phenomena to reveal themselves, to show through. The mute comes to 'speak for itself' in the silence afforded by the absence of commentary. The *Denkbilder* are formal, textual experiments in which Benjamin endeavours to erase or decentre himself as an author and so 'leave the reader to his own devices'. In this respect, they clearly prefigure his later collection and use of quotations in the *Passagenarbeit*.

Second, the limitations of such an approach – and in particular his problematic relationship to the historical materialist enterprise at this point – are highlighted. In his rejection of theoretical structures, Benjamin does not so much eschew a Marxist perspective as conflate materialism with a commitment to immediacy. Yet, it is precisely this 'wide-eyed' approach which forbids a sufficiently sophisticated, thoroughgoing critical engagement with the phenomena of the urban complex. A tension that comes to animate Benjamin's cityscapes has its origins here: namely, the need to reconcile an approach that does justice to the phenomena under consideration (immanent) with one that retains critical insight and power (redemptive). In other words, the dilemma which increasingly confronts Benjamin centres on how to combine a 'heightened graphicness' (N2,6, Smith ed., 1989, p. 48) with a historical materialist perspective, how to read and write the city at the same time. This is the central methodological concern of the *Passagenarbeit*, and is clearly foreshadowed in the essay on Moscow. Benjamin subsequently attempted to reconcile the demands of concreteness and facticity with those of a critical theory of society through the marriage of elements of Surrealism and Marxism, through the integration of modernist and historical materialist perspectives.

It is not only formally and methodologically, but also thematically that the Naples and Moscow pieces are linked. Benjamin's concern with the relationship between (and juxtapositioning of) the new and the old, the archaic and the modern, is developed and given particular emphasis in his writings on the Soviet city. He contrasts modern, collective forms of social and economic organization with traditional modes of perception and activity, which he terms 'Asiatic'. His preoccupation with the forms of temporal and spatial organization is elaborated with regard to the new rhythms demanded by Soviet industrialization and the shifting patterns of the Muscovite street and interior settings. Above all, the relationships between private and public, the individual and the collectivity, the intellectual and the worker, are explored in the Moscow writings, thus reflecting the very quandary he sought to resolve during his brief residence there. In the remainder of this chapter I will consider Benjamin's examination of these themes.

Technology and modernization

The relationship between the metropolitan environment and modern technological development is a crucial theme in 'Moscow'. The revolutionary, progressive potential of new technological forms and their reactionary utilization for the purposes of capitalist accumulation and domination were to become important in Benjamin's later writings. Indeed, a principal concern of his subsequent cityscapes is the manner in which the urban setting constitutes a display case or stage for technological

accomplishments, scientific innovations and new industrial
products. The metropolis presents itself as the pre-eminent site of
progress. In his 'Arcades Project' Benjamin explores the technological fantasies of mid-nineteenth-century Paris, and, in particular, attempts to unmask world fairs as events dedicated to the
fetishistic celebration of commodity production and the domination of nature. In 'Moscow', however, Benjamin is keen to
emphasize the positive aspects of the connection between the
Revolution and technological innovation. Lacis played an important part in shaping this initial formulation. Benjamin notes that,
following an argument with her on 13 January 1927 over some
unspecified comments in the *Moscow Diary*:

> She spoke of how she herself had not understood Russia in the least
> at the outset, how she had wanted to go back to Europe a few weeks
> after her arrival because everything had seemed finished in Russia
> and the opposition was absolutely correct. Gradually she had
> realised what was in fact taking place here: the conversion of
> revolutionary effort into technological effort. Now it is made clear to
> every communist that at this hour revolutionary work does not
> signify conflict or civil war, but rather electrification, canal construc-
> tion, creation of factories. (*MOD*, p. 82)

Lacis's argument clearly had a considerable impact upon
Benjamin, for he incorporated the thrust of this version of
revolutionary practice in 'Moscow'.[29] A central concern of the
essay is the transformation of everyday experience in Moscow
resulting from new technological developments and the accom-
panying changes in industrial practices. In a letter of 5 June 1927 to
Hofmannsthal, Benjamin writes: 'I have concentrated less on
visual than on rhythmic experience, an experience in which an
archaic Russian tempo blends into a whole with the new rhythms
of the Revolution, an experience which, by Western standards, I
have discovered to be far more incommensurable than I had
expected' (*MOD*, p. 134).[30] In Moscow one encounters not a
decaying, underdeveloped capitalist economic structure, but a
particular form of technological development and collectivized
modernization. The Revolution is concerned with the wholesale
replacement of the old by the new. Benjamin's account of Moscow
is underpinned by an attempt to give voice to the experience of
transformation and the transformation of experience. In a letter to
Buber he writes:

> Moscow as it appears at present reveals a full range of possibilities in
> schematic form: above all the possibility that the Revolution might

fail or succeed. In either case, something unforeseeable will result and its picture will be far different from any programmatic sketch one might draw out of the future. The outlines of this are at present brutally and distinctly visible among the people and their environment. (*MOD*, pp. 6–7)

Moscow constitutes a 'theatre of the new', a site of the indeterminate that is neither hidebound by the ritual forms of the past nor yet resigned to the *ennui* of the always-the-same that Benjamin considers to be the hallmark of modern capitalist cities.[31] For him, the entire city of Moscow forms one giant scientific experiment. He writes:

Each thought, each day, each life lies here as on a laboratory table. And as if it were a metal from which an unknown substance is by every means to be extracted, it must endure experimentation to the point of exhaustion. No organism, no organisation, can escape this process. Employees in their factories, offices in buildings, pieces of furniture in the apartments are rearranged, transferred and shoved about. New ceremonies for christening and marriage are presented in the clubs as at research institutes. Regulations are changed from day to day, but street-car stops migrate, too, shops turn into restaurants and a few weeks later into offices. (*OWS*, pp. 185–6)

The confrontation between old and new in Moscow involves conflicting rhythms, contrasting perceptions of temporal order. The city is the locus of the traditional and enduring (which, paradoxically, involve spontaneity and unpredictability) and experimental and transient (which threaten to bring with them the repetitious and nothing-new). In 'Moscow', Benjamin notes that 'time catastrophes, time collisions are . . . the order of the day' (*OWS*, p. 190). He draws a distinction between 'Asiatic' and modern conceptions of time. The hallmark of the former is the failure or refusal to equate time with money. This results in a temporal 'intoxication'. Benjamin notes that in Moscow 'one is tempted to say that minutes are a cheap liquor of which they can never get enough, that they are tipsy with time' (*OWS*, pp. 189–90). Such a conception of time is later developed in Benjamin's writings on Paris with regard to the figures of the dawdling *flâneur* and the gambler. As yet unbounded by the discipline of modern temporal order, the Muscovite, like the *flâneur*, loses him or herself in the chance distractions encountered in the city. In Moscow, Benjamin notes, 'if on the street a scene is being shot for a film, they forget where they are going and why, and follow the camera for hours, arriving at the office distraught. In his use of time, the Russian will remain "Asiatic" longest of all' (*OWS*, p. 190). On the one hand, this 'Asiatic' perception is like that of the gambler for the immediate and instantaneous. The only intelligible unit of time in Moscow is 'at once', 'now'. On the other hand, the reality of this immediacy is continual deferment and postponement. Paradoxically, the 'at once' of Muscovite existence actually demands enduring patience and waiting. Benjamin writes: 'the real unit of time is the *seichas*. That means "at once". You hear it ten, twenty, thirty times and wait hours, days or weeks until the promise is carried out. Just as you seldom hear the answer "no". Negative replies are left to time' (ibid.). In the chaos of the 'Asiatic', time both contracts and expands, making 'each hour superabundant, each day exhausting, each life a moment' (ibid.).

These traditional forms are being supplanted by others, however. A vital element of the technological crusade in the Soviet capital is the development of a new mode of temporal understanding. Benjamin writes:

> A feeling for the value of time, notwithstanding all 'rationalisation', is not met with even in the capital of Russia. 'Trud', the trade union institute for the study of work, under its director Gastiev, launched a poster campaign for punctuality. . . . 'Time is money' – for this astonishing statement posters claim the authority of Lenin, so alien is the idea to Russians. (*OWS*, p. 189)

The 'new rhythms' of Soviet life are those of the machine-based modern industrial factory. The chaos of the 'Asiatic' is replaced by the regularity and constancy of factory time. By 1927, the Revolution had educated the Muscovite in the value of time and the notion of time as value. The Moscow of old, famous for its clock-*making*, gave way to new industrial practices entailing clock-*watching*.[32] The relationship between old and new perceptions of time in Moscow thus connects with another crucial theme of the cityscapes: the process of the commodification of time. In the great Soviet experiment, the 'Asiatic' perception is transformed into forms of commodity production in which the 'theatre of the new' is replaced by the repetition, predictability and boredom of the production line.

Moscow: prairie, village and labyrinth

The distinguishing feature of Moscow is that it scarcely appears to be a city at all. According to Benjamin, the city lacks the grand, monumental edifices that characterize the heart of the modern metropolitan environment. Instead, 'one- and two-storey buildings are typical of its architecture. They give it the appearance of a summer vacation colony' (*OWS*, p. 17). Lateral rather than vertical development is characteristic, and the skyline of the city is described by Benjamin thus: 'the roofs of Moscow are a lifeless wasteland, having neither the dazzling electric signs of Berlin, nor the forest of chimneys of Paris, nor the sunny solitude of the rooftops of great cities in the South' (*OWS*, p. 200). Lacking a concentrated, visibly distinguishable urban centre, Moscow consists instead of a vast, amorphous sprawl of low-rise structures. It is not so much a city as, Benjamin notes, borrowing Reich's phrase, 'a prairie of architecture',[33] more an undifferentiated landscape than an urban complex.

This peculiarly rural appearance of the city is the key element in Benjamin's physiognomical reading of Moscow. It is the paradox that reveals the true character of the city. The city's physical structure is indicative of the confrontation between the traditional and modern patterns of life found within it. Architecturally, Moscow is not so much a modern metropolis as a sprawling 'urban village'. The chaos of traditional patterns of spatial organization still predominates, although centralized urban planning is being implemented. Moscow remains nothing other than a 'gigantic village' (*OWS*, p. 191) inhabited by a 'peasant population' (*OWS*, p. 190). Benjamin writes: 'in the streets of Moscow there is a curious state of affairs: the Russian village is playing hide-and-seek in them' (*OWS*, p. 202). In the centre of the city, the home of the Revolutionary experiment, the traces of the city's peasant origins are half-concealed but none the less discernible. The Muscovite house betrays its rural ancestry: 'wooden staircases give the backs of the houses, which look like city buildings from the front, the appearance of Russian farmhouses' (*OWS*, p. 203).

Just as in Naples a grain of Sunday was present in each weekday, so in Moscow a remnant of the rural resides, albeit barely perceptibly, behind the city's architectural façades. There is a subtle distinction here, though. In Moscow the old exists behind or beside the new, not within it. The archaic and modern are juxtaposed, not merged. Coexistence, rather than the 'porosity' characteristic of Neapolitan society, is evident. The old does not so much permeate the new as persist incongruously alongside it. Benjamin notes that 'in the suburban streets leading off the broad avenues, peasant huts alternate with *art nouveau* villas or with the sober façades of eight-storey blocks' (ibid.). This is a particularly striking image. The peasant dwelling, the bourgeois modernist-inspired villa and the new purpose-built proletarian mass residence exist side by side. The traditional, the *avant-garde* and the collectivist co-habit in the vast 'summer vacation colony' constituted by Moscow. The archaic lingers in the uncolonized niches and crevices of the modern city. Although these enduring remnants of the pre-Revolutionary epoch occupy an increasingly anachronistic, marginal position within the city, they are not concealed within, but defiantly wedged between, the modernist and the modern in the suburbs. Benjamin writes of such districts:

> The village character of Moscow suddenly leaps out at you undisguisedly, evidently, unambiguously in the streets of its suburbs. There is probably no other city whose gigantic urban spaces have such an amorphous, rural quality, as if their expanses were always being dissolved by bad weather, thawing snow or rain. The street-car line ended in front of an inn situated in one of these expanses that was no longer urban and not yet quite rural. (*MOD*, p. 112)

While the suburbs are 'no longer urban and not yet quite rural', Moscow itself is no longer rural, yet not quite urban. Benjamin observes: 'nowhere does Moscow look like the city itself; at most, it resembles its outskirts' (*OWS*, p. 203).

Chaotic, amorphous and sprawling, Moscow is an architectural wilderness. Undistinguished, devoid of monuments and memorable edifices, dazzling, the snow-bound city is a space in which navigation is impossible. Like Naples, it has a labyrinthine quality. It is a space of disorientation in which one can easily lose oneself. Benjamin states:

> the city turns into a labyrinth for the newcomer. Streets that he had located far apart are yoked together by a corner like a pair of horses in a coachman's fist. The whole exciting sequence of topographical dummies that deceives him could only be shown by a film: the city is on its guard against him, masks itself, flees, intrigues, lures him to wander its circles to the point of exhaustion. (*OWS*, p. 179)

This is an intriguing passage for two reasons. First, the reference to the 'newcomer' (*Neuling*) is important. Benjamin is here giving voice to the experience and perception of a stranger to the city, an outsider. The visitor is reduced to a state of powerlessness before the unknown urban complex, and becomes lost within its labyrinthine structure.[34] There is also another 'newcomer' to the city, a stranger within its spaces: the child. Benjamin notes that in

Moscow, 'the instant one arrives, the childhood stage begins. On the thick sheet of ice on the streets walking has to be relearned' (ibid.). This theme of the outsider-as-child is noted by Szondi: 'the foreign surroundings do not just replace the distance of childhood for the adult; they turn him into a child again' (Smith ed., 1988, p. 22). The notion of the child as a marginal or peripheral figure in the urban setting finds its initial articulation in 'Moscow'.[35] It is here that the relationships between knowing and unknowing, the 'at first sight' and the 'habitually seen' find their first, tentative formulation in the equation of stranger and child. For both, the city is mysterious and unfathomable. The visitor to the city, like the child, is unable to decipher and read street signs and notices (Benjamin's knowledge of Russian was, we may recall, extremely limited). Moscow is the locus of an arcane, untranslatable language, a site of linguistic as well as spatial disorientation.[36]

Second, Benjamin's claim that the bewildering maze of streets in the Soviet capital can be known through film is significant.[37] It is the moving image that best captures the topography of the city. This is a fundamental insight for Benjamin, and film becomes the model for his cityscapes. The analysis and representation of the urban setting, the quintessential modern environment, is to be achieved through the newest artistic medium. According to Benjamin, film plays a key role in overcoming the distance which separates viewer and viewed, subject and object.[38] As a medium, it has an 'immediate quality' which destabilizes established ways of seeing and generates new insight and understanding. In the 'Work of Art' essay Benjamin states:

> In and of themselves, these offices, furnished rooms, bars, city streets, railway stations, and factories are ugly, incomprehensible, hopelessly sad. Or rather: they were so and seemed so, until film came along. Film then exploded this entire dungeon-world with the dynamite of the tenth of a second, so that now, among its far-flung debris, we set out on long adventurous journeys. (cited by McCole, 1993, p. 192[39])

In its use of close-up and slow motion, film transforms our perception of time and space, and reveals new facets of the city's forms and character.[40] Furthermore, film captures the fleeting, fluid character of the modern metropolitan environment. In their ability to freeze and redeem the momentary and fragmentary, the *Denkbilder*, as literary 'snapshots', aspire to be textual equivalents of the cinematographic, to mimic it. In 'Moscow', 'thought-pictures' lead to 'moving pictures', to a sense of motion that

Benjamin subsequently attempts to realize in his use of the montage principle and the concept of the dialectical image.

Benjamin's concern with perspective and proximity is manifest in another guise in 'Moscow'. The principal mode of transport is the sleigh, which exists in a variety of forms 'of the most diverse construction' (*OWS*, p. 203). The sleigh offers the perfect vantage-point from which to observe the daily life of the city. Riding in a small sledge (*izvozchik*):

> The passenger is not enthroned high up; he looks out on the same level as everyone else and brushes the passers-by with his sleeve. Even this is an incomparable experience for the sense of touch. Where Europeans, on their rapid journeys, enjoy superiority, dominance over the masses, the Muscovite in the little sleigh is closely mingled with people and things. . . . No condescending gaze: a tender, swift brushing along stones, people, and horses. You feel like a child gliding through the house on its little chair. (*OWS*, p. 191)

While the sleigh-ride offers the passenger a rather different set of 'moving pictures', it does, like film, facilitate a particular proximity to the life of the street. It permits immersion in, rather than an overview of, the hustle and bustle of the urban landscape. This immediacy is interestingly linked to the experience of the child. A central theme developed in the Berlin writings is the peculiar affinity of the child for the world of objects. As we will see in the next chapter, Benjamin argues that the child has, as a result of his or her playfulness, a closeness to things that is superseded in the adult by a sense of 'superiority' and a 'condescending gaze'. In its depiction of the child as, on the one hand, a stranger to the city and, on the other, a privileged witness to its spaces and artefacts, 'Moscow' prefigures key thematic elements in the Berlin writings of 1932. It is no coincidence that the essay on the Russian city begins: 'More quickly than Moscow one gets to know Berlin through Moscow' (*OWS*, p. 177). In the sprawling, snow-bound urban village of Moscow, Benjamin begins to retrace his steps to the city of his birth.

The other principal form of transport in the city, the streetcar, reflects the incongruous mixture of the modern and the antiquated in the urban environment. Benjamin writes: 'the complete interpenetration of technological and primitive modes of life, this world-historical experiment in the new Russia is illustrated in miniature by a street-car ride' (*OWS*, p. 190). To travel on the trams of the city, which are 'painted all over with pictures of factories, mass meetings, red regiments, Communist agitators' (*OWS*, p. 199), is above all, Benjamin notes, 'a tactical experience' (*OWS*, p. 190). One must learn to negotiate the jostling, shoving crowds who board and cram the streetcar to the 'point of bursting' (ibid.). Benjamin contrasts them with the conductresses, who stand 'fur-wrapped at their places like Samoyed women on a sleigh' (ibid.). An 'illustration in miniature', the account of the streetcar journey functions in 'Moscow' in exactly the same manner as does the description of the procession of the guilty priest in 'Naples': it is a monad, a crystallization of the totality of Muscovite life. As in the city itself, the revolutionary (the designs painted on the vehicles), the 'Asiatic' (the peasant-dressed women) and the modern (the scrambling metropolitan crowd) combine.

Moreover, the city is as full and congested as the streetcar. One of the chief hallmarks of modern metropolitan experience for Benjamin is the encounter with the anonymous, seething multitude that inhabits the city's streets. This is particularly acute in Moscow because of the narrowness of the city's pavements. Benjamin notes: 'nowhere else, except here and there in Naples, do you find pavements this narrow. They give Moscow a provincial air, or rather the character of an improvised metropolis that has fallen into place overnight' (*MOD*, p. 31). There are no great thoroughfares in Moscow along which the dawdling pedestrian may saunter, no boulevards with sufficient elbow-room to accommodate the dallying *flâneur*. Instead, the limited space on which to walk ensures that the city is cramped and overcrowded. Benjamin remarks that in Berlin 'the breadth of the pavements is princely. They make of the poorest wretch a *grand seigneur* promenading on the terrace of his mansion. Princely solitude, princely desolation. . . . In Moscow there are three or four places where it is possible to make headway without the strategy of shoving and weaving that one learns in the first week' (*OWS*, p. 178). The dense urban crowd necessitates the adoption by the pedestrian of a distinctive 'serpentine gait' (ibid.). It is not only the 'jungle of houses' that is 'impenetrable' in Moscow, then, but also the agglomeration of human bodies. For Benjamin, the metropolitan crowd itself thus comes to form a mobile labyrinth within the confines of the maze of the city, a theme he was to develop in his writings on Paris.

An important aspect of the vitality of Muscovite street life is the abundance of street-traders. Benjamin notes: 'what fullness has this street that overflows not only with people. . . . In Moscow goods burst everywhere from the houses, they hang on fences, lean against railings, lie on pavements' (ibid.). Benjamin's description of the street-vendor in 'Moscow' is one of a number of similarities with 'Naples'. In both cities street-trading is a dominant form of exchange. Even in Moscow in mid-winter, it is the street rather than any interior space that is the primary locus for the buying and selling of goods, as if, Benjamin notes, 'it were not twenty-five degrees below but high Neapolitan summer' (*OWS*, p. 181). The bazaar with its random, chaotic arrangement of artefacts is characteristic of the Muscovite market. The improvised, *ad hoc*, rather than the formally packaged and displayed, predominate. Of the Sucharevskaia market Benjamin writes: 'the people simply have their wares lying in the snow. One finds old locks, metre rulers, hand tools, kitchen utensils, electrical goods. Repairs are carried out on the spot; I saw someone soldering over a pointed flame' (ibid.). The peculiar assemblage of objects for sale is a metaphor for Moscow generally. The bizarre juxtaposition of diverse wares would indeed not be inappropriate in a Surrealist still life. It is this incongruity that doubtless appeals to Benjamin when he writes: 'shoe polish and writing materials, handkerchiefs, dolls' sleighs, swings for children, ladies' underwear, stuffed birds, clothes-hangers – all this sprawls in the open street' (*OWS*, pp. 181–2).

There is an uncanny similarity between the goods of the street-vendor and the jumble of obsolete commodities housed in the dilapidated shopping arcades of Paris. Such a connection is intriguing, because the Moscow texts contain one of the first references to the consumer palaces of the nineteenth century. Benjamin notes:

> The luxury that has lodged itself in this ailing run-down city like tartar in a diseased mouth: the N. Kraft chocolate store, the elegant fashion boutique on Petrovka, with its immense porcelain vases standing among the furs, hideous and frigid. . . . Arcades. They contain an utterly indigenous array of tiers and galleries which appear to be as deserted as those of the cathedrals. (*MOD*, pp. 22–3)

The contrast between the vitality of the street and the gloomy, decaying interior is striking. As in contemporary Paris, the luxury shops of the arcades linger in the city as grand junk-rooms, as ruins. There is a distinction to be drawn here, however. The decline of the Muscovite arcade is not a matter of fashion or of changes in bourgeois consumer tastes. In Moscow it is capitalism itself, not just its monuments and edifices, that has become a thing of the past. Bypassed by the Revolution, capitalism is itself becoming archaic.

The streets of Moscow constitute 'an environment that has been totally transformed' (*MOD*, p. 6). This metamorphosis has not affected one particular figure though: the beggar. Despite the Soviet experiment, the 'unchanging wretchedness' (*OWS*, p. 185) of the city's beggars remains. Benjamin is principally concerned in the Moscow writings with the beggar as an emblem of permanence, of the nothing-new. The beggars and the poor 'alone are dependable, remaining unchanged in their place while everything around them shifts' (ibid.). Indeed, Benjamin notes that the beggar's lot has paradoxically been made worse by the Revolution: 'begging has lost its strongest foundation, the bad social conscience, which opens purses so much wider than does pity' (ibid.). The beggar is a static figure in the transformed space of the urban complex, and as such is fundamentally indicative of the continuity of past and present, of the intersection of old and new. The 'always-the-same' of suffering and destitution embodied in the Soviet beggar looks forward to Benjamin's writings on Paris, in which a pessimistic conceptualization of history as ongoing catastrophe plays a central role. For Benjamin, poverty and misery, embodied in the figure of the rag-picker, function as important counterpoints to the concepts of civilization and progress.

Benjamin's *Denkbilder* are mosaics of urban images and incidents. This is perhaps most apparent in the depiction of the Muscovite street, where one encounters a series of conflicting and incongruous images: the modern metropolitan crowd thronging the streets of the city centre and the fur-clad tram conductress; the packed streetcar daubed with revolutionary slogans and images of Party leaders and the assortment of sleighs gliding swiftly and silently through the streets, close to people and things; the street-vendor with his or her hotchpotch of wares and the dismal, run-down edifices of the arcades and luxury boutiques. Like the metropolis itself, the *Denkbilder* are kaleidoscopic entities, filled to 'the point of bursting' with such constellations of old and new, archaic and modern, enduring and fleeting.

Autonomy and solidarity

In Moscow the private sphere has been abolished. The bourgeois interior setting, like the arcades and the luxury shops, is a thing of the past, archaic, a ruin. It has been broken down and restructured (re-functioned) to accommodate the new proletarian masses. Benjamin writes: 'Bolshevism has abolished private life. The bureaucracy, political activity, the press are so powerful that no time remains for interests that do not converge with them. Nor any space. Apartments that earlier accommodated single families in their five to eight rooms now often lodge eight' (*OWS*, p. 187). In 'Moscow' Benjamin expresses his detestation of the cluttered comfort of the late nineteenth-century bourgeois interior, a theme that recurs in 'One-Way Street' and the Berlin studies. He writes contemptuously:

> An essential feature of the petty-bourgeois interior . . . was completeness: pictures must cover the walls, cushions the sofa, covers the cushions, ornaments fill the mantelpiece, coloured glass the windows. (Such petty-bourgeois rooms are battlefields over which the attack of commodity capital has advanced victoriously: nothing human can flourish there again.) Of all that, only a part here or there has been indiscriminately preserved. Weekly the furniture in the bare rooms is re-arranged – that is the only luxury indulged in with them, and at the same time a radical means of expelling 'cosiness', along with the melancholy with which it is paid for, from the house. (*OWS*, p. 188)

While dismissive of the suffocating, lifeless bourgeois home, Benjamin is not altogether enamoured of the reconstructed Muscovite domicile. The interior has been transformed from the melancholy, desolate 'battlefield' of commodity fetishism into an army camp, a small town, a whole city in miniature. He notes: 'Through the hall door one steps into a little town. More often still, an army camp. Even in the lobby one can encounter beds. Indoors one only camps, and usually the scanty interior is only a residue of petty-bourgeois possessions that have a far more depressing effect because the room is so sparsely furnished' (*OWS*, pp. 187–8). The interior, like the tram, is packed to the 'point of bursting' with people. Living space is accordingly strictly rationed. Each person, Benjamin points out, is 'entitled by law to only thirteen square metres of space' (*OWS*, p. 188). Space does not merge and interpenetrate as in Naples, but is rigidly delineated and allocated. As a result 'there is no "homeliness"' (*OWS*, p. 189). The 'melancholy' of the bourgeois home has been replaced by austerity. The rooms 'look like infirmaries after inspection' (*MOD*, p. 26). These Spartan proletarian 'barracks' are tolerable only because the domestic setting no longer forms a dominant locus of activity. 'People can bear to exist in [the Muscovite mass residence] because they are estranged from it by their way of life. Their dwelling place is the office, the club, the street' (*OWS*, p. 188). There is no longer the possibility of retreat from the public sphere into personal solitude. The work places and meeting-halls of the city are the principal sites of interaction, 'even for private affairs' (*OWS*, p. 189).

This destruction of the private domain is indicative of a profound transformation of Muscovite life. The very notions of the private, the individual and the idiosyncratic have themselves been abolished and replaced by the collective, the mass, the centralized. In such circumstances, one of the abiding themes of the cityscapes, the relationship between the individual and the urban population, takes on a special significance. The fate of the individual – or more precisely, of the intellectual – in the radically changed conditions of Soviet cultural life is perhaps *the* central issue for Benjamin in his writings on Moscow. The texts produced in connection with his visit bear witness to his overarching interest in the roles of the writer and the artist in post-Revolutionary society. This problem was a poignant one for Benjamin at that time; for the trip was undertaken to resolve his own dilemma regarding the possibility of involvement in the new literary institutions generated by the Party organization. The fundamental issue that haunts the Moscow writings – and indeed comes to influence much of Benjamin's subsequent work – is the acutely personal one of defining the responsibilities and obligations of the politically committed artist in particular and the *avant-garde* artist in general.

Benjamin rhetorically poses the question thus: 'what figure does the man of letters cut in a country where his employer is the proletariat?' (*OWS*, p. 197). In Moscow in 1927 such a position was defined and prescribed with the utmost clarity: the writer is obliged to place him or herself at the service of the 'employer' – that is, the masses. Benjamin notes that under the Bolshevik regime 'free trade and free intellect have been abolished' (*OWS*, p. 189). The independent imagination is instead harnessed to the cause of State and Party. As a consequence, 'the intellectual is above all a functionary' (*OWS*, p. 198), serving, through immersion in the Prolecult movement, the tastes of the proletariat and committed to the development of a revolutionary consciousness among those previously denied access to cultural artefacts. The didactic role of art is stressed. In Moscow, Benjamin notes, the

Revolution has brought with it new forms of cultural and artistic opportunities and awareness, a new relationship between art and audience. He writes the following of the Tretiakov Gallery, for example:

> Nothing is more pleasantly surprising on a visit to Moscow's museums than to see how, singly or in groups, sometimes around a guide, children and workers move easily through these rooms. Nothing is to be seen of the forlornness of the few proletarians who dare to show themselves to the other visitors in our museums. In Russia the proletariat has really begun to take possession of bourgeois culture, whereas on such occasions in our own country they have the appearance of planning a burglary. (*OWS*, p. 183)[41]

The aloof bourgeois intellectual, the self-styled artistic genius, has no place within such a system. The relationship between the writer/artist and the struggles of the proletariat is further developed in the essay 'The Author as Producer' of 1934. Here Benjamin writes: 'the Soviet State does not, like Plato's Republic, propose to expel its writers, but it does . . . propose to assign them tasks which will make it impossible for them to parade the richness of the creative personality, which has long been a myth and a fake, in new masterpieces' (*UB*, p. 97). Benjamin argues that the literary quality of a text and its political significance are intimately connected. A correct 'political tendency' (content) is inextricably bound up with a progressive 'literary tendency' (form). The adoption of radical literary techniques in conjunction with the use of innovative technology (newspapers, pamphlets, photographs) is vital for the progressive author. The writer's commitment to proletarian struggle derives not so much from sympathy with the sufferings of the working class, but from the recognition of his or her own position within the production process. Benjamin writes of the intellectual, the 'man of mind', thus:

> This man, says Döblin, should find his place at the side of the proletariat. But what sort of place is that? The place of a well-wisher, an ideological patron. An impossible place. And so we come back to the thesis we proposed at the beginning: the place of the intellectual in the class struggle can only be determined, or better still chosen, on the basis of his position within the production process. (*UB*, p. 93)

The progressive writer does not stand 'at the side of' the working class, but within it as a literary worker, a technician, a producer of cultural artefacts. He or she refunctions and transforms established literary forms, and is in turn changed 'from a supplier of the production apparatus, into an engineer who sees his task in adapting that apparatus to the ends of the proletarian revolution' (*UB*, p. 102). In the 'Work of Art' essay the following year, Benjamin reiterates this concern with technique, technology and progressive artistic practice. The capacity of modern technology to reproduce and replicate artworks brings with it the demise of 'aura', the traditional power of the original. To speak of an 'original' photograph or film as opposed to a copy makes no sense. For Benjamin, the multiplicity of the photographic image is the basis of a new, engaged, mass art-form. In 'Moscow', Benjamin notes that 'everything technical is sacred here, nothing is taken more earnestly than technique' (*MOD*, p. 55). Technique and technology – these have become the fundamental dimensions of progressive practice in post-Revolutionary Moscow. Benjamin's preoccupation in the mid-1930s with proletarian cultural forms and the pedagogical practice of radical artworks finds its initial stimulus here.

Benjamin is both drawn to the Prolecult movement and simultaneously dismayed by its primitive, rudimentary products. For example, on 29 December 1926 he went with Reich to see the Soviet actor Ilyinsky in a 'terrible film' (*MOD*, p. 52). The following day he wrote:

> It is extremely significant that a very run-of-the-mill Russian film actor, Ilyinsky, an unscrupulous, inept imitator of Chaplin, is considered a major comic here simply because Chaplin's films are so expensive that one doesn't get to see them here. . . . Russian film itself, apart from a few outstanding productions, is not all that good on the average. It is fighting for subject matter. Film censorship is in fact very strict. (*MOD*, pp. 54–5)

Film, the very medium that Benjamin advocated some ten years later as *the* critical proletarian medium, is of poor quality and subject to strict government control in Moscow. In the Prolecult, 'correct political tendency', rather than artistic or literary quality, unfortunately prevailed. It should have come as no surprise to Benjamin that his solitary attempt to produce material for the new Soviet encyclopedia was rejected by the compilers as unfit for proletarian consumption. His response to the eradication of the 'free intellect' from the context of the Soviet cultural experiment veers between the utmost enthusiasm and utter disillusionment.

On 8 January 1927, for example, he noted in *Moscow Diary* that 'the entire scheme of existence of the Western European intelligentsia is utterly impoverished in comparison to the countless constellations that offer themselves to an individual here in the space of a month' (*MOD*, p. 72). The next day's entry, however, has a rather different tone: 'Further considerations: join the Party? Clear advantages: a solid position, a mandate, even if only by implication. Organised, guaranteed contact with other people. On the other hand: to be a Communist in a state where the proletariat rules means giving up your private independence. You leave the responsibility for organising your own life up to the Party' (*MOD*, p. 73).

The 'free intellect' of the 'Western European intelligentsia' is no longer 'impoverished' but contains within it the 'seductiveness of the role of the trail-blazer' (ibid.). The Communist Party offers only practical advantages and securities, not intellectual stimulation and satisfaction. Benjamin is caught between his own 'private independence' and the allure of working for the collectivity, between his apparently irreconcilable desires for autonomy and solidarity. He poses his dilemma in Moscow in the following terms: 'whether one is going to remain in the hostile and exposed, uncomfortable and draughty spectator area, or whether one is going to adopt some sort of role in the commotion on stage' (*MOD*, p. 72). Benjamin felt an affinity for the Party and the Revolution, but this was eventually outweighed by his reservations. The Moscow writings show 'the self-styled convert in the initial moments of his first encounter with a revolutionary world that claims his instinctive sympathies and yet does not assuage the strong doubts of the middle-class introvert' (Demetz ed., 1978, p. xxviii). It was also to be his last encounter. He never joined the Communist Party or returned to Moscow. On 1 February 1927 he boarded the train for Berlin, and went back to the 'uncomfortable and draughty spectator area' he had so nearly forsaken.

2

Urban Memories: Labyrinth and Childhood

Introduction

Two cities were the principal loci of Benjamin's life and work: Berlin, the city of his birth, and Paris, the city that became his adopted home from 1933 until his untimely death in 1940. Benjamin was born in Berlin on 15 July 1892 into a prosperous, upper-middle-class, assimilated Jewish family. His mother, Paula (née Schoenflies), came from a prosperous East Prussian family, and his father, Emil, worked for a Berlin auction house as a merchant. The Benjamins resided in the city's comfortable, desirable West End district, and Walter's childhood was a period of relative affluence. The eldest of three children, he attended the local Kaiser-Friedrich-Schule in Charlottenberg. In 1904, he was sent (primarily on health grounds – he was a sickly child) to a progressive educational institution in Thuringia, the Haubinda Landerziehungsheim, where he remained until Easter 1907. Here he met, and was profoundly influenced by, the pedagogic reformer Gustav Wyneken. Benjamin joined the radical wing of the then popular Youth Movement and took an active role in the propagation of its romantic call for cultural regeneration through youth, regularly publishing material in its journal *Der Anfang*.

In his early years at university in Freiburg (1912–13) Benjamin continued to be actively engaged in the Youth Movement, and was eventually elected president of the Free Students' Union in Berlin during the summer of 1914.[1] Benjamin was later to break completely with the Youth Movement and with Wyneken, on

account of the latter's enthusiastic support for the war. Exempted
from military service on medical grounds, Benjamin spent the
early war years in Munich and Berlin where, on 17 April 1917, he
married Dora Sophie Kellner. Shortly afterwards, he left Germany
to study at the university in Bern, and he was to spend some three
years in Switzerland before returning to post-war Berlin.
Although the Weimar years were years of repeated and lengthy
absences from Berlin (Benjamin's travels took him not only to
Capri and Moscow but also to Paris, the south of France,
Scandinavia, Riga, and San Remo), he always returned there.[2]
Benjamin himself was in no doubt as to the importance of Berlin
both personally and intellectually. In a letter to Scholem (17 April
1931) he states candidly: 'Where is my production plant located? It
is located (and in this, too, I do not harbour the slightest illusions)
in Berlin W., W.W. if you like. The most sophisticated civilisation
and the most "modern" culture are not only part of my private
comfort; some of them are the very means of my production'
(Scholem, 1982, p. 232). The continued growth of the Nazi
movement in Germany during the next two years rendered
Benjamin's position in the city untenable, and after a brief visit to
the island of Ibiza he finally moved his 'production plant' to Paris
around 18 March 1933.[3] He was never to return to his native city.

Given his impending flight from the city that had played such a
pervasive and prominent role in his life and work, it is hardly
surprising that Benjamin devoted much of his attention in 1932 to
recording his relationship with Berlin. His 'Berlin Chronicle' and
'A Berlin Childhood Around 1900' may be understood on one
level as such labours of 'love at last sight'.[4] But these personal
reminiscences were not his only works about Berlin at this time. A
large number of his radio broadcasts for children (both in Berlin
and Frankfurt)[5] were concerned with the architectural features,
history and inhabitants of the German capital. The Berlin essays
and these radio scripts are testimonies to the city that was once
such an intimate part of his being and that was now home to
forces that threatened to destroy him. In his Afterword to 'Berlin
Childhood', Adorno notes that 'the shadows of Hitler's regime'
(*BK*, p. 169) fall across all the images contained in this text.

Furthermore, the period around 1932 was a particularly gloomy,
pessimistic, desperate one, even by Benjamin's own melancholy
standards. Scholem refers to this period in Benjamin's life as one
of 'crises and turning points'.[6] While staying on the island of Ibiza
in 1932, Benjamin contemplated suicide on more than one
occasion. Indeed, 'Berlin Chronicle' is pervaded by the idea of

suicide. In many respects it may be seen as a monument to the suicide in 1914 of his close friend from the days of the Youth Movement, Fritz Heinle.[7] Benjamin's reflections upon the city of his childhood are underlain by the figure of Heinle, who becomes a metaphor for Benjamin's own youthful dreams of cultural renaissance, for the optimism and naïveté of a generation that was to exterminate itself on the battlefields of France and Belgium. In examining the Berlin essays of 1932, one must be aware of the three 'ghosts' that seem to haunt them: that of Heinle and the horrors of the First World War; that of the adult Benjamin, disillusioned and exiled, preparing to take his own life; and the looming spectre of National Socialism and its attendant atrocities. The catastrophes and sufferings of the past, present and future are located within the spaces of the city. Pervaded by the notion of death, these texts were written from its very threshold.

Autobiography, estrangement and enlargement

Benjamin wrote the first draft notes of his 'Berlin Chronicle' during January and February 1932. The first indication of the project is contained in a letter to Scholem of 28 February 1932. Benjamin writes: 'Sometimes it seems to me as though something else is coming in to being behind my back – in the form of some notes I have been making for the past few weeks on appropriate (or, rather, usually inappropriate) occasions concerning the history of my relationship to Berlin' (Scholem, 1982, p. 180). From these sketches Benjamin composed the 'Chronicle', between April and July 1932, on the island of Ibiza. He then moved to Nice, where he wrote his will and contemplated suicide. The crisis passed, however, and he spent the rest of the summer in Italy. It was there that he reworked the 'Chronicle' (using some fifty-two pages of the original material and incorporating some passages previously published in 'One-Way Street') for publication as a book to be entitled 'A Berlin Childhood Around 1900'. On 26 September 1932 he noted his progress in a further letter to Scholem:

> I write all day and sometimes even into the night. But if you imagined an extensive manuscript you would be mistaken. It is not only a short manuscript but also one in small sections: a form repeatedly prompted by the materially endangered, precarious nature of my production, as well as by considerations of its commercial exploitability. In this case, to be sure, this form seems absolutely

necessary to me because of the subject. It is in short a series of notes
I shall title 'A Berlin childhood around 1900'. (Scholem, 1982, p. 190)

Although Benjamin's hopes of finding a publisher for these
fragments were to be frustrated, he none the less continued to
work on them in a much less intensive fashion for several years,
during which time he changed the order of the pieces, cut old and
incorporated new sections, and wrote a short Foreword for them.
Like the ever-expanding *Passagenarbeit*, the Berlin texts remain as
works-in-progress, eschewing completeness while rewarding
'endless interpolations'.

The essays on Berlin are short, autobiographical prose pieces, in
which he presents a series of images and impressions of his life as
a child (and as a youth in the 'Chronicle') growing up in the city of
Berlin around the turn of the century. The essays themselves seem
to invite, yet also confound, such a banal, superficial reading,
however. Although Scholem describes 'Berlin Chronicle' as
'purely biographical' (1982, p. 191), and Sontag regards it as the
'most intimate document of Benjamin's yet to be published' (*OWS*,
p. 40), one should not be tempted into regarding these texts as
concerned merely with recounting personal details. They are
intricate and perplexing. Benjamin himself explicitly denies the
purely autobiographical character of the 'Chronicle' and 'Childhood' writings. He writes:

> Reminiscences, even extensive ones, do not always amount to an
> autobiography. And these quite certainly do not, even for the Berlin
> years that I am exclusively concerned with here. For autobiography
> has to do with time, with sequence and what makes up the
> continuous flow of life. Here, I am talking of a space, of moments
> and discontinuities. (*OWS*, p. 316)[8]

In the Foreword Benjamin later attached, he reaffirms this:

> In this endeavour those biographical features, which appear more
> readily in the continuity than in the depths of experience, retreat.
> With them go the physiognomies – those of my family and of my
> friends. Instead, I have sought to capture the images which the
> experience of the big city left in a child of the middle class. (*GS* VII,
> p. 385)[9]

Benjamin's 'autobiographical' writings on Berlin are explorations
of the interplay between memory and setting, time and place.

They present images of a certain class at a particular moment as experienced by a child and as subsequently filtered through the memory of an adult. Their inspiration was the delicate web of childhood memories found in Marcel Proust's *À la recherche du temps perdu*[10] and, in particular, the notion of the *mémoire involontaire* (sudden, spontaneous recollection). For Proust, such remembrances are not the intentional consequence of some controlled, directed mental activity. Rather, they flow from the elusive moment of illumination in which a sensation in the present suddenly and fleetingly calls to mind an earlier, forgotten experience with its train of associations and impressions, only for these to be forgotten once more. The smell and taste of madeleines dipped in tea, the scent of various flowers – in Proust's work, these ephemeral stimuli awaken long-dormant memories of childhood encounters, loves and sorrows. The Berlin essays similarly interlace past and present, child and adult. They focus above all on how the objects and settings of the urban environ-ment (Tiergarten, Kaiserpanorama, Siegessäule, Pfaueninsel, Blu-meshof) are perceived and transformed by the child's imagination and recalled in adulthood.[11] Benjamin's texts seek to capture not only the forgotten times of childhood but also the hidden crevices of the metropolis. They are portraits of a turn-of-the-century Berlin childhood in general.[12]

They are not autobiographical sketches as such, but instead constitute recollections of particular locations and specific times, memories of the city and of the recent past. Thus 'Berlin Chronicle' and 'Childhood' were intimately connected with the ongoing but becalmed 'Arcades Project' which Benjamin had begun a few months after his return from Moscow in 1927. Menninghaus writes: 'Berlin and Paris are mythological spaces; the reconstruction of childhood experience and the materialist physiognomy of an entire epoch are the modes of representation oriented to them' (1986, p. 33).[13] Adorno also stresses this point when he observes that the 'Berlin Childhood' essay 'belongs in the vicinity of the pre-history of modernity with which Benjamin concerned himself during the last fifteen years of his life, and forms the subjective counterpart to the mass of materials which he gathered for the projected work on the Parisian Arcades' (*BK*, p. 168). The Berlin texts were theoretical and methodological experiments for the 'Arcades Project', models of historical analysis and writing which sought to explore the relationships between metropolitan environment, individual memory and collective history. How does the city transform memory? How does memory give form to the urban complex? Could the narration of an individual past critically illuminate the history of an epoch?[14] These complex questions underpin Benjamin's Berlin writings. His 'autobiographical' fragments are thus exercises in critical historiography rather than wistful nostalgia.

In his Afterword to the 1962 collection of Benjamin's cityscapes, Szondi links 'Berlin Childhood' with Benjamin's *Denkbilder*, for, as he points out, the 'motives underlying them scarcely differ from those that marked the book of reminiscences' (Smith ed., 1988, p. 19). For Szondi, the principal connection lies in the concept of 'distance', a journeying to and encounter with the remote either in time or in space. Szondi notes that 'anyone who describes his own city must travel into the past instead of into the distance' (Smith, ed., 1988, p. 19).[15] Szondi contends that the key to understanding Benjamin's urban studies (including the Berlin ones) is to recognize that they constitute attempts to 'convey the experience of alienation and of being a foreigner' (Smith ed., 1988, p. 26). Benjamin draws upon impressions and images of the city from childhood in order to become a stranger, a foreigner once more, in a space he knows so well as an adult. He encounters Berlin again 'for the first time' – that is to say, in the manner in which he experienced the unfamiliar cities of Naples, Moscow and Marseilles.

In his 1928 essay 'Marseilles', Benjamin states that 'childhood is the divining rod of melancholy, and to know the mourning of such radiant, glorious cities one must have been a child in them' (*OWS*, p. 211).[16] Benjamin 'knows' the city of Berlin, yet takes his reader back to the period of 'not knowing'. Szondi comments: 'gone, therefore, is our familiarity with streets and houses, though they may still surround us; we see them with a doubly alien view: with the view of the child we no longer are and with the view of the child to whom the city was not yet familiar' (Smith ed., 1988, p. 20). To know the city as a place of sorrow and wonderment, one must have been a child in it; yet this knowledge is retrospective in character, the product of hindsight. Only in the fullness of time does truth unfold, revealing itself to the understanding. Szondi writes:

> The adult's glance does not yearn to merge with the child's glance. It is directed toward those moments when the future first announced itself to the child. . . . Everywhere in the city, in the streets and parks, the Berlin book is on the trail of such shocks, the memories of which are preserved by the child until the adult can decipher them. (Smith ed., 1988, pp. 20–1)

In Moscow, Benjamin becomes a 'child' in a foreign city. In Berlin, he becomes a 'foreigner' in the city of his childhood. He transforms the urban setting by presenting it to the reader as it is perceived 'at first sight', as yet unobscured by familiarity and habit. The child becomes a lens that creates distance between viewer and viewed, subject and object. Observing the city from the vantage-point of the child is like looking at it through the wrong end of a telescope. Szondi contends that this creation of distance is a necessary condition for producing an account of the city. He writes: 'the journey into the past is a journey into the distance as well. For without distance there can be no description except that of mere *reportage*' (Smith ed., 1988, p. 20).

Szondi's account is a persuasive, insightful one, but it fails to do justice to the actual complexity of the material, perhaps. He overlooks the intricate, ingenious (indeed, also ingenuous perhaps) relationship between the gaze of the child and that of the adult.[17] He makes three only partially correct assumptions: first, that the child's gaze is used by Benjamin primarily to create an (unproblematic) sense of distance; second, that the child is a 'non-knowing' subject whose naïve misperception, 'at first sight', serves merely as a method of defamiliarization; third, that this sense of distance is a device to facilitate description of the city. I would contend that Szondi thereby fails to take into account the critical dimensions of Benjamin's thought and the subtle interplay of perspectives, and also underestimates the significance of the 'at first sight' and the playful activities of the child in the city.

In his essay on Moscow, Benjamin explicitly says that distance in time and space are not to be equated. In relation to the burgeoning cult of Lenin, he observes that 'in the optic of history – opposite in this to that of space – movement in the distance means enlargement' (*OWS*, p. 207). As events and figures recede into the past, they may come to increase rather than diminish in stature. Benjamin writes: 'remembrance advances from small to smallest details, from the smallest to the infinitesimal, while that which it encounters in these microcosms grows ever mightier' (*OWS*, p. 296). The remembrance of childhood is particularly significant in this respect. Benjamin sees the child as in some way 'closer' to objects, as enjoying a privileged proximity to the world of things. One may recall the Muscovite riding on a small sleigh being compared to the child 'gliding through the house on its little chair' (*OWS*, p. 191) because both are 'closely mingled with people and things' (ibid.). At the beginning of the 'Chronicle' Benjamin reiterates this theme when he observes that 'the child, in his solitary games, grows up at closest quarters to the city' (*OWS*, p. 293). In play the child does not stand back from and contemplate the object, but takes hold of it and, mimetically, becomes part of it.[18] The child, then, has a particularly intimate connection with things. Benjamin presents us with the images and impressions of childhood not to create a sense of distance, but rather to recapture those times when things were closest to us. He does not create distance to make the world 'smaller' and easier to perceive and describe as a whole; rather, he makes himself 'small' and his surroundings thereby 'larger'. He travels into the distance of time in order to move closer to things. It is a process of 'enlargement'.[19] Benjamin's recollections of his childhood in Berlin are thus a voyage to the land of Brobdingnag, the land of giants in Swift's *Gulliver's Travels*.

Szondi, then, is half-right. Benjamin does generate a sense of distance for the sake of perspective and representation; but he also intends thereby to bring one closer to the objects, spaces and inhabitants of the urban setting. The city is made closer and larger (the 'optic of history' and the smallness of the child) and at the same time distant and smaller (it becomes 'foreign'). Benjamin offers a subtle, intricate interplay of perspectives in which closeness is paradoxically achieved through distance. The city is rendered strange not so much through a simple effect of distance, but rather through the continual movement or fluctuation of vantage-points. There is flux between the minutely detailed close-up and the distant observation. Benjamin's images of the city are not static but dialectical in character. His 'doubly alien view' is precisely the sense of distortion produced by being too close to an object on the one hand and too far from it on the other.[20]

Szondi contends that Benjamin defamiliarizes the urban environment by presenting it through the eyes of the child, who is in a state of innocence, of 'not-yet-knowing'. This sets up a series of fixed dichotomies or oppositions: adult–child; knowledge–naïveté; hindsight–'at-first-sight'. It is my contention, however, that Benjamin does not offer such a straightforward set of hierarchical orderings. Rather, the child provides a disruptive vision which disconcerts the stable, distant adult gaze. For Benjamin, the 'not-knowing' of the child is another, sometimes insightful, way of knowing. As he notes in 'Marseilles', to know a city one must have been a child in it. The child, as a consequence of his or her proximity, has a distinctive, special knowledge of, and experience in, the metropolis, which the adult must endeavour to redeem. Benjamin's childhood recollections do not offer a contrast between the omniscient adult and the ignorant and/or innocent child, but between alternative, distinctive modes of seeing and knowing. The perception of the child challenges that of the adult, who in turn dismisses it as mistaken. Yet for Benjamin, the apparently error-filled knowledge of the child may serve, unintentionally, to reveal hidden facets of the cityscape, and may even come to unmask the false appearance of things, the mythic façades that hold the adult observer enthralled.

The case of Benjamin's Aunt Lehmann provides an example of how the child's misrecognition constitutes an insightful counterpart to the perception of the adult. Benjamin recounts that his Aunt Lehmann used to live on Steglitzer Strasse, but that as a child he misrecognized this name as *Stieglitz* ('goldfinch'). He writes: 'on account of this aunt . . . Steglitzer Strasse could henceforth, for me, never be named after Steglitz. A goldfinch in its cage bore greater resemblance to this street harbouring the aunt at her window than the Berlin suburb that meant nothing to me' (*OWS*, p. 301). In 'Berlin Childhood' Benjamin elaborates this: 'and did not this aunt live like a talking bird in its tree? Often, when I went in there, it was filled with the twitterings of this small black bird, who had flown about the nesting sites of the district where its scattered kin had resided' (*GS* IV, p. 249). The metaphor of the bird, which is the product of the child's mistake, reveals a much richer picture of the solitary old aunt, now living alone after the departure of her children. The conditions of her life are shown more vividly by the misnomer. In its tendency to equate name and named, word and thing or person, the perception of the child becomes in some sense a privileged mode of knowing. The city is a space of naming in which the purely denotative language of the adult is transformed by the 'at first sight' of the child into the magical language of the metaphorical.[21]

Stüssi begins her study of the Berlin writings with a consideration of the following paradox. Benjamin writes:

> Not to find one's way in a city means little. But to lose oneself in a city as one loses oneself in a forest requires practice. Then the street names must call out to the lost wanderer like the snapping of dry twigs, and the small streets of the city-centre must reflect the time of day as clearly as a mountain hollow. I have learned this art of straying only recently. (*GS* IV, p. 237)

Stüssi argues that here Benjamin transforms 'not-knowing' into an art, something that requires 'practice' and expertise. To become lost is an achievement rather than a failure, for it generates a particularly astute or heightened perception of the surrounding environment. Cityscape becomes landscape. This is an imperative for the lone wanderer in the city, and is a key feature of the child's misrecognition.[22] Stüssi notes how the child's perception defamiliarizes the city, transforms it into a place of disorientation. She writes: 'this paradoxical art of unknowing itself creates a no less strange setting: the city as landscape. . . . To those for whom the city appears as nature, it is not closer and more familiar, but rather thoroughly unnatural and strange' (1977, p. 12). In losing one's adult self, one becomes a child again (one who is 'lost' in the metropolis), and acquires once more that intimate connection with things that is the privilege of the child. Stüssi remarks that 'what we usually regard as a sign of inability and impotence is commended here as a method of mastery' (1977, p. 11).

The 'at first sight' plays a critical role in Benjamin's consideration of the city. In a section of 'One-Way Street' entitled 'Lost-Property Office' he writes:

> What makes the very first glimpse of a village, a town, in the landscape so incomparable and irretrievable is the rigorous connection between foreground and distance. Habit has not yet done its work. As soon as we begin to find our bearings, the landscape vanishes at a stroke like the façade of a house as we enter it. It has not yet gained preponderance through a constant exploration that has become habit. Once we begin to find our way about, that earliest picture can never be restored. (*OWS*, p. 78)

Benjamin's writings on Berlin are attempts to restore this earliest image, the initial impression, the 'at first sight' of a city he was seeing for the last time. He seeks to give voice to that perception which is as yet untainted by the destructive power of habit. He states: 'it is true that countless façades of the city stand exactly as they stood in my childhood. Yet I do not encounter my childhood in their contemplation. My gaze has brushed them too often since, too often have they been the *décor* and theatre of my walks and concerns' (*OWS*, p. 315).

The recovery of the 'at first sight' is an imperative for Benjamin, for it constitutes the critical, dereifying gaze. The work of habit engenders indifference, unconcern, disinterest. The metropolis appears unchanging, always-the-same. Habit brings with it petrification, boredom and forgetfulness.[23] The familiar is the forgotten, and the forgotten is the reified. Adorno, in a letter to Benjamin of 29 February 1940, writes: 'all reification is a forgetting: objects become thing-like in that moment in which they are captured without all their elements being present; when something of them is forgotten' (Berlin Archive, folder 30, p. 26). Benjamin attempts to remember the city when it was still strange, hence memorable. He does not 're-seek lost times' in order to generate a space in which description is possible, but instead tries to recapture the lost perspective, the pre-habitual gaze of the child. His purpose is not to describe the urban complex through the eyes of the child, but to dereify it through his or her special, incisive, yet 'mistaken' knowledge. Distance is not created simply for the purpose of description, as Szondi argues; rather, there is an interplay of distance and proximity in order to facilitate criticism. For Benjamin, 'criticism is a matter of correct distancing' (*OWS*, p. 89). His childhood recollections seek to dereify and redeem the objects and spaces of the city that have become frozen and forgotten in adulthood. The recovery of the 'at first sight' of the Berlin metropolis is an act of critical redemption.

Metropolis, memory and monument

In her study, Stüssi systematically explores each episode of 'Berlin Childhood' in order to 'illumine the encoded imagery . . . from within through an interpreting reading' (1977, p. 245).[24] She takes as her principal point of departure Benjamin's comment that the Berlin writings 'constitute individual expeditions into the depths of memory' (Scholem, 1982, p. 190), and emphasises the redemption of the forgotten *promesse de bonheur* of childhood. The task of memory is to retrieve the buried hopes, aspirations and dreams of the child that have been frustrated during the course of adulthood. The past is not something that is over and done with. It accompanies the adult – indeed, pursues him or her in the form of the 'little hunchback', of whom Benjamin speaks in the final section of 'Childhood'. But childhood itself, Stüssi argues, is no state of blissful innocence: 'in each chapter one can show that childhood is no safe origin, whose restorative reconstruction would be an appeasement for the homeless adult. The child is homeless too, paradise is already lost to the child, though the adult tends to see it in childhood' (1977, p. 246). The child stands bewildered, awaiting the future. The intimations and premonitions of the life yet to come are perceived by the child, but he or she is unable to name or decipher them. Only with the hindsight of adulthood will comprehension be possible, for meaning is achieved and apprehended only retrospectively. The significance of the past comes to light only in its relation to a particular present. Benjamin's Berlin writings are a complex play, therefore, upon notions of past, present and future. The half-forgotten past plagues the present, while the unknown ('forgotten' is the word Stüssi uses) future, murky and indistinct, haunts the past, the time of childhood. Benjamin re-seeks lost time, but this search is oriented and extended toward the future. He redeems the past for the sake of things to come. Memory is not closed, Stüssi argues; rather, it leads out into the open. Benjamin's enterprise is Janus-faced rather than nostalgic.

In Stüssi's study, however, at least one fundamental aspect seems to be underplayed. In her emphasis upon memory and childhood, she tends to neglect the role of the city. Although she considers the notions of the labyrinth and the *flâneur* – in particular, she regards Benjamin as a *flâneur* in the 'labyrinth of memory' – she fails to stress the fact that Benjamin is engaged in representing an *urban* childhood, and does not adequately connect the Berlin texts with his earlier city portraits. This would seem to be an important oversight, because Benjamin's writings on his native city are profoundly concerned with the elucidation of the child's perception of the buildings, localities, spaces and inhabitants of the modern city. Benjamin seeks, after all, to give voice to a *Berlin* childhood, to recount a *Berlin* chronicle. In Stüssi's study, the urban complex appears to form little more than a backdrop. My contention is that the city must be placed very much in the foreground. Sontag recognizes the need for such an approach when she writes: 'in the "Berlin Childhood" and the "Berlin Chronicle", Benjamin merges his life into a setting. The successor to the Baroque stage set is the Surrealist city: the metaphysical landscape in whose dreamlike spaces people have a "brief, shadowy existence" ' (*OWS*, p. 13). Benjamin's writings on Berlin are not explorations of memory *per se*; indeed, Benjamin precisely rejects the possibility of an ahistorical conception of remembrance. Instead, these texts seek to sketch and examine the particular relationship between memory and the metropolis.

The city is not simply a space remembered by Benjamin. It is, rather, the intricate interweaving of the memory of a particular site and the site of that memory which occupies Benjamin. Remembrance and metropolis become porous; they interpenetrate. He notes of a certain occasion:

> I wish to write of this afternoon because it made so apparent what kind of regimen cities keep over imagination, and why the city,

where people make the most ruthless demands on one another, where appointments and telephone calls, sessions and visits, flirtations and the struggle for existence grant the individual not a single moment of contemplation, indemnifies itself in memory, and why the veil it has covertly woven out of our lives shows the images of people less than those of the sites of our encounters with others and ourselves. (*OWS*, p. 318)

Benjamin presents a historical, dialectical conception of the character and work of remembrance. Memory shapes, and is in turn shaped by, the urban setting. Benjamin depicts the character of modern remembrance and the remembrance of the modern. This interplay of time and space lies at the heart of the Berlin writings. Benjamin appears to offer three interconnected models of the relationship between memory and cityscape: city and memory as labyrinth, shock and the *mémoire involontaire*, and the urban archaeologist.

Memory and labyrinth   The motif of the city as labyrinth is already familiar. The past, too, is convoluted. Benjamin muses: 'I have long, indeed for years, played with the idea of setting out the sphere of life – *bios* – graphically on a map. First I envisaged an ordinary map, but now I would incline to a general staff's map of the city-centre, if such a thing existed' (*OWS*, p. 295). He later adds the following:

I was struck by the idea of drawing a diagram of my life, and knew at the same moment exactly how it was to be done. With a very simple question I interrogated my past life, and the answers were inscribed, as if of their own accord, on a sheet of paper that I had with me. A year or two later, when I lost this sheet, I was inconsolable. I have never since been able to restore it as it arose before me then, resembling a series of family trees. Now, however, reconstructing its outline . . . I should, rather, speak of a labyrinth. (*OWS*, pp. 318–19)

In his writings on Berlin, Benjamin seeks to map out his early life, to chart his childhood experiences in the urban setting. He gives memory and his past life (the temporal, the historical) spatial representation. Memory itself is represented as 'city-like'. The dense networks of streets and alley-ways are like the knotted, intertwined threads of memory. The open spaces of the urban environment are like the voids and blanks of forgotten things. Lost times are like overlooked places. Berlin is formed in, and gives form to, memory. The city itself becomes the medium for

Benjamin's urban recollections. Memory and the city both
constitute labyrinthine figures, without beginning or end, in
which one may make 'endless interpolations' (*OWS*, p. 305).[25]
Benjamin links time and space in two ways: the journey into the
past is a voyage into the distance, and movement in memory is
like that in a labyrinth. These may initially be seen as complementary images, but they are actually antithetical. To move in a
labyrinth is a circling around in which one revisits the same
places. And yet, such motion indirectly leads towards the heart of
things. To journey into the distance is to be a traveller; to journey
within a labyrinth is to be a *flâneur*, one who wanders without
destination, one who is able to lose him or herself in the
metropolis. For Benjamin, time is not a linear progression. The
past is not left behind as one moves on, but, like spaces in a
labyrinth, is continually encountered again, returned to, though
approached from different directions. Motion in the city and in
memory is a persistent going nowhere in particular that constitutes a perpetual rediscovery.[26]

Benjamin's motif of the labyrinth is the key to understanding his
peculiar autobiography. The past is a labyrinth in which memory
endlessly circles, in which objects are repeatedly encountered as if
for the first time. Similarly, the Berlin texts themselves are not
linear narratives. They are not concerned with the representation
of progression or development, but are themselves labyrinthine in
character. Stüssi accurately notes that 'each chapter of the "Berlin
Childhood" is a labyrinthine figure: there is no development, the
goal remains hidden. Memory is the recollection of unfinished
moments' (1977, p. 245). In Benjamin's writings on Berlin, the
labyrinth of the modern city and that of the work of memory are
inscribed in the formal properties of the texts themselves. He
presents a labyrinth (the city) within a labyrinth (memory) within
yet another labyrinth (the text).[27] To remember the city and to
write about it, one must lose oneself in mazes that correspond to
the very structure of the metropolis itself.

Shock and the mémoire involuntaire   In his 1936 essay 'The Story-
teller: Reflections on the Works of Nikolai Leskov', Benjamin cites
the following German motto: 'When someone goes on a trip, he
has something to tell about' (*ILL*, p. 84). The journey upon which
Benjamin embarks in his Berlin texts is a voyage not into the
distance but within the confines of a labyrinth: it is a circling, a
continual return. Benjamin cannot 'tell his tale'; he is unable to
relate his life experiences in a direct or coherent manner, because

he has gone nowhere. The Berlin essays are labyrinthine figures, rather than simple linear narrative structures. Furthermore, they are discontinuous and fragmentary. For Benjamin, the story-teller is a figure of the past, since the capacity to remember one's tale and the ability to narrate it unproblematically have vanished in the modern epoch. Benjamin describes the teller of tales thus: 'His gift is the ability to relate his life; his distinction, to be able to tell his entire life. The storyteller: he is the man who could let the wick of his life be consumed completely by the gentle flame of his story. This is the basis of the incomparable aura about the storyteller' (*ILL*, pp. 108–9). The story-teller is dependent upon the faculty of conscious recollection, the bringing back of past experiences at will (the *mémoire volontaire*). But in the maelstrom of modern urban life, such conscious recollection becomes impossible. For Benjamin, the shocks and multiple stimuli encountered in the city cannot be assimilated by the individual, and are redirected into the sphere of the unconscious. Abrasive urban encounters leave scars on the unconscious, imprints of what has been forgotten, yet not forgotten, hidden but not lost. Half-obliterated by consciousness, half-preserved by the unconscious, the fragmentary, disparate data of the *mémoire involontaire* remain for Benjamin the principal traces of a person's past to survive the rigours of the modern epoch and the demise of conscious recollection. He writes:

> the important thing for the remembering author is not what he experienced, but the weaving of his memory, the Penelope work of recollection. Or should one call it, rather, the Penelope work of forgetting? Is not the involuntary recollection, Proust's *mémoire involontaire*, much closer to forgetting than what is usually called memory? And is not this work of spontaneous recollection, in which remembrance is the woof and forgetting the warf, a counterpart to Penelope's work rather than its likeness? For here the day unravels what the night has woven. (*ILL*, p. 204)

The story-teller spins yarns. For Benjamin, Proust's great achievement was his ability to weave a text from the threads of remembering and forgetting. In the Berlin essays, Benjamin seeks to follow Proust's pattern,[28] and attempts to recover the shocks of the urban setting which have scarred the child's unconscious and whose traces linger in the adult's mind. These texts are fundamentally engaged in the redemption of those moments when the city first announced itself to the child, with the shock of the new.

I have sought so far to indicate two models of the relationship between the modern urban setting and memory: time as space, memory and the city as labyrinthine structures; and the experience of the modern as shock, fragmentation, the ruination of conscious memory and the pre-eminence of the Proustian *mémoire involontaire*. Some aspects of these models are complementary: losing and finding one's way, the 'at first sight' (shock, memorable) and the habitually seen (adult familiarity, forgetting and reification). Others are contradictory. In the first, Benjamin is able to map out his past, give it coherent representation, even if this takes the form of a labyrinth. In the second, memory is unpredictable, incoherent, broken and fortuitous. Benjamin offers both the labyrinth (a whole or totality) and the fragment (the decomposed whole or ruin). Both are critical counterpoints to the notion of linearity, but they should be carefully distinguished. Their relationship and interplay are articulated by Benjamin in his third model, that of the archaeologist.

Urban archaeology   It is in the figure of the archaeologist that Benjamin most clearly interweaves memory and the city, and articulates the central purpose of the Berlin essays. The notion of repeated excursions into the same spaces and moments again finds expression. He writes:

> Language shows clearly that memory is not an instrument for exploring the past but its theatre. It is the medium of past experience, as the ground is the medium in which dead cities lie interred. He who seeks to approach his own buried past must conduct himself like a man digging. This confers the tone and bearing of genuine reminiscences. He must not be afraid to return again and again to the same matter; to scatter it as one scatters earth, to turn it over as one turns over soil. (*OWS*, p. 314)

The task of the archaeologist is to dig beneath the surface of the modern city and the modern sensibility it engenders, to unearth the evidence of past life and the shocks that have become lodged in the depths of the unconscious. Benjamin's archaeology seeks to disinter the childhood experiences buried within the adult. It is an archaeology of the experience of the modern city dweller and of modernity itself, an act of discovery which embraces both personal and collective history. In the Berlin texts Benjamin seeks to 'excavate and remember' the city. This is a complex undertaking. He notes:

True, for successful excavations a plan is needed. Yet no less indispensable is the cautious probing of the spade in the dark loam, and it is to cheat oneself of the richest prize to preserve as a record merely the inventory of one's discoveries, and not this dark joy of the place of the finding itself. Fruitless searching is as much a part of this as succeeding, and consequently remembrance must not proceed in the manner of a narrative or still less that of a report, but must, in the strictest epic and rhapsodic manner, essay its spade in ever-new places, and in the old ones delve to ever-deeper layers. (*OWS*, p. 314)

In the metaphor of the archaeological excavation, the labyrinth (excavation plan, continual return to the same spot), conscious recollection (cautious probing, fruitless searching) and *mémoire involontaire* (unexpected discovery) are revealed as complementary rather than contradictory moments.

The 'dark joy of the place of finding' is in accord with the sorrowful character of the undertaking. In his *Trauerspiel* study Benjamin notes that 'the downward gaze is characteristic of the saturnine man who bores into the ground with his eyes . . . for the melancholic the inspirations of mother earth dawn from the night of contemplation like treasures from the interior of the earth' (*OGTD*, pp. 152–3). The true archaeologist is no treasure-hunter, though. For him or her, a shard of pottery, a broken comb, a worn-out shoe may have greater worth than the gold and silver treasures of the past. To retrieve the commonplace, the mundane and the unremarkable is his or her task. The fragments found serve above all to illuminate the lives of those in the past who are unrecorded and unremembered in the present. It is the archaeologist who recognizes that beneath our feet are the countless bones and remains of those who have no monument, no landmark to indicate their passing. The archaeologist is concerned with the forgotten dead, those whose traces have been concealed, who are thus 'hidden' from history.[29] In his notes for the 'Theses on the Concept of History' Benjamin insists that 'historical construction is dedicated to the memory of the nameless' (*GS* I, p. 1241). The goal of the Berlin essays is not only to rediscover the forgotten *promesse de bonheur* of childhood, but also to remember the forgotten dead, the unremembered shades who haunt the city.

The work of the past is unfinished; it continues in the present.[30] For Benjamin, redemption of the unremembered dead constitutes a vital political praxis. The thwarted aspirations and desires of past generations, the utopian moments and impulses sedimented in the past and preserved by memory and tradition, must be redeemed, refashioned and refunctioned for use in the continuing political struggles. Remembrance is the impetus for revolutionary action. Benjamin notes that the transformation of the world through the revolutionary proletariat is 'nourished by the image of enslaved ancestors rather than that of liberated grandchildren' (*ILL*, p. 262).[31] He seeks to give voice to those whom oppression and time have reduced to silence. His is a peculiarly urban archaeology, for this work has a desperate quality to it. The urban archaeologist is engaged in a race against time, a frantic act of rescue before the site is given over to the prevailing interests of builders and developers. The imminent danger of destruction by contemporary powers animates and gives a sense of urgency to the activity of the urban archaeologist, who must salvage all he or she can before the site vanishes without trace. In a similar fashion, Benjamin is concerned with the redemption of lost things and lost times before they are irrevocably destroyed. In the 'Theses on the Concept of History' he writes: 'even the dead will not be safe from the enemy if he wins' (*ILL*, p. 257). Benjamin's goal is to rescue the utopian impulses of the past not only from the oblivion of forgetting, but also from obliteration and appropriation by 'the enemy', the National Socialists. For Benjamin as urban archaeologist, the city of Berlin constitutes an unmarked grave of the unremembered dead, a place on the point of desecration by the forces of modern barbarism and amnesia.

Benjamin's examination of the character of the city as it appears in memory (the remembered city) and that of memory as it appears in the city (urban memory) coalesce in his conceptualization of the monument, the edifice or structure erected in the city precisely to commemorate the past. The monument is a manifestation of, and focus for, the celebration of those who have triumphed in the past.[32] Benjamin writes: 'whoever has emerged victorious participates to this day in the triumphal procession in which the present rulers step over those who are lying prostrate. . . . There is no document of civilisation that is not at the same time a document of barbarism' (*ILL*, p. 258). The monument is precisely such a 'document'. It presents itself as an object of adoration, an unchanging and timeless reminder of former splendour and achievement. The monument is doubly mythic: in its evocation of a false history and in its proclamation of its own permanence. The monument is a petrified myth. To break its spell, it must be critically unmasked as a historical form, embodying particular articulations of past and present.

In his essay on Moscow, Benjamin writes: 'scarcely one of these broad spaces bears a monument. (In contrast, there is hardly one in Europe whose secret structure was not profaned and destroyed by a monument in the nineteenth century)' (*OWS*, p. 203).[33] For Benjamin, the nineteenth century was an epoch preoccupied with the construction of monuments. In Berlin the statues of the recent past are important markers of childhood experience. In the 'Tiergarten' section of 'Berlin Childhood', Benjamin recalls the statues of Friedrich-Wilhelm, Queen Luise and Prince Louis Ferdinand. These figures appear aloof and 'timeless'. Their blank eyes do not return the gaze cast upon them by the child, but remain lifeless. The statues are auratic, 'distant' despite their physical proximity. They are sources of enchantment demanding humble reverence and servile obedience. Above all, Friedrich-Wilhelm and Queen Luise, as 'representatives of the nineteenth century' (Stüssi, 1977, p. 13), are idols erected by the modern bourgeoisie after their own image. The statues are expressions of the self-aggrandizement of the nineteenth-century bourgeoisie, artefacts to be critically deciphered by the urban physiognomist.

The monument is to be revealed as a transient rather than an enduring structure. Its significance is not fixed and final, but is subject to political changes in the present, to transformation and ruination. The clearest example of this is found in Benjamin's account in 'One-Way Street' of the Egyptian obelisk in the Place de la Concorde in Paris. He writes: 'What was carved in it four thousand years ago today stands at the centre in the greatest of city squares. Had it been foretold to him – what a triumph for the Pharaoh! The foremost Western cultural empire will one day bear at its centre the memorial of his rule' (*OWS*, p. 70).[34] Once the symbol of Egyptian rule, Pharaoh's monument now proclaims the colonial power of France. The meaning of the monument changes in the course of its own history. Monuments to victory are inevitably transformed in time into those of defeat. As an object falls into a state of ruination, the pretensions which accompanied its construction crumble, and its truth is unfolded. The monument has an 'afterlife'[35] which negates the original intention. While the city's proud monuments most clearly articulate the glorification of history, in their 'afterlife', these same structures come to unmask the modern metropolis as the locus of mythic delusion.

The clearest example of Benjamin's critical analysis of the monument is his chapter in 'Berlin Childhood' on the Siegessäule, the 'Victory Column' erected in Berlin to celebrate and commemorate victory in the Franco-Prussian War (1870–1) and the establishment of the German Empire. This monument was the focal point for the parades and festivities of Sedan Day.[36] Benjamin notes: 'when I was little, one could not imagine a year without Sedan Day. After Sedan, only parades remained' (*GS* IV, p. 240). For Benjamin, the pomp and pageantry of 'eternal Sedan Day' (*GS* IV, p. 242) and its grotesque, pretentious monument involved the distortion of the past rooted in the glorification of war and military conquest. The Siegessäule demands cultic adoration, presenting itself as eternal, as an enduring monument to the heroism of Imperial Germany. Accordingly, Benjamin is concerned with it as evidence of the fleeting and transient, the brutal and inhuman. He writes of the Siegessäule thus: 'it stood on the broad square like the red date on a tear-off calendar' (*GS* IV, p. 240). Stüssi notes: 'the apparently naive image of the tear-off calendar establishes itself here as a corrosive critique of the false eternal claim of the column (1977, p. 94). For Benjamin, the monument is not to the boastful omnipotence of Imperial Germany, but is rather an emblem of the cruelty and barbarism of war. He writes caustically: 'with the defeat of the French, world history appeared sunk in its glorious grave with the column as its marker' (*GS* IV, p. 241). The monument of the birth of Imperial German civilization is at the same time a monument to the brutality of its founding violence. Benjamin contrasts the figures of victory with the reliefs of carnage inside the column: 'so this gallery was the Inferno, the exact counterpart to the ring of mercy [*Gnadenkreises*] which surrounded the shining figure of Victory above' (*GS* IV, p. 242). The Siegessäule is 'an aestheticisation, even a deification of barbaric history' (Stüssi, 1977, p. 95). Like the Pharaoh's obelisk, the Siegessäule is an ironic monument for Benjamin. What is the status of this monument in 1932? The symbol of German victory over the French in 1870–1 can have only a paradoxical significance after the German defeat of 1914–18 and the ensuing collapse of the Imperial system. The Siegessäule and the parades of Sedan Day remain as indictments of the smug complacency of a short-lived, myopic social order. By the end of the First World War, the monument to omnipotence had become a monument to impotence.

The monument constitutes a pervasive, mythic but also paradoxical structure in the city. It is a product of human labour, yet seeks to exert dominion over its manufacturer (it is fetishistic and alienating); it purports to glorify civilization, yet represents only brutality and barbarism; it stands for military victory, yet at every moment is threatened with being transformed into an emblem of vainglory and ruin. The modern city endeavours to present itself through its monumental façades and structures as the zenith or culmination of progress. The past is as much a part of the 'phantasmagoria' of modernity as the commodities and dream-like architecture of the cityscape. For Benjamin, however, such monuments, read critically, unveil the metropolis as the locus of self-deception and folly, ignorance and inhumanity, myth and myopia. The city is composed of nothing more than the ceaselessly piled up ruins of the past.

This destructive moment of critical, physiognomical reading is balanced by a constructive impulse. To the monuments of the city Benjamin counterpoises his own monuments. His essays on Berlin are attempts to erect a different set of monuments, to capture an alternative version of history within the city, a vision of the past that dwells on the sorrowful, the fragile, the ephemeral. Benjamin's 'childhood monuments' (Brodersen, 1990, p. 14) suggest transience, impermanence, mortality; they are monuments to the forgotten dead. Of these, the most important is that to Benjamin's young friend Fritz Heinle. The meeting-house where Benjamin and the other members of the radical wing of the Youth Movement met was also the place where the bodies of Heinle and Seligson were found after their joint suicide in 1914. This constitutes nothing less than a holy place for Benjamin. It is a shrine not only to the young lovers, but also to Benjamin's own youthful aspirations of cultural renaissance. It is a monument to a betrayed generation. Benjamin writes:

> today this point in space where we chanced then to open our Meeting House is for me the strictest pictorial expression of the point in history occupied by this last true elite of bourgeois Berlin. It was as close to the abyss of the Great War as the Meeting House was to the steep slope down to the Landwehr Canal, it was as sharply divided from proletarian youth as the houses of this *rentiers'* quarter were from those of Moabit, and the houses were the last of their line just as the occupants of those apartments were the last who could appease the clamorous shades of the dispossessed with philanthropic ceremonies. In spite – or perhaps because – of this, there is no doubt that the city of Berlin was never again to impinge so forcefully on my existence as it did in that epoch when we believed we could leave it untouched, only improving its schools, only breaking the inhumanity of their inmates' parents, only making a place in it for the words of Hölderlin or George. It was a final, heroic attempt to

change the attitudes of people without changing their circumstances. (*OWS*, p. 307)

For Benjamin, the space formerly occupied by the meeting-house remains as a monument to the romantic, bourgeois reformism of his youth, heroic in both its earnestness and folly. It is the landmark that separates the exuberant attempt to win the hearts and minds of the well-meaning bourgeoisie from the commitment to the transformation of the material conditions of the proletariat through revolution.

The meeting-house is not the only monument erected by Benjamin in Berlin. There are smaller shrines: his grandmother's house in Blumeshof and the surrounding neighbourhood have become 'an Elysium, an indefinite realm of the shades of deceased but immortal grandmothers' (*OWS*, p. 330). This is a half-affectionate, half-scornful monument to the previous bourgeois generation that locked itself away in gloomy interiors crowded with obsolete commodities. Blumeshof comes to be a memorial to the misguided bourgeois sense of security, to its misplaced notion of comfort and well-being, to the folly of dismal, claustrophobic lives spent accumulating now outdated, ridiculous objects. Benjamin also refers to Luise von Landau, a girl in his class at school who died in childhood. It is to her, not the imperious Queen Luise, that Benjamin offers his love among the statues of the Tiergarten. He writes of Luise von Landau thus: 'each time I passed the Lützow Ufer, my eyes sought her house' (*OWS*, pp. 331–2).

Benjamin sets up a series of personal counter-monuments: to the Siegessäule (the glorification of war), he contrasts the meeting-house (the horror of war); to the Tiergarten statues of Friedrich-Wilhelm and Queen Luise (the self-adoration and immortality of the bourgeoisie), he counterpoises the house of his grandmother (the dingy bourgeois junk-room, its precious objects obsolete) and that of Luise von Landau (frailty and transience). For Benjamin, each building, each space in the city, has its own half-forgotten tale to tell. The city is the 'discovery site of the personal past' (Stüssi, 1977, p. 59). For the urban physiognomist, the city is a series of monuments. Like the *mémoire involontaire*, it interweaves forgetting and remembering. The cityscape stimulates recollection; it serves as a mnemonic device. For the physiognomist, as for the archaeologist, such personal monuments, fleetingly recognized by the remembering adult, reveal the modern metropolis as the sprawling agglomeration of the multitudinous houses of the dead. He writes:

> Noisy, matter-of-fact Berlin, the city of work and the metropolis of business, nevertheless has more, rather than less, than some others, of those places and moments when it bears witness to the dead, shows itself full of the dead; and the obscure awareness of these moments, these places, perhaps more than anything else, confers on childhood memories a quality that makes them at once as evanescent and as alluringly tormenting as half-forgotten dreams. (*OWS*, p. 316)

Benjamin's 'autobiographical' writings on Berlin focus on the dialectic between the modern metropolis and memory. He seeks to give voice to the interplay between the city and the remembering subject through an exploration of the manner in which the urban setting shapes, and is in turn shaped by, the work of remembrance. The metropolis is a vital site for Benjamin's archaeology, because it is within the city that one encounters those cultural forms and artefacts which seek to define the past and articulate its relationship with the present. In the urban setting a particular, persuasive version of the past is constructed and elaborated. History appears as progress, as continual development, the ever-new. The past is dead and finished, and is to be subject either to obliteration by the bulldozer or linear organization and display within the confines of the museum. The myth of history as continuous, as perpetual improvement, is bound up with that of history as triumphant procession. This vision of a sequence of glorious, heroic occurrences is given concrete form in the monument. In the metropolis, the past is to be eradicated, catalogued, or glorified.

In the Berlin texts, Benjamin endeavours to unmask each of these visions of the past as mythic. His archaeological practice is concerned to show that the past is not complete and unalterable, but rather that it is the task of the present to redeem the forgotten dead. Benjamin's 'spatialisation' of time rejects any notion of history as continuity, and instead reveals the past as broken and fragmentary, as labyrinthine not linear. History is not developmental but catastrophic in character, not glorious advance but sorrowful endurance. Benjamin redeems a series of personal memorials that give voice to a very different history, one which proclaims the sufferings of the past and the persistence of barbarism in the present. For Benjamin, the task of the historical materialist as remembering subject is to 'brush history against the grain' (*ILL*, p. 259). Benjamin offers us the 'flipside of history' (Stüssi, 1977, p. 209) in the form of the individual remembrance of the past.

Benjamin endeavours to transform autobiography into history, memoirs into memorial.[37] His goal is to bear witness to the dead. He himself recognized the hazards and limits of such an approach. The act of individual remembrance provided an inadequate model for socio-historical analysis. The examination of nineteenth-century Parisian society would demand a different theoretical framework. In his letter to Gretel Adorno of 16 August 1935, Benjamin notes that 'the ur-history of the nineteenth century, which is reflected in the gaze of the child playing on its threshold, has a quite different face from that which it engraves upon the map of history' (*GS* V, 1139, cited by Buck-Morss, 1989, p. 280). In the 'Theses' of 1940, Benjamin advocates not the redemption of a unique past, but a 'unique experience with the past' (*ILL*, p. 264). The labyrinthine structures of the Berlin texts, of the modern city remembered, remain as literary fragments or ruins of a critical experiment that Benjamin ultimately came to perceive as a failure.

Attic and junk-room

It is with trepidation that Benjamin returns to the scenes of his childhood. He writes of the Berlin West End thus: 'if I chance today to pass through the streets of this quarter, I set foot in them with the same uneasiness that one feels when entering an attic unvisited for years. Valuable things may be lying around but nobody remembers where. And in truth this dead quarter with its tall apartment houses is today the junk room of the West End bourgeoisie' (*OWS*, p. 309). The remembered child bears witness to the claustrophobic character and dismal locations of bourgeois life. In 'Berlin Chronicle' Benjamin notes that as a child of middle-class parentage he was 'a prisoner of the old and new West' (*GS* IV, p. 287) of the city. Unable to venture out alone, the child was enclosed 'where the class that had pronounced him one of its members resided in a posture compounded of self-satisfaction and resentment that turned it into something like a ghetto held on lease. In any case, he was confined to this affluent quarter without knowing of any other' (*OWS*, p. 300).

Largely free from material want, such a sheltered life produced its own myopia. Poverty and misery were hidden away in other locations in the city. Benjamin notes: 'the poor? For rich children of his generation they lived at the back of beyond' (ibid.). The middle-class child's knowledge of the city's 'wider expanses' (*OWS*, p. 293) is acquired slowly through various expeditions accompanied – indeed, encumbered – by particular guides to the city: parent, relative, nursemaid. Benjamin writes ruefully: 'one thing, therefore, can never be made good: having neglected to run away from home. From forty-eight hours' exposure in those years, as in caustic solution, the crystal of life's happiness forms' (*OWS*, p. 48). For Benjamin, the bourgeois child experiences the city as a strictly delineated, bounded space. The city is divided into permitted and forbidden zones by invisible walls, imperceptible boundaries and thresholds that the child does not know, but which he or she longs to, yet must not, cross. The primary experience of the bourgeois child in the city is that of incarceration within a class-determined territory, and, in particular, in the gloomy family domicile, the bourgeois interior. The critique of the interior is consequently a fundamental theme in Benjamin's various writings on Berlin. The interior appears in three guises: as hiding-place, 'junk-room', and 'dead space'.

The bourgeois interior is a loathsome, desolate refuge from social activity in the public sphere. The 'privatization' of life is identified by Benjamin as a characteristic feature of nineteenth-century bourgeois life. He writes: 'Bourgeois existence is the regime of private affairs. The more important the nature and implications of a mode of behaviour, the further removed it is from observation here. Political conviction, financial situation, religion – all seek these hideouts' (*OWS*, p. 100).[38] This is particularly apparent with regard to sex, sexuality and the body. In 'One-Way Street', Benjamin argues that the interior is the locus in which the erotic and the sensual are confined. He notes: 'mundane life proclaims the total subjugation of eroticism to privacy. . . . The shift of erotic emphasis to the public sphere is both feudal and proletarian' (*OWS*, p. 101).[39] The hallmark of the modern bourgeoisie is the public denial of sensuality, of the reciprocity of gaze, of human interactions and relationships. Physical contact in public spaces is limited to the unpleasantness of being jostled in the metropolitan crowd. Sexuality is confined to the shadowy recesses of the most private of settings. Benjamin notes that 'the family is the rotten dismal edifice in whose closets and crannies the most ignominious instincts are deposited' (*OWS*, pp. 100–1). In its flight into the 'dismal edifice' of the bourgeois family and its stale, stagnant home, the erotic is robbed of its vitality and integrity. For Benjamin, the bourgeois interior is a sterile environment haunted by the dark spectres of repressed desire. Passion is denied, and sexuality reduced to the endurance of a joyless physicality. The interior is the prison-house of the erotic.

Desire and sexuality are transposed on to objects. Eroticism is transformed into commodity fetishism.[40] The interior is the locus of the phantasmagoria of modernity.[41] Benjamin writes:

> The inventory that filled these many rooms . . . could today be accommodated without incongruity in the shabbiest of second-hand furniture shops. And if these ephemeral forms were so much more solid than those of the *art nouveau* that superseded them – what made you feel at home, at ease, comfortable, and comforted in them was the nonchalance with which they attached themselves to the sauntering passage of years and days. . . . Here reigned a species of things that was, no matter how compliantly it bowed to the minor whims of fashion, in the main so wholly convinced of itself and its permanence that it took no account of wear, inheritance, or moves, remaining for ever equally near to and far from its ending, which seemed the ending of all things. (*OWS*, p. 328)[42]

The 'comfort' of the apartment derives from its sense of permanence and endurance. The interior seeks to establish itself, like the other monuments of the city, as 'timeless', impervious to changing socio-economic conditions, as something that will remain 'always-the-same'. Benjamin notes the smug complacency of the bourgeois domicile: 'with what words am I to circumscribe the almost immemorial feeling of bourgeois security that emanated from these rooms? Paradoxical as it may sound, the idea of that particular protectedness seems to relate most directly to their shortcomings' (ibid.). Confident of their own enduring comfort and privilege, the modern bourgeoisie articulate their self-satisfaction through the objects and spaces they possess. For Benjamin, this is the most precise example of their myopia and supreme folly.

The truth of the apartment and its contents, like that of the Egyptian obelisk in Paris or the Siegessäule, is apparent only in its afterlife. The revelation of fashion as the 'always-the-same' finds its counterpart here as the permanent is unmasked as the transient. The commodities that fill the interior are 'ephemeral forms' rather than enduring ones. They have deteriorated and decayed, while the interior remains pompously and blindly 'convinced of itself and its permanence'. The bourgeois interior, like the arcade, is home to objects which, though once fashionable and desirable, are now obsolete and ridiculous. Such artefacts have become worthy occupants of the 'shabbiest of second-hand furniture shops', the arrogant illusions of the bourgeois domicile thus critically revealed by the final destination of its contents: the junk-shop. The bourgeois apartment might adopt the guise of heroic immortality, but it actually constitutes nothing more than a site of decay and disintegration. The middle-class interior is home to the ruination of things.

Benjamin writes of his grandmother's residence in Blumeshof thus: 'when I think of this house . . . I am met on its threshold by a nightmare' (*OWS*, p. 329). The interior is a morbid, macabre setting. He writes:

The furniture style of the second half of the nineteenth century has received its only adequate description, and analysis, in a certain type of detective novel at the dynamic centre of which stands the horror of apartments. The arrangement of the furniture is at the same time the site plan of deadly traps, and the suite of rooms prescribes the fleeing victim's path. (*OWS*, p. 48)

The middle-class domicile, the site of the 'most ignominious instincts', is, according to Benjamin, the crucial locus of the nineteenth-century detective story. This space 'fittingly houses only the corpse. "On this sofa the aunt cannot but be murdered." The soulless luxuriance of the furnishings becomes true comfort only in the presence of the corpse' (*OWS*, p. 49). Strangely, however, Benjamin argues that although the interior is the space of the dying and the lifeless, the dead body itself is absent. He writes regarding his grandmother's abode in Berlin thus:

Poverty could have no place in these rooms where even death had none. They had no space for dying – which is why their owners died in a sanatorium, while the furniture went straight to the second-hand dealer. Death was not provided for in them – that is why they were so cosy by day, and by night the theatre of our most oppressive dreams. (*OWS*, pp. 328–9)

The bourgeois interior of the late nineteenth century is, on the one hand, the quintessential site of the dying, yet, on the other, the setting from which the dying are unceremoniously removed. It is the scene of the murder and the appropriate home for the corpse, but the body itself is absent.[43] This paradox is intelligible as follows. While the interior is for Benjamin the domain of decay and demise, any association with the natural history of the human body, its gradual disintegration and eventual death is denied. The interior becomes 'ageless', the sense of 'bourgeois security that emanated' from the middle-class home stemming from 'timelessness', from the denial of transience. The space of death, the murder, simultaneously becomes that of immortality, of permanence.

Benjamin's analysis of the interior highlights the bourgeois fear and detestation of the physical and corporeal. The erotic is hidden in the 'closets and crannies' of the middle-class apartment, while the dying are removed and confined to the hospital. Whereas in Naples the deformed body of the beggar was publicly on display, in Berlin, physical decay is taken away from the perceptual realm of everyday life. The dead body must be placed in its own particular space, away from the gaze of the living. Bourgeois order demands that everything be in its appointed place: the convict in prison, the insane in an asylum, the sick in hospital, the dying in a hospice, the dead in a mortuary, the poor at the 'back of beyond'. The 'abnormal' and disturbing are thus rendered invisible.[44] In 'The Storyteller' Benjamin writes:

> in the course of the nineteenth century bourgeois society has, by means of hygienic and social, private and public institutions, realised a secondary effect which may have been its subconscious main purpose: to make it possible for people to avoid the sight of the dying. Dying was once a public process in the life of the individual and a most exemplary one; think of the medieval pictures in which the deathbed has turned into a throne toward which the people press through the wide-open doors of the death house. In the course of modern times dying has been pushed further and further out of the perceptual world of the living. . . . Today people live in rooms that have never been touched by death, dry dwellers of eternity, and when their end approaches they are stowed away in sanatoria or hospitals by their heirs. (*ILL*, pp. 93–4)[45]

Death is cast out of the bourgeois interior, and sexuality is consigned to its miserable recesses. The vitality of the living and the integrity of the dead are simultaneously denied in this space. As a result, it becomes lifeless, sterile and inhuman. Although the site of the 'murder scene', the interior is not so much a space of death as itself 'dead space'. It is a site of imprisonment with its own incarcerated subject: the child.

Cityscape and playground

Buck-Morss accurately observes: 'imagery of the child's world appears so persistently throughout Benjamin's opus that the omission of a serious discussion of its theoretical significance in practically all commentaries on Benjamin is remarkable' (1989, p. 263). Benjamin does not posit an idyllic view of childhood, nor does he advocate any naïve or foolish return to 'childhood'; rather 'only he who can view his past life as an abortion sprung from compulsion and need can use it to full advantage in the present' (*OWS*, p. 76). Remembrance of the child's perception of things awakens a new understanding, however. As Szondi suggests, to view the city through the eyes of the child is to defamiliarize and therefore recognize it. The Berlin essays are attempts to recover the 'at first sight' of the child. This apparent misperception of the world may come to provide a more insightful image of reality, and serve to problematize the habitual, forgetful vision of the adult. Furthermore, whereas the adult seeks a position of superiority from which to view the world, the child enjoys a privileged proximity. As has already been suggested with reference to Benjamin's 'Moscow' essay, the child has a special, distinctive relationship with the spaces and objects encountered in the urban environment. He or she is 'closely mingled' with people and things. The child's perception and playful activity are marked by a distinctive, intimate connection to, and immersion in, the surrounding world.

Although this *promesse de bonheur* of childhood is to be recovered, childhood itself is not a period of blissful happiness or innocence. The child has a series of hopes, desires and expectations which are systematically denied and frustrated in the urban setting.[46] As a child, Benjamin is a prisoner of particular class locations and conventions. Cut off from the other districts of the urban environment, the quintessential childhood experiences recounted by Benjamin are those of loneliness and boredom, isolation and solitude.[47] The city promises excitement, diversion and adventure, yet provides these only in small measure. It is a locus of the broken promise of happiness. Benjamin writes: 'the city promised me something new each day and by evening it was left wanting' (*GS* IV, p. 291).[48] The metropolis contains only the always-the-same, the nothing-new, the boring. The child is an 'enslaved ancestor' whom the recollecting adult must redeem. The Berlin writings constitute a prehistory of the modern subject, the disappointed, frustrated, metropolitan individual. Benjamin presents an archaeology of the modern bourgeois self.

It is through play that the child encounters and transforms his or her surroundings. The notion of play is a fundamental, differentiated one in Benjamin's work. The key aspect of this is the relationship between play and myth: the playful child both participates in and negates myth. Playfulness contains within it utopian impulses, eschewing the division between subject and object and creating reciprocal and non-hierarchical relationships with the world of things. Play is spontaneous and creative, a counterpoint to the tedium and exploitation inherent in instrumental labour. It is the domain of freedom from compulsion. For Benjamin, the playfulness of the child comes to unmask the desolate, alienated reality of the bourgeois mode of existence within the city. The 'magic' of the child's imagination (disruptive, subversive) is the antithesis of the mythology of the adult (fetishistic, reifying).

Play is itself embroiled in the mythic, however. In a review of Karl Groeber's 1928 *Kinderspielzeug aus alter Zeit. Eine Geschichte des Spielzeugs* Benjamin writes:

> Finally a study of this kind must look into the law that, above all individual rules and rhythms, reigns over the whole world of play: the law of repetition. We know that, for a child, this is the very soul of play, that nothing makes him/her happier than 'once more'. The dark urge for repetition is hardly less powerful here in play, hardly less cunning in its work, than is the sexual drive in love. (*GS* III, p. 131)

Repetition is the key motif in Benjamin's understanding of mythic consciousness, and it holds sway in the sphere of play. The child's desire is 'not twice but always again, a hundred times, a thousand times' (ibid.). In a section of 'One-Way Street' entitled 'Child on the Roundabout', Benjamin uses the image of the carousel to illustrate this connection. He writes: 'his beast is devoted: like a mute Arion he rides his silent fish, or a wooden Zeus-bull carries him off as an immaculate Europa. The eternal recurrence of all things has long become child's wisdom to him, and life a primeval frenzy of domination' (*OWS*, p. 73). Play is both mythic and demythifying. Hence, as Buck-Morss points out, 'at no time did

Benjamin suggest that the child's mythic understanding was itself truth' (1989, p. 277). Rather, his concern with the activity of the playful child within the metropolitan environment stems from his desire to unravel the mythic from within. The Berlin essays, like the early phases of the *Passagenarbeit*, are 'dialectical fairytales' which seek to 'disenchant' the modern city through 'enchantment'.

Play as transgression   Play appears in three main guises in the Berlin writings: as transgression, mimesis and collection. For the child, the city is strictly divided into areas which are permitted (the middle-class 'ghettos' of the old and new West End) and those which are forbidden (the proletarian districts, the 'back of beyond'). A recurrent theme of the Berlin texts is Benjamin's desire to cross topographical (hence class) thresholds. He writes, somewhat crassly, 'a feeling of crossing the threshold of one's class for the first time had a part in the almost unequalled fascination of publicly accosting a whore in the street' (*OWS*, p. 301). To recognize yet disregard the invisible boundaries of the cityscape – this is the desire of the child and the regret of the adult. It is intimately bound up with straying, with losing oneself in the labyrinthine streets of the city. To surrender oneself to the pleasure of distraction, to allow oneself to be led by fancy and caprice, is the fundamental basis of the heedless wanderings of the dawdling *flâneur*. To lose oneself requires practice, because it demands that one overcome imposed prohibitions and inhibitions. The child is an apprentice in this 'art of straying', in the still self-conscious crossing of the spatial limits of his or her class.

The child also seeks to overcome the claustrophobia of the 'gloomy parental apartment' (*OWS*, p. 74) through the clandestine crossing of its thresholds. In 'Möbel und Masken', a review of the paintings of James Ensor, Benjamin writes: 'pale light breaks through heavily draped windows into the interior of those chaotic rooms crammed with furniture where we, as children, were often close to suffocating – as if in the entrails of a reptile' (*GS* IV, p. 478, cited by McCole, 1993, pp. 215–16). Though trapped within the tedious 'dead space' of the middle-class apartment, the child magically transforms this setting into a city in miniature[49] with its own compartments, boundaries and forbidden spaces: cupboards, boxes, containers and drawers. In the section of 'One-Way Street' entitled 'Pilfering Child', which was later to be rewritten for inclusion in 'Berlin Childhood' under the title 'Cupboards', Benjamin stresses the thrill and excitement of surreptitiously raiding the larder. Here a double liberation is evident: the child penetrates the secret spaces of the interior, and the 'stolen' objects are freed from their enclosure, their place within the bourgeois order of things. The child is a rescuer, a redeemer of things. Benjamin writes humorously that the strawberry jam was as 'grateful and tempestuous as one who has been abducted from the parental home' (*OWS*, p. 72).[50]

Play and mimesis   It is not only the spaces of the city that are transformed in the child's imagination, but also the artefacts encountered in them. In his 1933 essay 'On the Mimetic Faculty', Benjamin argues that mimesis, imitation, is a fundamental dimension of play. He writes: 'children's play is everywhere permeated by mimetic modes of behaviour, and its realm is by no means limited to what one person can imitate in another. The child plays at being not only a shopkeeper or teacher but also a windmill and a train' (*OWS*, p. 160). This is most evident in Benjamin's account of the child playing hide-and-seek.[51] In hiding, the child assumes the characteristics of, and indeed becomes part of, the place of concealment. Benjamin writes:

> Standing behind the doorway curtain, the child becomes himself something floating and white, a ghost. The dining table under which he is crouching turns him into the wooden idol in a temple whose four pillars are the carved legs. And behind a door he is himself a door, wears it as his heavy mask and as a shaman will bewitch all those who unsuspectingly enter. (*OWS*, p. 74)[52]

The child perceives and operates in the ancient domain of sensuous correspondences, a sphere which vanishes with the rise of modern civilization.[53] Benjamin notes: 'the gift, to recognise correspondences, is nothing other than a faint remnant of the old compulsion, to become similar and behave similarly' (*GS* IV, p. 261). The child still possesses what the modern adult will lose. The proximity of the child to objects is based on a particular interaction with the material world and a sense of reciprocity. The child keeps faith with an archaic, magical mode of relating to things which Benjamin counterposes to the instrumentalism and quest for domination of the adult.

The child recognizes connections that the adult wishes to deny. In a passage of 'One-Way Street' entitled 'Gloves', Benjamin notes both the human fear of animals and the desire for domination:

> In an aversion to animals the predominant feeling is fear of being recognised by them through contact. The horror that stirs deep in

man is an obscure awareness that in him something lives so akin to the animal that it might be recognised. . . . He may not deny his bestial relationship with animals, the invocation of which revolts him: he must make himself its master. (*OWS*, pp. 50–1)

The child seeks a non-hierarchical relationship with nature, identity and harmony rather than mastery. Correspondences are perceived: 'just as one forms a picture of a person's nature and character by their dwelling and by the district where they live, so I did with the animals of the Zoological Gardens' (*GS* IV, p. 255). Indeed, in the plight of the imprisoned animal, the child may come to recognize his or her own experience of entrapment within the bourgeois ghetto and incarceration in the interior. The child, like the animal in the zoo, is named by others,[54] the former by 'the class that pronounced him one of their own'. Benjamin himself was particularly drawn to the fish-otter, an animal that inhabited 'the least used' and 'deadest region of the gardens' (*GS* IV, p. 256), just as he was a resident of the junk-room of the Berlin West End, the 'dead space' of the bourgeois district of the city.

Within the confines of the bourgeois apartment, the child is engaged in mimetic play with the dead objects he or she finds there. This magical relation must be carefully distinguished from the mythical adult perception of material things. The child participates in neither the self-abasement of human beings before things (commodity fetishism) nor their domination (instrumentalism), but instead seeks a playful reciprocity. For the child, new commodities and fashions are a source of embarrassment and humiliation. Benjamin writes:

In those early years I got to know the 'town' only as the theatre of purchases. . . . In the ignominy of a 'new suit' we stood there, our hands peeping from the sleeves like dirty price tags, and it was only in the confectioner's that our spirits rose with the feeling of having escaped the false worship that humiliated our mother before idols bearing the names of Mannheimer, Herzog and Israel, Gerson, Adam, Esders and Maedler, Emma Bette, Bud and Lachmann. An impenetrable chain of mountains, no, caverns of commodities – that was 'the town'. (*OWS*, p. 327)[55]

While the adult is engaged in the fetishization, the 'false worship' of the commodity and those who purvey it, the child views the commodity only with a sense of horror and disgust. The adult humiliates him or herself before the commodity; the child is humiliated by it.

Play and collecting   According to Benjamin, the child inverts the value system of the adult world: what is prized by the adult brings misery to the child, whereas what the adult despises is precious to the child. He writes: 'the world is full of the most unrivalled objects for childish attention and use. And the most specific. For children are particularly fond of haunting any site where things are being visibly worked upon. They are irresistibly drawn by the detritus generated by building, gardening, housework, tailoring or carpentry' (*OWS*, p. 52). The child is concerned with the by-products, the unwanted and discarded objects found in the urban landscape. Benjamin notes:

> In waste products they recognise the face that the world of things turns directly and solely to them. In using these things they do not so much imitate the works of adults as bring together, in the artefact produced in play, materials of widely differing kinds in a new, intuitive relationship. Children thus produce their own small world of things within the greater one. (*OWS*, pp. 52–3)

The old-fashioned and cast-off are rescued by the child and reassembled in his or her own world in miniature. The demolition site, the space where the old is torn down to make way for the new, is transformed into a site of playful (re)construction. The child gathers up and saves the fragments found in the modern metropolis, and reassembles them in new constellations. Play consequently entails the activities of both the rag-picker and the collector.[56] The rag-picker, a figure of urban destitution and poverty, earns his or her living by gathering and recycling the detritus found in the city. The child, like the rag-picker, salvages the remnants of the old from obliteration.

As a collector, the child has a special relationship with the world of objects. Benjamin notes: 'the happiness of the collector, the happiness of the solitary: to be *tête-à-tête* with things' (Q°7, *GS* V, p. 1036). Collection is an act of renewal rather than possession. Benjamin points out that as a child, 'it was not my intention to keep the new but to renew the old. To renew the old by making it my own, the novice's. This was the work of the collection that was accumulating in my drawer' (*GS* IV, p. 286). The object, redeemed and renewed by the child, is arranged in new configurations and contexts. Benjamin writes: 'each stone he finds, each flower picked and each butterfly caught is already the start of a collection, and every single thing he owns makes up one great collection' (*OWS*, p. 73). In the child's collection, Benjamin notes, 'his drawers must become arsenal and zoo, crime museum and crypt' (*OWS*, p. 74).[57] The collection is not an ordered series of artefacts, however, but a motley agglomeration of random finds, of *objets trouvés*. Haphazard acquisition and disorderliness are the hallmarks of this assemblage. Benjamin notes: ' "to tidy up" would be to demolish an edifice full of prickly chestnuts that are spiky clubs, tinfoil that is hoarded silver, bricks that are coffins, cacti that are totem-poles and copper pennies that are shields' (ibid.).

Through the playfulness of the child, the broken and forgotten object is transformed into something new, something valuable. For the child every object in this hotchpotch of artefacts may come to represent or stand for something else. A preoccupation with the multiplicity of the fragment is the hallmark of the allegorical gaze. Stüssi perceptively notes: 'the child's collection is an assemblage of allegorical fragments, wrenched from their original context, which become highly significant in the eyes of the child' (1977, p. 207). It is the melancholy gaze of the allegorist which reduces the object to a ruinous condition, which breaks the mythic spell of appearance and totality. Through collecting, the remembered child liberates everyday things from the fate of the commodity, just as the remembering adult redeems apparently insignificant moments from the oblivion of amnesia. The child is the finder and keeper of lost things who complements the adult's remembrance of lost times.[58] The child is the urban archaeologist *par excellence*, an image of redemption, an allegory of the allegorist. Benjamin's writings on the child in the city, his act of remembrance, forms a re-membering (a reconstitution) of lost times, a recollection of the collector, a redemption of the figure of redemption.

This conception of the child as the finder and redeemer of lost objects is intimately linked with his or her special relationship with nature. In 'One-Way Street', Benjamin offers a critical denunciation of the destructive impact of modern capitalist industry on nature. He writes:

> An Athenian custom forbade the picking up of crumbs at the table, since they belonged to the heroes. If society has so degenerated through necessity and greed that it can now receive the gifts of Nature only rapaciously, that it snatches the fruit unripe from the trees in order to sell it most profitably, and is compelled to empty each dish in its determination to have enough, the earth will be impoverished and the land yield bad harvests. (*OWS*, p. 60)

Nature is ravaged by contemporary humankind. In the modern period, human beings do not live in thrall to the elements, or in a sense of balance or equilibrium. Benjamin notes in 'The Story-teller': 'Leskov tells us that the epoch in which humankind could believe itself to be in harmony with nature has expired. Schiller called this epoch in the history of the world the period of naive poetry. The storyteller keeps faith with it' (*ILL*, p. 97). 'Naïve poetry', the lyrical and pastoral, are incongruous with, and anachronistic within, modern capitalist society. The quest for harmony with the natural world is replaced by an instrumental, manipulative attitude. Modernity involves the unequivocal subjugation of nature to human mastery. Technology becomes the instrument wielded by a callous, indifferent humankind in its arrogant domination. Benjamin writes:

> The mastery of nature, so the imperialists teach, is the purpose of all technology. But who would trust a cane wielder who proclaimed the mastery of children by adults to be the purpose of education? Is not education above all the indispensable ordering of the relationship between generations and therefore mastery, if we are to use this term, of that relationship and not of children? And likewise technology is not the mastery of nature but of the relation between nature and humankind. (*OWS*, p. 104)

Like the story-teller, the child, who also fears the 'cane wielder', has a conception of a beneficent natural environment, and seeks not to disturb, rob or dominate it, but to find pleasure in its generosity.

Benjamin recounts an illuminating episode in this regard. Told that he would be able to find peacock feathers lying in the grass on Pfaueninsel (Peacock Island), the young Benjamin discovers nothing. He writes: 'had I found the feather I craved in the grass, I should have felt as if I were expected and welcome at this spot' (*OWS*, pp. 343–4). The disappointment felt at this failure 'would not have been so great had it not been Mother Earth herself who had inflicted it upon me' (*OWS*, p. 344). The child does not wrench the fruit 'unripe from the trees' (*OWS*, p. 60), but patiently searches for what nature has left unbidden. The child wants only that for which nature no longer has need. His or her wish is to discover the unrequested rather than control the uncooperative. Benjamin notes that 'finds are to children what conquests [*Siege*] are to adults' (*GS* IV, p. 298). The child seeks in play what the adult extracts through labour, violence and brutality. In the *Passagenarbeit*, Benjamin identifies his concern with the development of a harmonious, playful relationship with nature with the utopianism of Charles Fourier. With the end of capitalist domination,

> human labor . . . will cast aside its characteristic exploitation of nature. Human labor will then proceed in accord with the model of children's play, which in Fourier is the basis of the *travail passionné* of the *harmoniens*. To have situated play as the canon of a form of labor that is no longer exploitative is one of the greatest merits of Fourier. Labor thus animated by play aims not at the production of value, but at an improved nature. And Fourier's utopia presents a model for it, one that can in fact be found realised in children's play. . . . In it, activity would be the sister of the dream. (J75,2, *GS* V, p. 456, cited by Buck-Morss, 1989, p. 276)

The reference to dreaming is significant. In play, the child remains true to the desire for reconciliation and harmony with the world. Benjamin writes: 'the childhood experience of a generation has much in common with the dream experience. . . . Each epoch has this side turned toward the dream, the child side' (K1,1, *GS* V, p. 490). The unfulfilled aspirations and hopes of the child are dream-like in two senses: they are expressive of genuine utopian longing, and they are repressed and forgotten in adulthood.

The child in the metropolis is a figure of utopian dreaming in the very space of the frustration, inversion and distortion of dreams; for this is the pre-eminent locus of the myths of modernity.[59] It is here that play is transformed into toil, curiosity into fetishism, reciprocity into tyranny, spontaneity into drudgery. The natural history of the human subject is denied. Sexuality and eroticism are locked away in the bourgeois interior. The dying and deceased are removed and confined to special locations. The corpse disappears from the everyday perceptual realm so that the modern individual is not confronted and disturbed by the horror of physical decay. As 'dry dwellers of eternity', the middle classes seek to preserve a sense of the permanence of their values and order, of their own immortality. Just as they avoid the sight of their individual demise, so the bourgeoisie endeavour to render the proletariat invisible. The rich and the poor are segregated in their own 'ghettos', so that the former need not witness the consequences of the capitalist order. Benjamin writes: 'the bourgeoisie no longer dares to look in the eye the order of production that it itself has set into motion' (D9,3, *GS* V, p. 175, cited by Buck-Morss, 1989, p. 283).[60] The poor are situated out of sight and out of mind. This invisibility is temporal as well as spatial. The poor vanish from history. They are both hidden and forgotten. The modern city is not only the site of the disappearance of the poor in the present, but also the space in which they become imperceptible in the past. In the metropolis, the oppressed occupy the 'back of beyond'; in history, they are the forgotten dead. The monuments and museums of the urban complex bear witness to a partial, mythic conception of history as triumphal procession and ongoing progress. The city presents itself as the culmination of a glorious civilizing process.

Memory and the metropolis are interwoven. Benjamin's critical historiography is formed through the interplay of the adult-as-recollector (producer of a new history of humankind) and the child-as-collector (creator of new relationships between social, natural and material domains). The former, as an archaeologist, strips the urban monuments of their pretensions and illusions. He or she uncovers a different past buried in the cityscape, an alternative set of personal monuments to the unremembered dead. These sites of remembrance reveal history as continual tyranny, barbarism and suffering. Above all, the adult remembers and redeems the forgotten desires and thwarted aspirations of his or her own childhood. Locked in the tedious middle-class ghetto and the dismal parental apartment, the child transforms the objects and spaces he or she encounters through magical play. While not free from mythic compulsion, the playful child endeavours to establish an intimate, harmonious set of relations with both the natural world and the social environment. As collector, he or she rescues despised and disregarded objects and renews them in vital, magical configurations. Playfulness and dreaming are part enchantment, part disenchantment, of the adult world. To remember the child is to redeem for the present the redeemer of things. In play, the child keeps faith with, and is the custodian of, the dreams of humankind. The recollection of childhood is a fundamental imperative for Benjamin, because it recalls those forgotten dreams, those buried utopian impulses which must be recovered and realized in the present. The Berlin texts constitute an archaeology of hope.

3

Dialectical Images: Paris and the Phantasmagoria of Modernity

Introduction

From the humblest of beginnings in 1927, Benjamin's analysis of the shopping arcades of nineteenth-century Paris (the *Passagen-arbeit*) underwent fundamental, episodic transformation, and became a vast, sprawling, amorphous study, an absorbing passion that increasingly claimed all his intellectual energy.[1] Indeed, the 'Arcades Project', the culmination of his writings on the theme of the metropolis, the zenith of his cityscapes, remained unfinished at the time of Benjamin's tragic death in 1940, and forms only 'a charmed circle of fragments' (*OWS*, p. 48). While it is tempting to describe and mourn the *Passagenarbeit* as a literary 'ruin', such a characterization would be misleading: for a ruined building was once a complete one. Its structure, formerly whole and intact, has decayed and disintegrated. The 'Arcades Project', by contrast, never formed a coherent entity. It comprises, and was never anything more than, a mass of quotations and references, various working notes, and a collection of assorted drafts, sketches and *exposés*. If the *Passagenarbeit* is a ruin, it is, like the *Trauerspiel*, a purpose-built one.[2]

Alternatively, the *Passagenarbeit* may be celebrated as work-in-progress. In 'One-Way Street', Benjamin stresses the significance of such unfinished business when he observes that, 'to great writers, finished works weigh lighter than those fragments on which they work throughout their lives' (*OWS*, p. 47). Looked at in this light, the 'Arcades Project' may be seen as a disorderly construction site comprising a vast pile of building blocks interspersed with a few scattered sets of opaque, repeatedly redrawn blueprints for assembling them. The *Passagenarbeit*, then, is both ruin and building site. In the spirit of the 'porosity' which Benjamin identified in 'Naples', it is the place where construction and ruination interpenetrate and become indistinguishable from one another.

The form and character of the 'Arcades Project' are not just problems when it comes to examining it, but also critical keys to its interpretation. Both ruin and building site are urban, architectural metaphors that capture its design. Indeed, my central argument is that the experience of the metropolis itself is self-consciously embedded in the formal properties of the text of the 'Arcades Project', and that it is thus fruitful to regard the study itself as 'city-like'. In other words, the *Passagenarbeit* is best understood not as a description of the urban (text-about-city), but as itself fundamentally urban in character (text-as-city). I intend to clarify this rather odd statement in the following way. First, I will trace the history of the *Passagenarbeit*, the process of its faltering construction, then I will consider aspects of the contemporary debate over its status as a text. After indicating the central features of Benjamin's methodological approach and the primary content of his substantive concerns, I will explore some of the principal categories of the Paris writings: namely, the concepts of phantasmagoria and dreaming, commodity fetishism and fashion, and the 'dream-architecture' of modernity. In the next chapter, the focus of attention will shift to Benjamin's analysis of Baudelaire and allegory, the urban population as crowd and mass, and the 'heroism' of modern life.

The decisive inspiration for the 'Arcades Project' is conventionally regarded as Louis Aragon's surrealistic text *Le Paysan de Paris* ('The Paris Peasant'), published in 1926. In this work Aragon explores the soon to be demolished Passage de l'Opéra and the so-called mythology of modernity in a series of dream-like visions of the metropolitan environment. Benjamin was extremely enthusiastic about this work. In a letter to Adorno of 31 May 1935 he writes: 'there stands at its beginning Aragon: *The Paris Peasant*, of which at night in bed I was never able to read more than two or three pages because my heartbeats became so strong that I had to put the book down' (*GS* V, p. 1117). One should be careful not to overstate the importance of Aragon's book, however, for a number of reasons. First, Benjamin was excited by Aragon's study not because it stimulated a set of new themes and ideas in him, but because it articulated and gave voice to a series of pre-existing ones.[3] The *Passagenarbeit* clearly draws upon methodological insights (a concern with fragments, imagistic representation and concreteness, the montage principle) and substantive themes (forms of architecture, the notion of myth, commodities and patterns of consumption) that he had pioneered in his earlier cityscapes and 'One-Way Street'. Moreover, Benjamin's initial, and for some most significant, engagement with Surrealist ideas (the 1925–6 essay 'Dreamkitsch') only considers works pre-dating *The Paris Peasant*.[4] It is also important to realize that Benjamin's attitude to Surrealist themes and elements was never uncritical. He was at pains to distance himself from the ecstatic, celebratory tendencies of the Surrealists, and rejected Aragon's participation and pleasure in the very *mythologie moderne* he identified. For Benjamin, the intoxication of the city must not be allowed to befuddle the senses or hinder critical engagement. Benjamin does not adopt Aragon's stimulating vision of the metropolis, but rather employs it as a counterpoint to his own more sober, and more melancholy, historical gaze. Surrealist motifs waned in importance for Benjamin in the 1930s, and were supplanted, first by Proust's *mémoire involontaire* and later by Baudelaire's allegorical poetics.

Benjamin's original intention was to write a short essay on the Parisian arcades with Franz Hessel. To this end he composed a short sketch (simply entitled 'Passagen'[5]) between April and October 1927, and wrote a few further pages of notes by the end of the year (*GS* V, pp. 991–1038). On 30 January 1928 Benjamin, writing to Scholem from Berlin, stated that the arcades study would be 'the work of just a few weeks' (*GS* V, p. 1083). In this letter Benjamin also noted a revised provisional title for the study: *Pariser Passagen: Eine dialektische Feerie* ('Paris Arcades: A Dialectical Fairy-Tale'). Some seven years later he noted (in a letter to Adorno of 31 May 1935) that this title was intended to capture 'the rhapsodic character of the representation' (*GS* V, p. 1117). On 18 April 1928 he informed Kracauer that 'the arcades are on the agenda [*auf dem Tapet*] day in and day out' (*GS* V, p. 1085). Four days later, in a letter to Max Rychner, he mentions the arcades study 'on which I have been working for several months and which must be completed by the [time of my] prospective return to Paris' (ibid.). In the light of such comments by Benjamin during the early part of 1928, it is important to take note of the limited expectations and ambitions he had for the work.[6]

During the course of 1928, though, the parameters of the 'essay' began to expand. On 5 May of that year Benjamin states in a letter to Hofmannsthal: 'I am working further and almost exclusively on the "Paris Arcades" ' (*GS* V, p. 1086). By the end of the month, Benjamin's increasing concern with the Paris material finds expression in a letter to Scholem (24 May 1928), in which the 'Arcades Project' is said to howl 'in my nights in the manner of a small beast if I do not daily take it to drink at the most distant sources' (ibid.). With reference to the Paris work, Benjamin informs Scholem on 30 October 1928 that 'I have had to expand it more and more' (*GS* V, p. 1089). It is evident that by the end of 1928 the 'small beast' was steadily and inexorably becoming a huge monster.

Early 1929 saw Benjamin's essay on the Surrealist movement,[7] which he describes in a letter to Scholem of 15 March 1929 as 'a "paravent" in front of the "Paris Arcades" ' (*GS* V, p. 1090). On 21 March he voiced his total immersion in the work on Paris in a letter to Kracauer: 'I am at the Arcades – "to me it is as though in a dream, as though it were a part of me" ' (*GS* V, p. 1091). The ongoing importance of the revised *Passagenarbeit* during the winter of 1929–30, which Benjamin spent in Paris, is stressed in a letter to Scholem of 20 January. The work on Paris, he writes, 'is the theatre of all my struggles and all my ideas' (*GS* V, p. 1094).

The early 1930s saw Benjamin caught up in financial and personal crises. In a letter to Scholem of 28 October 1931 Benjamin writes: 'I could only think of accomplishing the work if my activity were secured for two years, which, for the last few months, it has never been even for as many weeks' (*GS* V, p. 1095). His precarious financial position was exacerbated by the worsening socio-political conditions in Germany. The growing power of the Nazis led to Benjamin's emigration in 1932, when he moved briefly to Ibiza before settling in Paris. Given such traumatic upheavals, it is not surprising that the 'Arcades Project' took on a 'subterranean' character (Frisby, 1988, p. 195) during this time. However, Benjamin did manage to produce what he regarded as a 'prolegomenon' to the *Passagenarbeit*, his 'Small History of Photography' of 1931,[8] and his enthusiasm for the project did not wane. As soon as he reached the relative security of Ibiza in May 1932, he described the overall content of the Paris enterprise as that 'in which, if not for others then certainly for me, the most important directives lie' (*GS* V, p. 1095).

The possibility of producing an overarching interpretation, a coherent, integrated piece of work out of the material he had assembled, appeared, if still desirable at this point, remote. The more he worked on the prospective study, the more distant its completion seems to have become. His comment to Scholem in a letter from Nice of 26 July 1932 may be seen as characterizing his entire literary activity: 'though many – or a sizable number – of my works have been small-scale victories, they are offset by large-scale defeats' (*GER*, p. 14). This may also be a reference to Benjamin's other historical project of the moment: 'Berlin Chronicle' and 'Berlin Childhood', for these essays are precisely such 'small-scale victories'. In these writings the analysis of the recent past, the 'prehistory' of the nineteenth century, is articulated in terms of the 'autobiography' and memoirs explored in the previous chapter. The Berlin texts constituted historiographic experiments in the representation of the metropolis as the preeminent locus of myth. They were models which Benjamin recognized as inadequate, however, for the now apparent large scale of the 'Arcades Project'.

Benjamin resumed work on the *Passagenarbeit* during the early spring of 1934. Benjamin writes to Adorno on 9 March 1934: 'life has once again come into the Arcades. . . I am in the study room [of the Bibliothèque nationale] practically the whole day' (*GS* V, p. 1100). By the end of March, this renewed labour had supplied the study with both a 'provisional chapter organisation' and a 'new visage' (letter to Gretel Adorno, *GS* V, p. 1103). While visiting Brecht in Skovsbostrand Per Svendborg in Denmark during the autumn of 1934, Benjamin notes his intention to approach the Paris material 'with significantly changed points of view' in a letter to Scholem of 17 October (*GER*, p. 144). Shortly after this, Benjamin, writing from San Remo, informs Horkheimer: 'I was occupied further with this material in the summer and today the clear structure of the book stands before my eyes' (*GS* V, p. 1105). The remainder of 1934 seems to have been devoted to this reorganization and restructuring of the Paris notes, as Benjamin remarks in a letter to Alfred Cohn of 19 December: 'I have begun to go through my studies for the Arcades precisely and systematically' (*GS* V, p. 1111).

Benjamin's resumption of concerted work on the *Passagenarbeit* prompted Horkheimer in early 1935 to request an *exposé* of the project for the Institute for Social Research (based in Geneva prior to its eventual relocation in New York). Benjamin's response was enthusiastic. In a letter to Scholem of 20 May 1935 he notes that in this *exposé* 'the work has entered a new phase, in which for the first time it bears more resemblance – even if from afar – to a book'

(*GER*, p. 158). He adds: 'the title "Paris Arcades" has finally been discarded and the draft is entitled "Paris: The Capital of the Nineteenth Century"; privately I call it *Paris: capitale du XIXe siècle*' (*GER*, p. 159). While Horkheimer's response was encouraging,[9] Adorno's was not. At the beginning of August 1935 Adorno sent a detailed, much discussed critical response to Benjamin's draft. Adorno's critical reception of the central categories of the study (commodity fetishism and the dreaming collectivity) focused above all on what he regarded as Benjamin's dangerous proximity to the reactionary theories of Carl Jung and Ludwig Klages. Adorno was concerned that Benjamin's version of the commodity as a 'wish-image' lodged in a dreaming collective mind bore an unfortunate resemblance to their doctrines of ahistorical or trans-historical archetypes and the collective unconscious.[10]

Benjamin, who in the autumn of 1935 was preparing material for his essay 'The Work of Art in the Age of Mechanical Reproduction',[11] was responsive to Adorno's critique. During a visit to Paris the following year, Adorno suggested that Benjamin write a critical study of Jung and Klages in order to uncover and delineate the fundamental differences between the 'archaic image' and the 'dialectical image'. Benjamin confessed his unfamiliarity with the work of Jung, but warmed to the proposal,[12] and prepared a bibliography.[13] In a letter to Horkheimer of 28 March 1937 he states: 'what made this proposal of two and a half months ago plausible, and what attracts me still, is the chance to clarify those pages of my planned book that least satisfied me in the 1935 *exposé* via an investigation of Klages and Jung' (*GS* V, p. 1157). This is reiterated and specified in a letter to Scholem on 2 July 1937: 'it is my desire to safeguard certain foundations of the "Paris Arcades" methodologically by waging an onslaught on the doctrines of Jung, especially those concerning archaic images and the collective unconscious' (*GER*, p. 197). A week later, however, this projected critique of the 'devil's work' (*GER*, p. 203) of Jung was apparently postponed or dropped. Benjamin writes to Fritz Lieb (9 July): 'I am now turning to a study of Baudelaire' (*GS* V, p. 1162).

In his writings on Baudelaire, Benjamin sought to formulate a model in miniature of, and for, the larger Paris study,[14] incorporating in the process some of its 'philosophical contents' (letter to Pollock of 28 August 1938, *GS* V, p. 1167) in new configurations.[15] He gave specific details of the themes of the projected Baudelaire study in a letter to Horkheimer of 16 April 1938.[16] The book was to be divided into three sections entitled

'Idea and Image', 'Antiquity and Modern', and 'The New and the Always-the-Same'. The first of these was to be concerned with the meaning and structure of allegory in *Les Fleurs du mal* and with Baudelaire's theory of correspondences. Whereas Baudelaire was to appear in 'monographic isolation' (*COR*, p. 557) in this initial section, the second part was to emphasize his position within the literary and social milieu of mid-nineteenth-century Parisian society. This middle section was to explore the interpenetration of modern and archaic, with particular reference to the urban crowd and the city as labyrinth. 'The third part', Benjamin states, 'treats the commodity as the fulfilment of Baudelaire's allegorical vision' (*COR*, p. 557). This was to include an analysis of *art nouveau* and of the figure of the prostitute as the embodiment of the commodity. In a consideration of the notions of novelty, the always-the-same and eternal recurrence, the 'historical config-uration' made up of Baudelaire's *Les Fleurs du mal*, Blanqui's *Éternité par les Astres* and Nietzsche's *Will to Power* was to be identified and explored.

Benjamin began this undertaking during mid-1938 by writing the second section (itself subdivided into three parts: 'The *Bohème*', 'The *Flâneur*' and 'Modernism'); he sent it forthwith to the Institute in New York for publication in its journal (the *Zeitschrift für Sozialforschung*). But Adorno, took a rather dim view of Benjamin's 'Paris of the Second Empire in Baudelaire', arguing that the work lacked theoretical underpinning and drew a simplistic equation between, on the one hand, the material circumstances and historical events of the time, and, on the other, Baudelaire's poetry. He considered such a deterministic vision undialectical. The crucial absence of any adequate form of mediation resulted, Adorno claimed, in a shallow immediacy and bald facticity. The work was dismissed as 'located at the crossroads of magic and positivism' (*AP*, p. 129). Despite a spirited rejoinder to these criticisms and a plea from Benjamin for the essay to be published in order to facilitate open debate, it remained unpublished, a fact for which Adorno has been justly rebuked. Benjamin rewrote the manuscript a few months later under the new title 'On Some Motifs in Baudelaire'. Although this may be regarded as a slightly inferior work, lacking the originality and precision of insight of the first text, it none the less met with a considerably more favourable response from Adorno and, accordingly, was published in January 1940.[17]

Benjamin's last few months saw the composition of the now famous 'Theses on the Concept of History'. These unfinished fragments, which drew upon and elaborated elements found in *Konvolut* N, were intended to form an introduction or preface to the 'Arcades Project'. The *Passagenarbeit* was left by Benjamin with his friend George Bataille when he fled from Paris in mid-1940 before the advancing Nazi forces, and was lodged for safe keeping during the war years in the Bibliothèque nationale. But Benjamin never returned to it; he committed suicide at Port Bou on the Franco–Spanish border on 26 September 1940.

The diverse assortment of papers and notes produced by Benjamin in connection with his Paris studies over the last thirteen years of his life were gathered by Rolf Tiedemann for publication in 1982 under the title *Das Passagen-Werk*, a name that has not been free from criticism.[18] This two-volume work contains Benjamin's first notes and early sketches from the late 1920s,[19] the mass of quotations and other fragments organized by Benjamin into separate folders (*Konvoluts*) designated by letter (A–Z and a–z) and a subject heading ('Fashion', 'Arcades', 'Iron Construction', 'The Streets of Paris', etc.), and two versions (one in French) of the 1935 *exposé*. The raw materials for the Baudelaire studies are largely to be found in *Konvoluts* J ('Baudelaire') and M ('The *Flâneur*'). The 'Arcades Project' is not so much an unfinished text as a series of texts in various stages of completion. It is neither a coherent nor a single piece of writing, but rather an agglomeration or plethora of interconnected, related enterprises, begun at various times, dropped, taken up with renewed zeal, transformed and eventually abandoned in favour of something else. Adorno 'worked through it exhaustively' (cited by Buck-Morss, 1983, p. 212), and decided that, in the absence of a theoretical or conceptual framework to facilitate construction, the literary jigsaw puzzle could not be assembled. 'If it were possible at all,' Adorno states, 'only Benjamin could have accomplished it' (cited ibid.).

Since the publication of the texts, a number of scholars have come to view such lamentations over the impossibility of construction as fundamentally misplaced. Lloyd Spencer, for instance, plausibly points out that 'it has become common to lament that Benjamin did not live to synthesise the fragments of his thought. He would never have synthesised them, but only further elaborated them' (*CP*, p. 30). Buck-Morss goes somewhat further when she writes:

> In the *Passagen-Werk* Benjamin has left us his note-boxes. That is, he has left us 'everything essential'. Lamentations over the work's

incompleteness are thus irrelevant. Had he lived, the notes would not have become superfluous by entering into a closed and finished text. And surely, the card file would have been thicker. The *Passagen-Werk* is as it would have been: a historical lexicon of the capitalist origins of modernity, a collection of concrete factual images of urban experience. (1986, p. 99)

In the views of Spencer and Buck-Morss, there was to be no synthesis, only the ceaseless piling up of ever more fragmentary and disparate elements.[20] The unfinished text has been transformed from a vice (incomplete, impossible to interpret) into a virtue (open, a site of 'endless interpolations'). Speculations as to what Benjamin might or might not have done aside, the key issue remains: *given* the condition and character of Benjamin's Paris texts, what provides the most useful and/or most interesting interpretive framework for analysis?

While it is clear that, as Buck-Morss states, 'any argument based on the *Passagen-Werk* is necessarily tentative due to its extremely ambiguous status as a text' (1983, p. 211), it is evident that the 'Arcades Project' elaborates and extends Benjamin's abiding preoccupation with the critical interpretation of features of urban life. Benjamin's writings on Paris are best understood in relation to his other cityscapes, for they contain further articulation and elaboration of the themes and methods pioneered in the *Denk-bilder*. The *Passagenarbeit* is concerned with the city as the site of myth, the commodity and consumption, the interpenetration of architecture and social activity, the organization and relationship between public and private realms, and the problematic interaction between the urban masses and the marginal figures of the metropolitan landscape. Benjamin's methodological concerns and innovations are developed and refined: physiognomic reading, facticity and concreteness, and an imagistic historiography. The task of giving voice to the ephemeral and fragmentary character of metropolitan experience is pursued through the formulation of montage and the dialectical image. Adorno notes: 'politics and metaphysics, theology and materialism, myth and modernity, intentionless material and extravagant speculation – all streets in Benjamin's cityscape converge in the plan of the book on Paris as they do in the city's *Étoile*' (1990, pp. 19–20).

Adorno's urban metaphor is apt; for when one unravels the relationship between the mode of representation and the object of analysis, unfolding the connections between form and content, it becomes apparent that the *Passagenarbeit* incorporates precisely those metropolitan experiences it seeks to describe. The text is city-like. In its pages one may linger in the structures and spaces of the urban complex, the arcades and world exhibition centres, the museums and railway stations, the boulevards and the Métro. One may browse among the heterogeneous objects (the commodity, fashion, the designs of *art nouveau*) assembled by Benjamin the collector in this, his greatest collection. One may laugh scornfully at the once fashionable but now quaint and obsolete artefacts one may chance to find. One may admire oneself in the looking-glass city and the mirror-like eyes of the passers-by. One may saunter among the milling urban populace that presents itself in various guises, as crowd, as collective, as mass, but always as customers. One is introduced to a variety of urban characters: the dandy, *flâneur*, idler, fop, prostitute, rag-picker and poet. One encounters the often absurd, and always pompous, social and literary commentators of the Parisian journals and newspapers. One meets the more distinguished figures of the epoch, both political (Marx, Fourier, Saint-Simon, Blanqui) and literary (Hugo, Baudelaire). It is a panoramic vision of the city. Thus, 'Arcades Project' seems an inappropriate name for this mass of material, first, because it in no way constituted a single unified project, and second, because by the time of Benjamin's death, the texts specifically concerned with the arcades formed only a fraction of the writings. As Tiedemann observes: 'if it had been completed it would have become nothing less than a materialist philosophy of the nineteenth century' (Smith ed., 1988, p. 261).

The range of material is wide and daunting. I wish to explore only a small selection of this vast pile of fragments, in the hope that this may provide the keys to the whole. In this chapter I will explore Benjamin's understanding of the objects, architectural forms and spaces of the city itself. A consideration of his view of the modern metropolis as the pre-eminent site of myth introduces the central categories of dreaming and awakening. I will then examine the two key instances of urban phantasmagoria: the commodity and the so-called dream-houses of modernity. In the next chapter I will be concerned with the figures that populate the urban setting, and in particular Benjamin's account of Baudelaire, the motif of the crowd, and the heroism of modern life. This is not to suggest any thematic division between the city and its inhabitants. It is simply to impose some analytical order on the chaos of Benjamin's materials. It is an attempt at a map to help the wanderer pick his or her way through the seemingly endless literary sprawl, a guide to some of the salient features and hidden connecting alley-ways of this most complex of cityscapes.

Modern mythology and urban dreamscape

For the Surrealists Louis Aragon and André Breton, the metropolis was bewitching. With its kaleidoscope of lights and perspectives, its cacophony of sound and noise, its mass of diverse artefacts and distractions, the city was a site of the perpetual stimulation, the intoxication of the modern. Benjamin writes of the Surrealists: 'at the centre of this world of things stands the most dreamed-of of their objects, the city of Paris itself' (*OWS*, p. 230). The city was a dreamscape of the magical and mysterious. To surrender oneself to such enticements, to roam the enchanted metropolis in pursuit of desire and distraction – such motives inspired the *Paysan de Paris* and *Nadja*. 'Walking tipsily' in the metropolis, Aragon notes, 'I set about forming the idea of a mythology in motion. It was more accurate to call it a mythology of the modern. And it was under this name that I conceived it' (1987, p. 130). This rapture, this mythology, had its own idols, altars and rituals. These were neither the gods of old nor natural phenomena. Aragon states: 'So it seemed to me right away that nature could play no part in this mythical conception of the modern world to which I was becoming attached . . . Although supplanting the old myths of nature, the new myths cannot really be set up in opposition to them, for they draw their strength, their magic from the same source, and so have an equal right to be considered myths' (1987, p. 137). The myths of modernity do not arise from the compulsions of nature, but rather pay homage to the creations of humankind: the commodities, buildings and machines of the cityscape. Aragon provides the following description of one of these 'modern idols', the petrol pump:

> Painted brightly with English or invented names, possessing just one long, supple arm, a luminous faceless head, a single foot and a numbered wheel in the belly, the petrol pumps sometimes take on the appearance of the divinities of Egypt or of those cannibal tribes which worship war and war alone. O Texaco motor oil, Esso, Shell, great inscriptions of human potentiality, soon shall we cross ourselves before your fountains, and the youngest among us will perish from having contemplated their nymphs in naphtha. (1987, p. 132)

The Surrealist recognition of the metropolis as the locus of myth and the cult of the commodity was fundamental for the *Passagenarbeit*. Benjamin also possessed that eye for the bizarre, the arcane and the absurd within the everyday which characterized the Surrealist gaze.[21] For Benjamin, Paris is the home of the phantasmagoric: the so-called dreaming collectivity and the architectural forms it spawned, commodity fetishism and fashion, and the concept of 'progress'. In the 'Arcades Project', Benjamin seeks to trace the archaic and most ancient in the heart of the ultimate site of modernity, to discover mythic forms and compulsive repetition precisely where progress, enlightenment and novelty proclaim themselves most loudly. For him, the *Passagenarbeit* presented and constituted the 'prehistory' (*Urgeschichte*) of modernity. He writes:

> 'Prehistory of the nineteenth century' – this would have no interest, if we understood it to mean that prehistoric forms are to be rediscovered among the inventory of the nineteenth century. The concept . . . has meaning only where this century is to be presented as the original form of prehistory, that is, as a form in which all of prehistory groups itself anew in images peculiar to the last century. (N3a,2, Smith ed., 1989, p. 51)

The modern was to be revealed not merely as the continuation and rearticulation of such forces, but as the fundamental culmination of the mythic, as its most refined and pervasive form.

In the initial phases of the *Passagenarbeit* Benjamin explores the mythic character of the metropolis with reference to a particular, and distinctive, constellation of motifs drawn from the idiom of psychoanalysis (with which Benjamin was not especially familiar) and Surrealism: sleeping, dreaming and awakening. For Benjamin, the modern period is one of sleeping. He writes: 'capitalism was a natural phenomenon with which a new dream sleep came over Europe and with it, a reactivation of mythical powers' (K1a,8, *GS* V, p. 494). The nineteenth century is a time-space (*Zeitraum*) and a time-dream (*Zeit-traum*) (K1,4, *GS* V, p. 491) with Paris as its ultimate focus. Just as the desires and wishes of the individual are frustrated and repressed in waking life only to reappear in disguised form in dreams during sleep, so the cityscape and the artefacts found therein are dream-like creations of the dormant collectivity. For Benjamin, as for Baudelaire, Paris is nothing other than a 'teeming city, a city full of dreams' (*CB*, p. 60). The dream-world of modernity, which proclaims itself as the end of the myth, is only its persistence in a new, intensified, historical form. The city is both the setting for and the product of the fantasies of the collective unconscious, the 'dreaming collectivity'. Wolin notes that:

> The dream for Benjamin becomes an autonomous source of experience and knowledge, a hidden key to the secrets and mysteries of waking life. In no uncertain terms, dreams become the repositories of the utopian visions of humanity whose realisation is forbidden in waking life; they serve as the refuge for those desires and aspirations that are denied to humanity in material life. (1986, p. 207)

For Benjamin, the edifices and the objects of the metropolis are utopian wish-images, frozen representations or objectifications of genuine wants and aspirations that remain unfulfilled or thwarted. The utopian impulses of long-dead generations lie embedded in the latest products and innovations of capitalist society. The arcades of the moderns are the distorted manifestation of the Arcadias of the ancients. Menninghaus notes that 'just as fetishism and ideology are a combination of false and true moments for Marx, so Benjamin recognises the realms of mythological images and dreams as a duality of "utopian" and "cynical element[s]" ' (1986, pp. 18–19). Abundance, progress, freedom from the dictates of compulsion and fate – these find distorted material form in the architecture, fashions and commodities of the nineteenth century. They are the fantastical materialization of the longing for liberation from myth. The phantasmagoria of modernity consists of entities which paradoxically contain the promise of the overcoming of the mythic. For Benjamin, the utopian dream elements must be liberated, redeemed and realized in the present. It is this that forms the basis of the *Urgeschichte* of the recent past.

Benjamin's notions of the collective unconscious, the dreaming collectivity and the commodity as wish-image caused Adorno considerable disquiet. In his critique of Benjamin's 1935 *exposé*, Adorno complains of the undifferentiated character of the notion of the collective dream (un)consciousness thus:

> who is the subject of the dream? In the nineteenth century it was surely only the individual; but in the individual's dream no direct depiction of either the fetish character or its monuments may be found. Hence the collective consciousness is invoked, but I fear that in its present form it cannot be distinguished from Jung's

conception. . . . It should be a clear and sufficient warning that in a dreaming collective no differences remain between classes. (*AP*, pp. 112–13)

For Adorno, the concept of the collective obscures the reality of class distinctions and class conflict in modern capitalist society. It postulates an untenable sense of identity and shared interest that radically contradicts the actual antagonistic character of class relations. A state of classlessness may be the content of the dream, but it is not the existing condition of the dreamer.[22]

Benjamin did not clarify these issues. His proposed solution to these problems, a critique of Jung and Klages, never materialized. Instead, Benjamin began his work on Baudelaire, in which this conceptualization of the mythic character of modernity as dream is absent. Myth remains as a corollary of the unconscious mind, but is now articulated with respect to forgetfulness. As pioneered in the Berlin writings, the modern metropolis constitutes the site of amnesia. Forgetfulness dooms the modern individual to that fundamental dimension of mythic consciousness and experience: repetition. The old appears as new precisely because the past has been forgotten. That which passes for novelty and invention is the ceaseless and tiresome parade of the always-the-same. Benjamin writes:

> It is not a question of the same thing happening again and again (*a fortiori* I do not speak of eternal return) but rather that the face of the world never changes precisely in that which is the latest, that this 'latest' remains in every instance always the same thing. This consitutes the eternity of Hell. To determine the totality of traits in which 'modernity' finds its expression would be to portray Hell. (S1,5, *GS* V, p. 676)

It is not that things recur, but that they do not change, that is crucial for Benjamin. History is the endless stream of the nothing-new; it is fundamentally at a standstill, not engaged in some cyclical motion. Benjamin writes: 'the idea of eternal recurrence transforms historical events into mass-produced articles' (*CP*, p. 36). Indeed, for Benjamin, Nietzsche's doctrine of eternal recurrence is part of the mythology of the nineteenth century, not the breaking of its spell.[23] Benjamin writes:

> The idea of eternal recurrence conjures out of the misery of the *Gründerjahre* the phantasmagoria of happiness. This doctrine is an attempt to combine the contradictory tendencies of desire: that of

repetition and that of eternity. This heroism is a counterpart to that of Baudelaire, who conjured the phantasmagoria of modernity out of the misery of the Second Empire. (D9,2, *GS* V, p. 175)

The key to modernity is ongoing sameness, the unchanging. Modernity, Benjamin writes, 'is a world of strict discontinuity, the ever-new is not the old which remains, nor the past which recurs; rather it is the one and the same intersected by countless pauses' (G°19, *GS* V, p. 1011).[24]

The corollary of the doctrine of eternal recurrence is to be found in the concept of progress. Benjamin notes: 'the belief in progress, in an endless perfectibility – an endless task in the moral sphere – and the idea of eternal recurrence are complementary. They are the indelible antinomies in the presence of which the dialectical conception of historical time is to be developed' (D10a,5, *GS* V, p. 178). Modernity presents itself as the always-new, as continual improvement, and the metropolis proclaims itself to be the zenith of civilization. Such a vision of the historical process found an accomplice in what Benjamin in his 'Theses on the Concept of History' terms 'historicism',[25] the historiographic principles of Gottfried Keller and Leopold von Ranke.[26] For Benjamin, historicism falsifies history in three main ways:[27]

1 The myth of historical closure. Historicism conceives of the past as unproblematically 'given', as a static object of contemplation, as that which simply was and is no more. Historicism claims to present a complete, all-encompassing 'universal history'.
2 The myth of historical empathy. Knowledge of the past is to be gained through the act of 'empathy'. One must place oneself retrospectively and imaginatively in the shoes of historical figures in order to gain insight into the world of the past.
3 The myth of historical progress. For historicism, while the past is indisputably finished, it is also unambiguously linked to the present through the chain of intervening occurrences. History is conceptualized as a continuum of events, as linear progress culminating in the present.

For Benjamin, 'historicism' posited an uncritical notion of the past as given and readily available. The past could be unproblematically related as it 'really was', unadulterated by present interests. It was historicist narration of the past which saw history as continuity and progress. Benjamin regarded such a reading of history as an ideological vision, a legitimation and vindication of both past and present social arrangements. The doctrine of progress involved misrecognition of the nothing-new and forgetfulness of ongoing suffering. For Benjamin, the catastrophic character of history must be stressed. He notes: 'definition of the present as catastrophe' (*GS* I, p. 1243) and adds: 'the catastrophe is progress, the progress is the catastrophe' (*GS* I, p. 1244). In its denial of the persistence of myth, historicism itself participates in the phantasmagoria of modernity.

In his later writings on Paris, the mythology of modernity is no longer articulated with respect to dreaming collectivities, but in terms of a new constellation of concepts: repetition, reification and progress. Benjamin's critical task involves an intricate, twin operation: first, to reveal the ever-new (fashion, *nouveauté*) as the always-the-same (the unchanging world of commodity production and corresponding alienation); and second, to unmask the always-the-same (bourgeois pre-eminence and the persistence of the mythic itself) as nothing other than the transitory and temporary. One paradox is thereby transformed into another. The nineteenth century presents itself as the progressive and endlessly enduring, whereas for Benjamin it must be revealed as the static yet ephemeral. When 'history' itself becomes embroiled in myth, the task must be 'to brush history against the grain' (*ILL*, p. 259), to explode the illusion of progress and bring true liberation from the repetitions of the nineteenth century.

Historical awakening

Benjamin describes the task confronting him in the 'Arcades Project' as follows:

> To clear the fields, where until now only delusion ran rampant. Forge ahead with the whetted axe of reason, looking neither to the left nor the right, in order not to fall victim to the horror beckoning from the depths of the primeval forest. At a certain point, reason must clear the entire ground and rid it of the undergrowth of delusion and myth. Such is the goal here for the nineteenth century. (see N1,4, Smith ed., 1989, p. 44)

In this passage Benjamin appears to embrace the conventional dichotomy between myth and reason expounded by Enlightenment thought. Human beings must free themselves from the 'primeval forest', the blind forces of nature and chaos, through the exercise of reason. For Benjamin, however, the task involved and the methods to be employed are far more complex than this. The 'whetted axe' of reason would prove less useful than nimble fingers for unpicking the knotted threads of myth and modernity. Elimination of the mythic is not to be achieved through 'reason' as such at all; rather, the disenchantment of the world is to take place paradoxically and precisely through enchantment. Enchantment disenchants modernity. It is this that constitutes Benjamin's 'dialectical fairy-tale',[28] the telling of which breaks the spell that holds us in thrall.[29]

In the 'Arcades Project', the Surrealist revelation of the metropolis as dreamscape was to be pursued and transformed into the critical negation of the myths of modernity. Benjamin writes: 'to win the energies of intoxication for the revolution – this is the project about which Surrealism circles in all its books and enterprises' (*OWS*, p. 236). The 'Arcades Project' was to engage in, rather than skirt, such an undertaking. For Benjamin, the Critical Theorist must not be lulled into complicity with the intoxication of the city, but resist its allure and unmask its barbarism. Aragon and Breton lingered in the realm of the mythic, whereas the task was to escape and negate it. This was the crucial flaw in the Surrealist project. Benjamin writes: 'profane illumination did not always find the Surrealists equal to it, or to themselves, and the very writings that proclaim it most powerfully, Aragon's incomparable *Paysan de Paris* and Breton's *Nadja*, show very disturbing symptoms of deficiency' (*OWS*, p. 227). In the dream-world of the metropolis, Benjamin conceptualizes this overcoming of the mythology of the modernity with reference to the motif of awakening and the critical power of history. He states:

> Setting off the slant of this work against Aragon: Aragon persistently remains in the realm of dreams, but we want here to find the constellation of waking. While an impressionistic element lingers on in Aragon ('mythology') – and this impression should be held responsible for the many nebulous philosophemes of the book – what matters here is the dissolution of mythology into the space of history. (see N1,9, Smith ed., 1989, pp. 44–5)

For Benjamin, the dreaming collectivity 'finds its expression in the dream, and its meaning in awakening' (K2,5, *GS* V, p. 496). Dreaming, like waiting, like boredom, is the prelude to great deeds. Benjamin notes: 'every epoch not only dreams the next, but while dreaming impels it towards wakefulness' (*CB*, p. 176). Benjamin's argument is that one must awaken from the dream in order to realize it. One must seize and utilize the utopian moments contained in the mythic (the genuine desires of the dreaming collectivity) to end myth (compulsion, repetition, fetishism).[30] Benjamin characterizes his *Passagenarbeit* thus: 'what follows here is an attempt at the technique of awakening' (K1,1, *GS* V, p. 490), and his inspiration for this is Proust rather than the Surrealists. Benjamin notes: 'Just as Proust begins his life story with the moment of awakening, so must every presentation of history begin with awakening; in fact, it should deal with nothing else. This one deals with awakening from the nineteenth century' (see N4,3, Smith ed., 1989, p. 52).

Awakening depends upon, and accompanies, historical recognition. For Benjamin, 'the utilisation of dream elements upon awakening is the canon of dialectics. It is an example for the thinker and an exigency for the historian' (N4,4, Smith ed., 1989, p. 53). Myth was to be 'dissolved' into history in two ways: through the exploration of the afterlife of the object, and via the notion of the dialectical image. The key to unlocking the secrets of modernity is to be found in obsolescence. Benjamin regarded the Surrealists, and Breton in particular, as the first to recognize the revolutionary potential and critical character stored up in the old-fashioned artefact, the commodity now shorn of both its use- and exchange-value.[31] The outmoded object defetishizes and demythifies the commodity and the processes of its production, exchange and consumption in the city. The posthumous existence of the object is the period of judgement which negates the original intention and meaning of the artefact. The 'truth content' of the object is revealed at the moment of its extinction. Ruination, the fracturing of the deceptive surface of the object, frees the critical, utopian moments buried within it. Lindner states: 'Benjamin valued Surrealism's discovery of the revolutionary energies of obsolescence. The fading of the nineteenth century is the historical condition for the setting-free of its relics as elements of a dream-world and a children's world' (Lindner, 1986, p. 26). The once fashionable artefact is transformed into the old, the despised, the cast-off and indeed the comical. Benjamin notes that Surrealism is nothing other than 'the death of the last century via comedy' (N5a,2, Smith ed., 1989, p. 56). For Benjamin, the modern is the already-old.[32] The old dressed up as the new is the essence of both fashion and the concept of progress. This insight is the possibility of the realization (the making real) of the actually new.

To recognize that one is asleep is to become conscious, to awaken from sleep. Benjamin's 'dialectical fairy-tale' is concerned with the bringing to fulfilment of the wish, of which the commodity is the 'wish-image'.

Only retrospectively, through the lens of an object's gradual demise, does its true character emerge. For Benjamin, 'afterlife' (*Nachleben*) unravels 'prehistory' (*Urgeschichte*) and is the negation of myth. He states: 'historical "understanding" is to be viewed primarily as an afterlife of that which has been understood; and so what came to be recognized about works through the analysis of their "afterlife", their "fame", should be considered the foundation of history itself' (N2,3, Smith ed., 1989, p. 47). Benjamin's critical understanding of the outdated artefact is intimately bound up with that of the significance of the afterlife of the monument discussed in the previous chapter. Indeed, Benjamin's preoccupation with the arcades, the monuments built by the bourgeoisie to house and display the fetishized commodities of consumer capitalism, fundamentally derives from the fact that they rapidly became obsolete and old-fashioned. From being the very height of fashion in the 1830s, the arcades rapidly lost their appeal, and fell into disrepair and relative neglect. They became home to curios and the quaint. Benjamin describes the arcades as 'residues of a dream-world' (*CB*, p. 176). If modernity is characterized by the fleeting and the momentary, its truth is to be found in its lingering remains. The architecture of the recent past, the ruins of the present, thus come to take on a special significance for Benjamin. The *Passagenarbeit* is preoccupied with the ruins of the dreams of the nineteenth century, with discovering those hopes and promises buried within its mythical façades and objects. The afterlife of the recent past provides for an archaeology of dreaming.[33]

Like the Surrealists, Benjamin looked for the most unusual things in the least likely places; like them, he sought to combine these diverse elements in original, provocative configurations.[34] Benjamin attempts to reveal and give voice to the experience and character of modern social forms through the rescue, examination and decipherment of the minutiae and detritus of urban existence. The trivial, the despised and the ridiculous are precious things to be salvaged, important clues to be deciphered. The activity of the rag-picker is the fundamental model for Benjamin's redemptive, historical practice. He insists that the historian 'give up claim to nothing' (N3,3, Smith ed., 1989, p. 51) but instead collect everything, so that it may be reassembled. He writes:

Every historical perception can be visualized by substituting the image of a pair of scales, one pan of which is weighted with what was, the other with a recognition of what now is. While the facts collected on the first pan can never be too trivial or too numerous, only a few heavy, massive weights need lie on the other. (N6,5, Smith ed., 1989, p. 57)

Benjamin's goal is reconstruction, but for this to occur, the artefact must first be liberated from the suffocation of its context. Benjamin states: 'the destructive or critical impetus in materialist historiography comes into play in that blasting apart of historical continuity which allows the historical object to constitute itself' (N10a,1, Smith ed., 1989, p. 66). Once freed from dependence on their original context, the heterogeneous, incongruous objects excavated from the urban site may be juxtaposed in alternative patterns to produce mutual illumination. Benjamin is fundamentally concerned in the 'Arcades Project' with the montage technique pioneered by Surrealism.[35] Montage is a central aspect of Benjamin's methodological intentions in the Paris writings: 'Method of this project: literary montage. I need say nothing. Only exhibit. I won't filch anything of value or appropriate any ingenious turns of phrase. Only the trivia, the trash – which I don't want to inventory, but simply allow it to come into its own in the only way possible: by putting it to use' (N1a,8, Smith ed., 1989, p. 47).[36] For Benjamin, the critical exploration of the nineteenth century must adopt a visual form, as 'history breaks down into images, not into stories' (N11,4, Smith ed., 1989, p. 67). Historical materialism is to become imagistic, pictorial, perhaps poetic. Benjamin poses the problem thus:

by what route is it possible to attain a heightened graphicness combined with a realization of the Marxist method? The first stop along this path will be to carry the montage principle over into history. That is, to build up the large constructions out of the smallest, precisely fashioned structural elements. Indeed to detect the crystal of the total event in the analysis of the small, individual moment. (N2,6, Smith ed., 1989, p. 48)

The iron skeleton of the arcade, assembled from thousands of precisely wrought, intricately interconnected individual components, is not only the object of analysis, but also provides a model for Benjamin's historiographic and textual practice.

Benjamin's architecture of history appeals to the sense of vision. His task is to illuminate the modern metropolis, to provide images of, and insights into, urban experience. The principal form of this historical vision, this bringing to light of the past, is the 'dialectical image'. This is rooted in Benjamin's rejection of 'historicism'. He writes: 'it is not that the past casts its light on the present or the present casts its light on the past: rather, an image is that in which the Then and the Now come into a constellation like a flash of lightning. In other words: image is dialectics at a standstill' (N2a,3, Smith ed., 1989, p. 49).[37] The dialectical image is a pause, a moment of interruption and illumination, in which past and present recognize each other across the void which separates them.[38] The metaphor Benjamin uses to illuminate this notion is that of the lightning flash, the sudden, unexpected moment of illumination: 'In the fields with which we are concerned, knowledge exists only in lightning flashes. The text is the thunder rolling long afterward' (N1,1, Smith ed., 1989, p. 43). This fleeting instant must be retained and preserved: 'The dialectical image is a lightning flash. The Then must be held fast as it flashes its lightning image in the Now of recognizability' (N9,7, Smith ed., 1989, p. 64).

A sudden flash, momentary illumination, and then the capturing of an image; the dialectical image is a historical snapshot or, better, a frozen film image. Konersmann perceptively notes:

> The metaphor of the photographic snapshot encapsulates and illustrates several of those attributes which characterise the conditions and modes of this historiography: the transience of the chance which presents itself; the suddenness with which the motif appears; the momentariness of the truth which is to be established; the fleetingness of the spatio-temporal constellation in which one must act; the visualisation of the past as an image which receives its illumination from references to the present. (Konersmann, 1991, pp. 73–4)

Indeed, the dialectical image perhaps receives its earliest formulation in the essay 'A Small History of Photography' when Benjamin writes:

> No matter how artful the photographer, no matter how carefully posed his subject, the beholder feels an irresistible urge to search such a picture for the tiny spark of contingency, of the here and now with which reality has so to speak seared the subject, to find the inconspicuous spot where in the immediacy of that long-forgotten moment the future subsists so eloquently that we, looking back, may rediscover it. (*OWS*, p. 243)

Just as the *Denkbild* in the early cityscapes sought to provide a literary snapshot of the urban complex, so the dialectical image seeks to capture historical movement, the changing visage of the metropolis in a textual freeze-frame.

The dialectical image is the point of intersection of the 'here and now' and the 'then and there'. The meaning of the past is determined by the particular constellation it enters into and forms with the present. The dialectical image recognizes the filtering or 'telescoping of the past through the present' (N7a,3, Smith ed., 1989, p. 60). Hence, Benjamin notes, 'the materialist presentation of history leads the past to place the present in a critical condition' (N7a,5, Smith ed., 1989, p. 60). The present becomes a battle-ground for the past. The past is not dead and buried, fixed for all time, but rather remains open and contestable. The dialectical image captures an instant from the past as it threatens to vanish.[39]

The dialectical image is the moment in which the forgotten is remembered. Benjamin notes: 'the image of the past flashing in the Now of its recognisability is, according to its wider definition, an image of remembrance' (*GS* I, p. 1243). It is here that the significance of the historical experiment undertaken in the Berlin writings becomes apparent. The dialectical image draws its inspiration from the Proustian *mémoire involontaire*. Spontaneous and unexpected, a moment in the present brings with it the fleeting recognition of an occurrence or sensation in the past. Benjamin writes:

> To articulate the past historically means: to recognise in the past that which comes together in the constellation of one and the same moment. Historical knowledge is only possible in a historical moment. Knowledge in a historical moment is, however, always knowledge of a particular moment. As the past coalesces as such a moment – forms a dialectical image – it enters the *mémoire involontaire* of humanity. (*GS* I, p. 1233)

The dialectical image, as a moment of remembrance, is the redemption of lost time to accompany that of despised things. Benjamin states: 'the dialectical image is to be defined as the *mémoire involontaire* of a redeemed humanity' (*GS* I, p. 1233). Benjamin's archaeological monadology and his attempt to make historical materialism imagistic are fundamentally concerned with the redemption of forgotten past moments, of the utopian impulses and stunted aspirations of dead generations, of the traces of those whom 'historicism' has consigned to silence.

Benjamin seeks, on the one hand, to give voice to that which has gone unsaid and, on the other, to allow others to speak. He wishes to show silently, without comment. He seeks to present the social world in its immediacy, devoid of the mediation Adorno insisted upon. In order to restore voice to the silent, to permit mute things to speak for themselves, Benjamin advocates the bald, direct presentation of the quotation. Wolin notes: 'through this method he sought to lend an autonomous voice to that which is otherwise denied one, that which is otherwise conceived of as mere fodder of the conceptual "will-to-knowledge": things themselves, objectivity as such' (Wolin, 1986, pp. 204–5). For Benjamin, 'to write history therefore means to *quote* history' (N11,3, Smith ed., 1989, p. 67). Ernst Bloch describes the *Passagenarbeit* as a text 'brimming with miscellany, a tortuous piece of work in which he even wanted to obliterate all traces of himself as author and let the mere documents speak for themselves' (in Smith ed., 1988, p. 343). Adorno notes that Benjamin's intention was to startle the reader, to bring about recognition through surprise. The latter sought 'to abandon all apparent construction and to leave its significance to emerge out of the shock-like montage of the material. Philosophy was not merely to have recourse to Surrealism but was itself to become Surrealistic' (Adorno, cited by Frisby, 1988, p. 188).

The montage principle was crucially based on the concept of 'shock'. Benjamin challenges more conventional notions regarding the form and content of philosophical discourse. Benjamin, ingeniously or ingenuously, rejects authorial control in order to provoke and disconcert the reader, to bring about recognition. His intention in using the montage principle is to startle, to make manifest that which lies hidden and forgotten, to bring the repressed unconscious to consciousness, to awaken the dreaming collectivity so that it might come to realize the content of the dream. Benjamin notes that 'the Now of recognizability is the moment of awakening' (N18,4, Smith ed., 1989, p. 80). The dialectical image is the instant of historical illumination, of remembrance and of 'the awakening of a knowledge not yet conscious of what has gone before' (N1,9, Smith ed., 1989, p. 45). The dialectical image is the alarm clock of history, which brings awakening from the dream-sleep of the nineteenth century. The moment of recognition is that of revolution.

The Paris writings constitute the fullest development of methods pioneered in the *Denkbilder*. Benjamin is concerned with the analysis and refunctioning of the fragment, the redemption of the obsolete as part of an 'archaeo-monadological' practice. Such ephemera and minutiae are to be arranged in new configurations.

These mosaics of modernity are based on the disruption of established contexts and the juxtaposition of diverse elements in order to startle the reader. They engender shock. Benjamin emphasizes the shifting, multiple perspectives offered by montage. Photography and film provide the model of representation. Benjamin stresses the importance of the fleeting moment of recognition, and elaborates the dialectical image as a pause in the flux of experience. He incorporates into the structure of the text precisely those facets of urban experience that he is describing. The preponderance of the fragmentary, the visual, of shock – the experience of the modern metropolis is embedded in the formal properties and methodological innovations of the *Passagenarbeit*. Above all, it is the arcade itself that serves as Benjamin's model: constructed from thousands of tiny, precise iron components, covered by glass to permit illumination from above, it is a ruin filled with the outmoded and the despised, and frequented by the shabby outcast. The 'Arcades Project', like the Berlin writings, can be seen as an attempt to write dialectically, or perhaps mimetically, to delineate the form and content of a reflexive critical theory of modern social life.

The commodity and the capital of capital

For Benjamin, Paris is both the capital of, and the centre of capital during, the nineteenth century.[40] It was home to the grandiose technological accomplishments and pompous imperial achievements of the epoch. The dreams of the past and of the present were intertwined in nineteenth-century Paris, and manifested themselves in the arcades and world exhibitions. Benjamin notes: 'the world exhibitions erected the universe of commodities. Grandville's fantasies transmitted commodity-character onto the universe. They modernized it. The ring of Saturn became a cast-iron balcony' (*CB*, p. 166). He adds: 'The phantasmagoria of capitalist culture attained its most radiant unfurling in the World Exhibition of 1867. The Second Empire was at the height of its power. Paris was confirmed in its position as the capital of luxury and fashion. Offenbach set the rhythm for Parisian life. The operetta was the ironical Utopia of a lasting domination by Capital' (*CB*, p. 166)[41]

Paris was filled with the finest commodities and latest innovations. It was the city of glass, which might one day, it was suggested, be enclosed by a vast glass dome to protect its citizens

from the unpleasantness of the elements;[42] the city of light and of
mirrors in which to admire oneself; the city of exhibitions,
extravagant display and conspicuous consumption.[43] The world
came to the French imperial capital in order to marvel at its world
exhibitions, peruse and appreciate its luxurious commodities, and
buy. Paris proclaims itself to be the ultimate 'theatre of purchases':

> One hears: 'La Ville de Paris, the largest shop in the capital' – 'Les
> Villes de France, the largest shop in the Empire' – 'La "Chaussée
> d'Antin", the largest shop in Europe' – 'Le coin de Rue, the largest
> shop in the world' – 'the world', in the whole world nothing larger;
> that ought to be the limit. But no; 'Les magasins du Louvre' are still
> to come and these bear the title 'the largest shop in the Universe'. Of
> all worlds!' (G2,1, *GS* V, p. 237)

As the principal site of commodity consumption, Paris is the
quintessential modern metropolis, the home of myth.

Tiedemann states that 'the concept of phantasmagoria that
Benjamin repeatedly employs seems to be merely another term for
what Marx called commodity fetishism' (Smith ed., 1988, p. 277).
Having stressed and extended the notion of commodity fetishism
in Benjamin's work, Tiedemann rather strangely then questions
the original centrality of the concept. He writes: 'This notion
surfaces only once in the first sketch [*GS* V, p. 1030]; it was then by
no means clear that commodity fetishism was destined to form the
central schema for the whole project. When Benjamin wrote the
first *exposé* in 1935, he was probably still unfamiliar with the
relevant discussion in Marx's writing' (Smith ed., 1988, p. 276).
While it is clearly important to recognize, as I have already
suggested, the shifting emphases and continual thematic transformations of the Paris writings, Tiedemann fundamentally
misses the point here. Although Benjamin's familiarity with
Marx's texts was limited during the early stages of the 'Arcades
Project',[44] he had been acquainted with the reifying, alienating
character of commodity production and consumption since his
visit to Capri in 1924. It was there, one may recall, that he read and
became fascinated with Georg Lukács's *History and Class Consciousness*. It is Lukács who provided Benjamin with the key insight that

> The problem of commodities must not be considered in isolation or
> even regarded as the central problem in economics, but as the
> central, structural problem of capitalist society in all its aspects. Only
> in this case can the structure of commodity relations be made to yield

a model of all the objective forms of bourgeois society together with all the subjective forms corresponding to them. (Lukács, 1974, p. 83)

For Benjamin too, exposition of the mythic forms of modernity was to have as its focus the critical analysis of the commodity and its fetishization under the conditions of modern consumer capitalism. The commodity contains within it all the tendencies of nineteenth-century Parisian social life. For Benjamin it was the fragment that held the key to, and disclosed the totality of, modern cultural forms. The commodity constitutes the monad-ological form for the prehistory of modernity.[45]

Benjamin appears to have understood commodity fetishism as a triadic structure. First, it was a delusion of consciousness, a myth of modernity. Second, it was concerned with the idolization of the object, the product of human labour returning as an alienating, dominating thing demanding devotion from its makers. Third, it denoted a distortion of sexual desire whereby the erotic was projected on to the inorganic. The first of these aspects has already been outlined. Wolin summarizes how Benjamin regarded commodity fetishism as an integral element of the prehistory of modernity when he writes:

> he sought to demonstrate how the phantasmagorical proliferation of new commodities which distinguished urban life under conditions of nineteenth-century capitalism . . . represented a return to the notion of *cyclical time* dominant in prehistoric life, insofar as the novelties themselves were thoroughly interchangeable. When viewed from the vantage point of consumption, full-scale commodity production signified the reversion to a Great Myth: the reproduction of the always-the-same under the semblance of the production of the perpetually new. (Wolin, 1982, p. 174)

Commodity fetishism was the principal characteristic of the dreaming urban collectivity. Benjamin writes: 'Fashion stands in the darkness of the lived moment, in the collective. Fashion and architecture (in the nineteenth century) counted toward the dream-consciousness of the collective. One must pursue it, as it manifests itself. For example, in advertising (O°11, *GS* V, p. 1028). The products of the nineteenth-century industrial complex and the luxury items and exotic products rapaciously seized with the expansion of the boundaries and ambitions of the Empire in some manner contained within them, or had as accretions clinging to them, the utopian impulses or moments of the past that demand redemption in the present. The commodities and associated architectural forms of the recent past constituted wish-images of the collective unconscious, artefacts that linger in the twentieth century as obsolete and ridiculous.

Benjamin's conception of commodity fetishism is not restricted to this notion of the products of capitalist industrial development as elements of a dream-world. It seems to parallel Marx's account in the 'Economic and Philosophical Manuscripts' of 1844 regarding the alienation of the human subject and human 'species-being' under the conditions of capitalist industrial production. The object, produced by the worker and in some way containing part of his or her being, confronts the worker, now the customer, after its circuitous route through the system of capitalistic exchange relations, as an alien entity, something that the worker no longer recognizes as the product of his or her labour. The object appears to have been generated magically, to be a divine creation. For Benjamin, the techniques of mass production involve the destruction of the tell-tale marks upon objects that recall their origin. Mass production, the manufacture of vast numbers of standardized artefacts that are indistinguishable from one another, erases the traces left upon objects by suffering human labour. In obliterating the traces of the worker, mass production denies the life of the worker.[46] Hence, the recovery of traces, the revelation of the history of the object, the recollection of the hardship and injustice that surround the birthplace of the commodity, are fundamental imperatives for Benjamin.[47] Mass production seeks to present itself as the magical creation of objects, manufacturing without tears. Paris as home of the commodity is also home of amnesia and reification.

As the Surrealists recognized, machines and the commodities they bring forth demand the subservience of humankind; they seek to exact humble devotion.[48] For Benjamin, a fundamental facet of the *culture* of the commodity is the *cult* of the commodity. The commodity is the idol of modernity. The city forms the space of 'the enthronement of the commodity and the glitter of distraction' (*CB*, p. 165). Commodity fetishism entails not simply the empowerment but also the deification of the industrial artefact, not only submission to and before it, but also reverent worship. Benjamin observes that 'when Baudelaire speaks of the "big cities' state of religious intoxication", the commodity is probably the unnamed subject of this state' (*CB*, p. 56). The modern metropolis, like the medieval city from which it arose, is a holy place, a site to which pilgrimage is made. The arcades, the boutiques and the department stores are shrines to the commodity; they are its temples, where one goes to pay homage.

Benjamin argues that the 'world exhibitions were places of pilgrimage to the fetish commodity' (*CB*, p. 165). The World Exhibitions in Paris in 1867 and at the Crystal Palace in London in 1851 are nothing other than the cathedrals of modernity, the ultimate monuments to faith in progress.

The dream-world of the nineteenth century arises not only from the deformation of utopian impulses and the adoration of cultic consumer goods, but also from the manipulation and displacement of sexual desire. As discussed in the previous chapter, the modern bourgeoisie is preoccupied with the interiorization or domestication of the erotic, with the denial of the body and the bodily.[49] Moreover, a key component of the fetishization of the commodity is the projection of the erotic impulse on to the inanimate object. Benjamin writes of the commodity thus: 'It stands in opposition to the organic. It prostitutes the living body to the inorganic world. In relation to the living it represents the rights of the corpse. Fetishisation, which succumbs to the sex-appeal of the inorganic, is its vital nerve; and the cult of the commodity recruits this to its service' (*CB*, p. 166). Desire and passion are redirected towards the lifeless manufactured products of capitalist industrial technology. Fetishism is that condition in which the sexual 'is as at home in death, as in living flesh' (B3,8, *GS* V, p. 118). Benjamin writes: 'fashion was never anything other than the parody of the multi-coloured corpse, the provocation of death [*des Todes*] through the woman' (B1,4, *GS* V, p. 111). The commodity is transformed into an object of sexual desire, and to consume is to consummate this desire. Commodity fetishism is nothing other than the eroticization of modern consumer arte-facts. Modern capitalism involves both the sexualization of the commodity and the commodification of the sexual.[50] As we will see in the next chapter, as one of the definitive figures of modernity, the prostitute represents for Benjamin the commod-ification of the woman's body.

The city is not only the space of the fetishization of the commodity, but also the centre of fashion. The commodity world presents itself as the source of a limitless variety and diversity, as the continually shifting and changing, as the focus of new tastes and styles, innovative forms and designs. Paris is the locus of the newest, the latest, the best. The concept of fashion draws strength from that of continuous improvement, things getting better: the most recent is by definition the superior. Fashion is, in the realm of commodities, what the notion of progress is in the domain of technology. Central to Benjamin's Paris writings is the revelation of the mythic character of 'progress' and the preoccupation with novelty. Benjamin draws on Simmel's 1904 essay on fashion as the quest for social differentiation. The possession of the most fashionable artefacts is indicative of one's high social standing. A fashion becomes 'unfashionable' once it is acquired by all, once its elite status has been undermined. To be fashionable is to be the *avant-garde* of the consumer world and to avoid the absurdity and horror of the obsolete object which fashion ironically itself produces. Simmel writes: 'as fashion spreads, it gradually goes to its doom . . . the charm of novelty [is] coupled to that of transitoriness' (Simmel, 1971, p. 302). Fleeting and transitory, fashion is the beauty of the ephemeral and, as such, the encapsulation of *modernité*. Yet – and this is the crucial point of departure for Benjamin's analysis – the newest is really only the rehashing of what has already been. For all its apparent innovation and originality, fashion, as Simmel points out, 'repeatedly returns to old forms . . . and the course of fashion has been likened to a circle. As soon as an earlier fashion has partially been forgotten, there is no reason why it should not be allowed to return to favour' (Simmel, 1971, p. 320).

For Benjamin, fashion forms only the semblance of the new, only the image and illusion of innovation and change. As the new is, however, indistinguishable from that which has already been, the new is the nothing-new. Mass production is the sustained manufacture and reproduction of identical, unchanging objects. Fashion is the endless production and consumption of the always-the-same dressed up in the deceptive attire of the ever-new. Frisby notes that 'the world of the circulation of the commodity is precisely the announcement of the new as the ever-same' (Frisby, 1988, p. 210). For Benjamin, the modern is 'the new in the context of the always-the-same [*immer schon Dagewesnen*]' (S1,4, *GS* V, p. 675). *Nouveauté* is consequently only 'the quintessence of false consciousness of which fashion is the tireless agent. This illusion of novelty is reflected, like one mirror in another, in the illusion of infinite sameness. The product of this reflection is the phantasmagoria of "cultural history" in which the bourgeoisie enjoyed its false consciousness to the full' (*CB*, p. 172). The definitive experience of the metropolitan environment is the never-ending encounter with the nothing-new, ceaseless repetition. It is the fundamental basis of the mythic character of modernity. The fetishization of the commodity and the charm of fashion are the key elements of the spell that holds the modern metropolis in thrall, half-dormant, half-bored.

The always-the-same of fashion is the origin of boredom. The decisive experience of the urban consumer is *ennui*. Fashion is paradoxically the attempt to escape the unendurable tedium of the nothing-new. It is the mirage of novelty. That which Baudelaire and Constantin Guys, the 'painter of modern life', regard as the 'pageant of fashion' (Baudelaire, 1986, p. 4) is nothing other than the dreary and dismal continuation of monotony.[51] The proliferation of commodities, fashions and styles is what produces the proliferation of the bored. Veuillot is one such figure quoted by Benjamin: 'the construction of the new Paris resurrects every style; the assemblage though, is not lacking in unity, for every style is that of boring genres, and of boring genres, the most boring . . . [the buildings] exhale boredom' (D2,2, *GS* V, p. 160). Boredom is the 'index for participation in the sleep of the collective' (D3,7, *GS* V, p. 164). The nineteenth century let itself be lulled to sleep, into the complacency of forgetfulness. Benjamin states that 'the dreaming collectivity knows no history' (S2,1, *GS* V, p. 678), and it is only through historical recognition that these phantasmagoric slumbers are to be broken. It is only with the end of capitalism, the something-new, that tedium will cease. Benjamin's analysis is an exhortation to remember and awaken, to bring the tedious period of waiting to an end.

Adorno was critical of Benjamin's articulation of the notion of commodity fetishism. He argued that in situating fetishism within the framework of the dreaming collectivity, Benjamin had transformed an objective economic fact into a subjective category located in individual and/or collective consciousness. Adorno writes: 'the fetish character of the commodity is not a fact of consciousness, rather it is dialectical . . . it produces consciousness' (AP, p. 111). Indeed, Adorno also roundly rejected Benjamin's version of the commodity as a frozen, inverted manifestation of a genuine utopian moment. The commodity market of the nineteenth century constituted for Adorno nothing other than an image of Hell. Although Benjamin states that 'the "modern" [is] the time of Hell' (S1,5, *GS* V, p. 676), clearly contained within it are the as yet unredeemed utopian elements that prefigure the time of Heaven. Benjamin is loathe to present a totalizing critique of modernity, offering instead a peculiarly and precariously balanced version of the phantasmagoria of modernity.

Benjamin wishes to rescue the utopian moments locked in the commodity, to remember the commodity's forgotten content. These moments become manifest in obsolescence. Benjamin's special concern with the obsolete object stems from his account of the significance of the afterlife of the object, and also from the fact that the obsolete is useless and valueless; it is the senile object. Obsolescence is the pitiful fate, or comic final condition, of the commodity. The outmoded thing is an object of scorn and ridicule. No longer the stimulator of sexual desire, the old-fashioned is nothing other than, as Benjamin astutely points out, the ultimate anti-aphrodisiac.[52] The obsolete object reveals the truth of the fetishized commodity; the old-fashioned discloses the reality of the fashionable.

The dream-houses of modernity

Paris is the city of dreaming, the site of modern enchantment filled with the fantastic objects and fashions that new technologies have magically conjured up before our eyes. Buck-Morss notes that 'living in Paris meant being wrapped in this dream, which left visible traces as the city's physical elements' (1983, p. 215). The most apparent and enduring of the dream-elements of the urban complex are not so much the products of capitalist industry, however, as the very buildings that comprise the city. For Benjamin, the arcade, the museum, the exhibition hall, the railway station and the other great monuments inspired by the dream, designed and constructed to the glory of iron (the Eiffel Tower) and glass (the Crystal Palace), are the most prominent, profound forms of the phantasmagoria of the modern epoch. Benjamin states that 'all collective architecture of the nineteenth century provides the home of the dreaming collectivity' (H°1, *GS* V, p. 1012).

The buildings erected during the nineteenth century exist in the twentieth as the clearest vestiges of, and primary clues for, the mythic character of modernity. Benjamin stresses that one must regard 'architecture as the most important evidence of latent "mythology". And the most important architecture of the nine-teenth century is the arcade' (D°7, *GS* V, p. 1002). The modern metropolis, and the maze of arcades in particular, constitutes the 'primordial landscape of consumption' (A°5, *GS* V, p. 993). The nineteenth century constructed 'architecture in which we, held in a dream, may still experience the life of our parents, our grandparents' (D2a,1, *GS* V, pp. 161–2). The fantasies of the epoch remain sedimented in the buildings it spawned, and these proved an index of dream-traces for the contemporary archaeologist excavating the residual ruins of modernity. Benjamin writes that 'Just as the rocks of the Miocene or the Eocene bear within them the impressions of the creatures of the epoch, so the arcades remain today in the great cities like caverns [filled] with the fossils of a vanished monster: the consumers from the pre-Empire period of capitalism, the last European dinosaur' (R2,3, *GS* V, p. 670). For Benjamin, the 'dream-houses' of the modern epoch – the museum, the railway station, and the constructions for the world exhibitions – are the ultimate settings for the phantasmagoria of the metropolis.

There are at least three principal facets to Benjamin's preoccupation with the Parisian arcades: form, function and afterlife. First, the construction of the arcade involved a particular alteration – or, rather, inversion – of space: the street, that which is exterior to the building, became interiorized, was made part of the building itself. Additionally, as the earliest instances of iron and glass architecture, they were the most innovative, the most 'modern' buildings of the city in the first few decades of the last century; the arcade was the pioneer of new architectural principles and materials. The arcade was a monument to technological innovation and progress. Second, the arcade was the home of the commodity, the prime locus for the consumption of luxury goods and exclusive merchandise. The arcade was the place where the bourgeoisie came to buy and the rest came to look at what they could not buy. The arcade was a monument to industrial power and imperial expansion. Third, Benjamin's fascination with the arcade springs from the fact that it fell out of favour during the second half of the nineteenth century. The home of fashion became unfashionable. The arcade became run-down, obsolete, a ruin. The ultimate space of modern prestige in the nineteenth century was demolished as anachronistic in the early twentieth. Benjamin, writing of the arcades at the precise moment in which these monuments to bourgeois consumerism were on the verge of extinction (Aragon's book is concerned with the imminent demolition of the Passage de l'Opéra), seeks to uncover the processes and import of the rise and fall of the arcade. The arcade contains within it the totality of the nineteenth century (as a monad) and, in the twentieth, its truth (as a ruin), both enchantment and disenchantment.

In his study of the history of the arcade as an architectural form, Johann Geist writes:

From antiquity to the eighteenth century there was a wide variety of structures seemingly related to the arcade. However, one must not conclude that they were its immediate predecessors. The arcade remains as an invention which responded to the specific needs and desires of a society in a specific era of its cultural and industrial development – namely, the need for a public space protected from traffic and weather and the search for new means of marketing the products of a blossoming luxury goods industry. (1985, p. 12).

The first arcades to be built in Paris date from the last days of the *ancien régime* and the early ones of the Revolution: the Galeries du Bois (1786–8?), Galeries du Palais Royal (1786), Passage Feydeau (1791) and the Passage du Caire (1799) being the earliest examples. The new century brought with it the completion of the Passage des Panoramas (1800), but it appears that the zenith of the arcade was the period 1818–45 with the construction of the Passage de l'Opéra, the Galerie Vivienne and the Galerie Véro-Dodat (1823, 1825 and 1826 respectively) in Paris and its proliferation in other cities, principally London, but also Bristol, Brussels, Lyons, Milan and, in 1826–7, Philadelphia.

The point of departure for Benjamin's investigation of the arcades is the following passage from a Parisian journal of 1852: 'These arcades, a new invention of industrial luxury, are glass-covered marbled-panelled passageways through blocks of houses, whose proprietors have combined in the venture. On both sides of these passageways, which receive their light from above, there are aligned the most elegant shops, so that such an arcade forms a city, a world in miniature' (A1,1, *GS* V, p. 83). The arcade was a street of luxury shops with the peculiarity that this 'street' was an interior rather than an exterior space. The arcade brought with it the interiorization of the life of the street, the space primarily occupied by the working and lower classes. For Benjamin, the process of interiorization is one of the 'embourgeoisiement' of space. He notes that a transformed spatial orientation occurs: 'in it the street pretends to recognize itself as an inhabited interior: as the living space of the collectivity, because the true collectivity as such dwells in the street' (A°9, *GS* V, p. 994). Whereas the street is the home of the collective, the arcade is the space of the dreaming collectivity.[53] The arcade was the interior disguised as an exterior, a place of exclusion and of the exclusive. It shut out unpredictable and unwelcome elements, both natural (the rain) and social (the poor). The arcade was both the hiding-place from, and an attempt to domesticate, that over which the bourgeoisie had little or no control. Thus it was for Benjamin a city, a dream-world, in miniature.

The arcade was the fantastical successor to the street and its subtle transformation. Benjamin observes that 'business and traffic are the two components of the street. Now in the arcade, the second of these withered; its traffic is rudimentary. It is only the luxuriant street of commerce, only functioning to awaken greed' (A3a,7, *GS* V, p. 93).[54] The arcade was not only a refuge for the dreaming collectivity, it was also the home of the dream-objects of the modern metropolis. It was the setting, or rather the stage, for the display and exhibition of the commodity. The arcade was the ultimate 'theatre of purchases'[55], the space where everything was to be bought and where one could buy every-thing. It was the site of urban desire, the eroticized object and the commodified body.[56] The arcades were the haunts of prostitutes, the eventual banning of whom was among the main factors in their waning popularity.

The arcade was the space of the fetishization of the commodity, the locus in which it was worshipped. This notion of the arcade as a holy place in the commodity cult(ure) of modernity is stressed on several occasions by Benjamin. He recognizes 'the arcade as the temple of commodity capitalism' (A2,2, *GS* V, p. 86) and the 'temple of Asclepius' (L3,1, *GS* V, p. 517), though it is equally the temple of Eros.[57] Benjamin extends this comparison to the architectural form of the arcades. He writes: 'the dream-house of the arcade rediscovers itself in the church. Overlapping of the construction style of the arcades and sacred architecture' (L2,4, *GS* V, p. 515). With its transepts, aisles and galleries, Benjamin notes that 'something sacred, a left-over from the church nave, lingers in these rows of commodities that constitute the arcade' (F4,5 *GS* V, p. 222). The department store was to replace the arcade as the sacred precinct of the omnipotent commodity. Benjamin remarks: 'concerning Baudelaire's "religious inebriation of big cities": the department stores are temples dedicated to this intoxication' (A13, *GS* V, p. 109).

The last arcade to be built in Paris was the Passage de Princes in 1860, but the days of the arcades' popularity were already numbered. Benjamin notes that, 'as long as the gas-lamps – certainly the oil-lamps – burned, they were fairy-palaces. . . . The decline began with electric lighting' (D°6, *GS* V, p. 1001). The prohibition of prostitutes, the rise of an 'open-air' cult[58] and the construction of the boulevards under the auspices of Baron

Haussmann during the Second Empire were the principal factors in the waning attraction of the arcades. The fashionable goods of luxury boutiques were replaced by the obsolete oddities of bric-à-brac shops. Once the most innovative building housing the most desirable artefacts, the arcade now became the ruinous setting for the outmoded, eccentric and comical. In the early twentieth century many of the increasingly derelict arcades were demolished.

As the attraction of the arcade rapidly declined for the customer, so its allure for the Surrealists and for Benjamin was born. Dimly lit, with 'sunless corridors', the arcade takes on a murky, mysterious quality for Aragon. The arcades form 'human aquariums', illuminated by 'a glaucous gleam, seemingly filtered through deep water' (1987, p. 28). A reminder – and remainder – of a lost epoch, this twilight world is the perfect setting for Aragon's *mythologie moderne*. He writes:

> Although the life that originally quickened them has drained away, they deserve, nevertheless, to be regarded as the secret repositories of several modern myths: it is only today, when the pick-axe menaces them, that they have at last become the true sanctuaries of a cult of the ephemeral, the ghostly landscape of damnable pleasures and professions. Places that were incomprehensible yesterday, and that tomorrow will never know. (1987, pp. 28–9)

The notions of afterlife and dialectical image combine in Benjamin's consideration of the derelict arcade. Benjamin observes that the historian 'recognises objects as they are in the moment of their extinction [*Nicht-mehr-Seins*]. The arcades are such monuments of the extinct' (D°4, *GS* V, p. 1001). The arcades became the perfect object of the dialectical image, that method concerned specifically with the pause between life and death. The dialectical image captures the last fleeting moments of the afterlife of the object, the precise instant of demise in which illusion withers and truth becomes manifest. On the brink of oblivion, the crumbling arcade reveals itself as the locus of dreaming. The dialectical image is the redemptive 'at last sight' of the ruined phantasmagoria of modernity.

The arcade was a sacred place dedicated to the revered commodity. The bourgeois holy of holies, however, the ultimate loci of self-congratulation of modern industry and technology, were the world exhibitions staged in London in 1851 and Paris in 1855 and 1867. Benjamin writes:

> The world exhibitions glorified the exchange-value of commodities. They created a framework in which their use-value receded into the background. They opened up a phantasmagoria into which people entered in order to be distracted. The entertainment industry made that easier for them by lifting them to the value of the commodity. They yielded to its manipulation while enjoying their alienation from themselves and from others. (*CB*, p. 165)

The world exhibitions 'erected the universe of commodities' (*CB*, p. 166). They were celebrations of progress, of the technological mastery of nature and of imperial power. The Crystal Palace, a name taken straight from the dream-world of the fairy-tale, and the Eiffel Tower, the definitive modern structure,[59] were the great monuments that marked and presided over the world exhibitions.

It was at these exhibitions that the splendours of modernity sought comparison with the marvels and wonders of antiquity. In an image reminiscent of Aragon's petrol pump deities, Benjamin cites A. S. Doncourt's (1889) reflections on the 1855 Paris exhibition: 'four locomotives guard the entrance to the machine annex, resembling those massive bulls in Nineveh, and those great Egyptian sphinxes seen at the entrances of temples. The annex was the land of iron' (cited in G8a,2, *GS* V, pp. 252–3). The 1867 exhibition produced even greater astonishment in onlookers. Benjamin notes that 'the exhibition palace on the Champs de Mars . . . was compared with the Colosseum' (G9,2, *GS* V, p. 253). The parody of ancient monuments was a continual theme. The setting of the commodity was to be in the image of the holy shrines of the ancients: 'the Egyptian exhibition of 1867 was held in a building which was designed after an Egyptian temple' (G9a,6, *GS* V, p. 255). For one writer of the time, Théophile Gautier, the 1867 exhibition hall looked like nothing on earth: 'it seems as though one has before one a monument erected on another planet, Jupiter or Saturn, after a taste which we do not know, and in colours to which our eyes are not accustomed' (cited in G9,2, *GS* V, pp. 253–4).

The world exhibitions were occasions for the concentration of the fantastic and the exotic, objects distant in both time and space. The most modern and the most ancient were combined. Paris dressed up as the cities of old, parodying in its monuments to modernity those recently discovered by the archaeologist Austen Layard at Nineveh, for example. Paris could play at being Babylon while the actual remains of such cities were being accumulated in the great Parisian museums, trophies of imperial expansion. This link with the museum is an important one, for the museum is another feature of the dream-architecture of the modern metropolis. Benjamin notes: 'the interior of the museum appears . . . as an increasingly massive interior. Between 1850 and 1890 the exhibition occupied the position of the museum. Comparison of the ideological basis of the two' (L1a,2, *GS* V, p. 513). While the world exhibition celebrated the achievements of modernity through the exhibition of the latest technologies and artefacts, the museum also sought to articulate a vision of history as progress. Benjamin remarks: 'the exhibition of industry as the secret construction design of the museum' (G2a,6, *GS* V, p. 239). In the museum the past is catalogued and transformed into an object of contemplation, robbed of its power.

Like the arcade, and the department store that succeeded it, the museum was a compartmentalized setting, in this case for the fantastical display of exotic objects, a display case for artefacts dedicated to the cult of progress. Whereas the museum contained the unique, auratic object, the department store housed the non-auratic, mass-produced commodity.[60] As Benjamin points out, however, 'there are connections between the department store and the museum, with the bazaar as a linking structure. The massing of works of art in the museum brings them closer to commodities' (L5,5, *GS* V, p. 522). There is an intimate connection, then, between the art museum and the sites of commodity display. Paris, the capital of the nineteenth century, witnessed not only the culture of the commodity but also the commodification of culture. The painting, the sculpture, formerly dependent upon patronage, became objects produced for sale, for the tastes and demands of the market. Art was judged on its exchange- or, more accurately, its exhibition-value. The work of art sought, above all, to appeal to the customer. Like the commodity, it awoke a desire that could be fulfilled through purchase and possession. The art gallery, which contained the utopian images and representations of past generations, became a site conditioned by the market forces of the nineteenth century, as the storehouse of past desires was transformed into a warehouse for their sale and consumption.

The other great dream-house of the nineteenth-century urban environment was the railway station. The 'representation of the connection of temple, railway station, arcade [and] covered-market' (E°8, *GS* V, p. 1002) was an early concern of the *Passagenarbeit*. There are a number of correspondences between the arcade and the railway station. The station was a temple to industrial and technological development in two senses. First, like the arcades, the great metropolitan railway stations were iron and glass constructions which embodied the most innovative architectural practices. Moreover, these edifices shared a similar fate. Home of the most modern, the railway station, like the arcade, has been superseded in the twentieth century. The glorious days of the railway station are over. The motorway and the airport are now the great gateways to the metropolis. Benjamin's account recalls Aragon's description of the abandoned arcade:

> in this age of motor cars and aeroplanes, only slight atavistic terrors still lurk beneath the blackened halls, and that comedy of farewell and reunion played out against the background of Pullman cars transforms the platform into a provincial stage. Once again the decrepit Greek melodrama is performed for us: Orpheus, Eurydice and Hermes at the railway station. (L1,4, *GS* V, p. 512)

The railway station is home to what Benjamin terms the 'dream-world of farewells' (H°2, *GS* V, p. 1012), the threshold which once housed the moments of 'at first' and 'at last sight'. Indeed, as the setting for what is about to disappear into the distance, the railway station is an appropriate edifice for redemption by the parting glance of the dialectical image.

Second, the station was home to objects of awe and wonder. The locomotive was the technological accomplishment of the age, the definitive symbol of progress. Appropriately, it was steam locomotives that functioned as guardian statues to the 'land of iron' at the World Exhibition of 1855. The railway station was the temple to the locomotive, a site sacred to the power of steam. The railway station was a cultic site, the ultimate monument to progress. Benjamin made the following cryptic note: 'arcade and station: indeed / arcade and church: indeed / church and station: Marseilles' (A°14, *GS* V, p. 995). It is in the *Denkbild* 'Marseilles' that Benjamin most explicitly inverts the sacred and secular spaces of the city. He depicts the church as the home of the profane and the station as a holy site in the modern metropolis. He writes of the cathedral in Marseilles thus:

> when all was complete, in 1893, place and time had conspired victoriously in this monument against its architects and sponsors, and the wealth of the clergy had given rise to a gigantic railway station that could never be opened to traffic. The façade gives an indication of the waiting rooms within, where passengers of the first to fourth classes (though before God we are all equal), wedged among their spiritual possessions as between cases, sit reading hymn-books that, with their concordances and cross-references,

look very much like international time-tables. Extracts from the railway traffic regulations hang on the walls, tariffs for the discount on special trips on Satan's luxury train are consulted, and cabinets where the long-distance traveller can discreetly wash are kept in readiness as confessionals. This is the Marseilles railway station. Sleeping cars to eternity depart from here at Mass times. (*OWS*, p. 211)

The railway station is a microcosm of the nineteenth century, for it is the space of waiting, the liminal space composed of waiting-rooms. The railway station is a site imbued with the expectation of new things, in an epoch of the always-the-same. It is a monument to the tedium of waiting.

The fantastic edifices of Paris constitute a 'dream-architecture' which both represents and houses the phantasmagoria of modernity. Arcades, exhibition halls, railway stations – these are the settings of the commodities, technical accomplishments and machinery which fascinated the nineteenth century. These build-ings are monuments to the self-perception and bombast of the epoch. In the twentieth century, these structures linger as stale, empty shells. The penetrating gaze of the urban physiognomist reads the history of the recent past from these crumbling edifices, as they shed their mythic façades and finally reveal the cata-strophic, ruinous course of history. The illusions and deceptions that imbued the epoch of high capitalism are laid bare and shrivel in the intense glare of historical illumination. The utopian impulses of the nineteenth century are fleetingly recognized and preserved by the dialectical image as the dreamscape of modernity turns to rubble.

4

Urban Allegories: Paris, Baudelaire and the Experience of Modernity

Baudelaire and the city as poetic object

Against the background of the ever-expanding 'Arcades Project', Benjamin sharpened his focus on – one might say, returned to – the writings of the poet and essayist Charles Baudelaire (1821–67).[1] By far the longest of the numerous *Konvoluts* compiled by Benjamin as part of the overall *Passagenarbeit* had Baudelaire as its theme and title (*Konvolut* J), and many of the other *Konvoluts* (M, 'The *Flâneur*'; O, 'Prostitution, Gambling'; and m, 'Idleness') drew upon the poet's motifs. It is not altogether surprising, therefore, that from around July 1937 Benjamin envisaged a separate book on Baudelaire distinct from, but intimately related to, the 'Arcades' material. The themes of the larger project were to be crystallized in the three-part Baudelaire study, which was to be a monad of the *Passagenarbeit*. Even this much more modest undertaking, however, never approached completion. Benjamin did, it is true, produce three pieces of work, but these were only a draft of the central section ('Paris of the Second Empire in Baudelaire'), a rewrite of the draft ('On Some Motifs in Baudelaire') and a rather strange assortment of notes and theses (somewhat obscurely entitled 'Central Park'). The Baudelaire book was indeed to prove a model of the *Passagenarbeit*; it was a mess in miniature.

While Benjamin considered that 'Brecht is probably the first important poet who has something to say about urban man' (*UB*, p. 61), it was Baudelaire who 'perceived the frailty at the heart of

Paris; in the Parisians he perceived only what that frailty had done to them' (ibid.). For Benjamin, the writings of Baudelaire offer the most precise and precious insights into nineteenth-century Parisian social life.[2] Wolin notes: 'Benjamin proceeded from the conviction that the allegorical poetics of Baudelaire constituted a privileged vantage-point from which to view the plight of a "self-alienated humanity" in the era of industrial capitalism' (1982, p. 231). Baudelaire presents the finest articulation of the experience (and often the pretentious self-delusions) of the modern individual in an urban setting based on his own vision of the task of the modern artist and as a consequence of his allegorical poetics.

In the conclusion of his review of the 'Salon of 1845', Baudelaire laments the absence of artistic works depicting contemporary themes. He writes: 'There is no lack of subjects, nor of colours, to make epics. The painter, the true painter for whom we are looking will be he who can snatch its epic quality from the life of today, and can make us see and understand, with brush or with pencil, how great and poetic we are in our cravats and our patent-leather boots' (Baudelaire, 1965, p. 32).[3] For Baudelaire, the task of the contemporary artist is to depict this 'pageant of fashionable life' (1965, p. 118), metropolitan life, in all its richness, vitality and fluidity. In his essay 'The Painter of Modern Life' (written 1859–60, first published in 1863) Baudelaire develops this theme of the spectacle of urban existence,[4] and finds an exponent of his long-awaited artistic style: Constantin Guys. Guys, a nonentity in the world of art, is praised by Baudelaire for his pen-and-ink sketches and water-colours. These are not painstaking studies of formally arranged or carefully posed subjects. Rather, these images are formed by swift brush-strokes which capture authentically the momentary and dynamic character of urban forms. The city creates and demands a new mode of representation, a new artistic sensibility and practice, corresponding to the transformed perception of the urban environment. This urban aesthetic, this appreciation of the ephemeral and fleeting, is what Baudelaire terms *modernité*. He states: 'by *modernité* I mean the ephemeral, the fugitive, the contingent, the half of art whose other half is the eternal and the immutable' (Baudelaire, 1986, p. 13). There is lasting beauty, that which survives as beauty through different ages, and there is *modernité*, the beauty of the novel and the transient. The painter of modern life has a specific task: 'he makes it his business to extract from fashion whatever element it may contain of poetry within history, to distil the eternal from the transitory'

(Baudelaire, 1986, p. 12). The sketcher of modern manners must not copy the *modernité* of earlier ages, but immerse him or herself in the modern. His or her inspiration is the turbulence of the street, not the serenity of the studio. The poet who coined the very term *modernité* to describe the beauty of the fleeting and transient and the critical essayist who sought to sketch the social manners and tastes of his class and epoch, Baudelaire is the lens through which Benjamin examines the fate of the individual in the mythological topography of nineteenth-century Paris. Benjamin regards Baudelaire as the figure who gives voice to the shock and intoxication of modernity; he is the lyric poet of the metropolis.

I will begin my analysis of Benjamin's Baudelaire studies with a consideration of the relationship between the concept of allegory and the commodity. I will then explore Benjamin's shifting understanding of the composition, character and consequences of the metropolitan population, the 'last European dinosaur' (a°3, *GS* V, p. 1045). For Benjamin, as for Baudelaire, the hallmark of modern urban experience is the encounter with the crowd. After that, I will examine the central category of 'shock' with regard to the disintegration of coherent experience (*Erfahrung*) and its replacement by the disjointed impressions of inner life (*Erlebnis*). Then I will analyse Benjamin's critical and problematic reconceptualization of Baudelaire's 'heroism of modern life'. The modern 'hero' is one who, while embodying the tendencies of modern capitalism to the highest degree, is simultaneously engaged in an inevitably doomed struggle against them. The heroism of modernity as endurance and as impotent rage takes the form of self-deception (the *flâneur*, the gambler) and self-negation (the prostitute, the worker and the rag-picker). For Baudelaire, the ultimate hero of modernity is the figure who seeks to give voice to its paradoxes and illusions, who participates in, while yet still retaining the capacity to give form to, the fragmented, fleeting experiences of the modern. This individual is the poet.

Benjamin's understanding of the relationship between economic production and the cultural sphere is the key to his preoccupation with Baudelaire from 1937. He writes: 'Marx describes the causal connection between economic system and culture. The expressive relationship is what matters here. The expression of an economic system in its culture will be described, not the economic origins of culture' (N1a,6, Smith ed., 1989, p. 46). Benjamin rejects any one-dimensional, deterministic account of the relationship between economic forces and cultural life, between the material base and the ideological superstructure of a society. Cultural forms and artefacts exist as expressions of underlying economic patterns, giving voice to them, but are not to be conceptualized as mere reflections of the forces and relations of production.[5] For Benjamin, Baudelaire's poetry directly expresses, and must be understood in relation to, the commodity culture of the nineteenth century. Buck-Morss observes: 'Benjamin . . . believes the allegorical in Baudelaire's poetry has an objective source: the social reality of commodity production which finds expression within it' (1989, pp. 223–4). In this sense, the allegorical poetics of Baudelaire are as intimately interwoven with the character and fetishization of the commodity as the arcades themselves. Indeed, for Benjamin there exists a particular elective affinity between the concept of allegory (which underpinned his *Trauerspiel* study) and the commodity form (the central category of the *Passagenarbeit*). Benjamin writes: 'the figure of the "modern" and that of "allegory" must be interrelated' (J6a,2, *GS* V, p. 311). The specific character of this rather peculiar relationship between poetic form and industrial product is central to an interpretation of Benjamin's Baudelaire studies.

Allegory is a mode of representation in which each element of what is said or depicted stands for something else. In allegory, the apparent or surface meaning is a veneer which conceals the actual, hidden sense. One narrative appears disguised as another; it is a palimpsest. Each object represented may have a host of competing possible meanings. A crown, for example, may serve as an allegorical device for monarchy, sovereignty, wealth, legitimate power, tyranny, the folly of worldly as opposed to divine authority, and so forth. Meaning is elusive and multiple. Benjamin points out that 'any person, any object, any relationship can mean absolutely anything else. With this possibility a destructive but just verdict is passed on the profane world: it is characterised as a world in which the detail is of no great importance' (*OGTD*, p. 175). The object, the detail, the forms of nature, in that they can mean anything and everything, come to mean precisely nothing. Allegory involves the hollowing out of meaning. Language becomes an expanse of empty signs 'signifying nothing'.

In the third section of his proposed book on Baudelaire Benjamin planned to examine the commodity as poetic object. For Benjamin, the commodity both exhibits characteristics similar to the allegorical – it is 'hollow' – and is the object of the allegorical gaze – as a result of which, it becomes a ruin. The commodity is in the realm of artefacts what the allegory is in the realm of words. It is an entity whose actual meaning, in this instance its use-value, has been emptied out, leaving an arbitrary, conventional exchange-value. In the allegory, the domain of nature, God's creation, is shown to be (in the post-Fall epoch) devoid of grace, and hence meaningless. This is matched by the denigration of the products of human labour through the process of commodification. Benjamin writes of Baudelaire's poetry: 'the fashions of meaning changed almost as quickly as the price of the commodity changed. In fact the meaning of the commodity is: price; as a commodity it has no other. Thus the allegory is in its element with the commodity' (J80,2/J80a,1, *GS* V, p. 466). Baudelaire's poetry constitutes a 'privileged vantage point' because of the shared emptiness of the allegory and the commodity. Benjamin writes: 'Baudelaire was isolated as an allegorist. He sought to explain the experience of the commodity by the allegorical' (J67,2, *GS* V, p. 438). He also notes: 'the commodity form comes to light in Baudelaire as the societal content of the allegorical gaze' (J59,10, *GS* V, p. 422). Buck-Morss observes: 'Baudelaire's allegorical representations were antithetical to the mythic form of the objects as wish-images. He showed, not the commodities filled with private dreams, but private dreams as hollowed out as the commodities' (1989, p. 182).

The commodity is the modern embodiment of the allegorical. With its emphasis upon exchange- and exhibition-value, the commodity is devoid of substance. Its fate within the cycle of production and the contingencies of fashion is to become out of date, old-fashioned, obsolete. The commodity thus exhibits another similarity to the allegory. Hollowed out and barren, the commodity is revealed as nothing other than a ruin. In the *Trauerspiel* study Benjamin states: 'In the ruin history has physically merged into the setting. And in this guise history does not assume the form of the process of an eternal.life so much as that of irresistible decay. Allegory thereby declares itself to be beyond beauty. Allegories are, in the realm of thoughts, what ruins are in the realm of things' (*OGTD*, pp. 177–8). Ruination, that which fashion and innovation achieve with the passage of time, is accomplished instantaneously in allegorical representation. The commodity, an empty shell, and the arcade which houses it[6] are revealed as transient, disintegrating forms. The experience of the commodity is that of ruination. The modern city, the site of the smug celebration of progress and the conquest of the natural world, is critically revealed through the allegorical gaze as the space of ruin. Benjamin writes:

in allegory the observer is confronted with the *facies hippocratica* of history as a petrified, primordial landscape. Everything about history that, from the very beginning, has been untimely, sorrowful, unsuccessful, is expressed in a face – or rather in a death's head. . . . This is the form in which man's subjection to nature is most obvious and it significantly gives rise not only to the enigmatic question of the nature of human existence as such, but also of the biographical historicity of the individual. This is the heart of the allegorical way of seeing, of the baroque, secular explanation of history as the Passion of the world; its importance resides solely in the stations of its decline. (*OGTD*, p. 166)

Allegory is concerned with the natural history of the object, the body and the world. It reveals the transitory or historical character of things, yet stresses their continuity, their ongoing existence. Allegory unmasks the ever-new as the always-the-same and the timeless as the temporary. It is thus allegory which provides those nimble fingers with which Benjamin seeks to unravel the mythic. He notes the need 'to clearly develop the antithesis between allegory and myth' (J22,5, *GS* V, p. 344). Allegory is precisely that mode of representation which brings about the 'dissolution of "mythology" into the space of history' (N1,9, Smith ed., 1989, p. 45).

Allegory appeals to the sense of vision.[7] The allegorical gaze is that of the physiognomist, and has both a destructive and a constructive moment. In emptying out meaning, allegory brings the ruination, the 'mortification' (*OGTD*, p. 182) of things. Allegory thus sees the object as it will appear in its 'afterlife'; it is a form of premonition. The allegorical gaze frees the utopian or dream element of the artefact (commodity or architecture) through the destruction of the context which held it captive. Benjamin writes: 'tearing things out of the context of their usual interrelations – which is quite normal where commodities are being exhibited – is a procedure very characteristic of Baudelaire. It is related to the destruction of the organic interrelations in the allegoric intention' (*CP*, p. 41).[8] Allegory also contains a positive, redemptive moment. Benjamin observes that: 'an appreciation of the transience of things, and the concern to rescue them for eternity, is one of the strongest impulses in allegory' (*OGTD*, p. 223). The world is reduced to ruins so that the rubble and fragments that result can be gathered up and reused. Benjamin notes that objects viewed through the optic of allegory 'are broken apart and conserved simultaneously. Allegory holds tightly to the debris' (J56,1, *GS* V, pp. 414–15). The *promesse de bonheur* contained in the phantasmagoria of the modern is thus redeemed. The allegorical gaze, like the magical gaze of the child-as-collector, is the salvation of the thing. Ruination and redemption – these are the Janus-faces of allegory. The allegorical vision as the overcoming of myth and the moment of historical redemption contains within it the qualities of the dialectical image, and hence becomes the fundamental basis of Benjamin's critical historiography.

The interconnections that Benjamin perceives between allegory and the commodity, and subsequently between the allegorical purpose of the poet and the historical-redemptive task of the Critical Theorist, underpin his analysis of Baudelaire. In stressing the centrality of the commodity, one must be careful that one does not, as Buck-Morss tends to, lose sight of its location and setting: the city as the space of ruin. Although she writes of Baudelaire (and one could well apply her comment to Benjamin also), 'it was precisely the splendor of the newly constructed urban phantasmagoria with its promise of change-as-progress that elicited in him the most prototypically melancholic allegorical response' (1989, p. 178), the urban dimension is somewhat underplayed in her interpretation. She tends to overlook the fact that it is not only the commodity that exists as a poetic object for Baudelaire, but also the city itself. The relationship between the allegorical and the urban must be stressed. Benjamin writes: 'no-one felt less at home in Paris than Baudelaire. The allegorical intention is alien to *every* intimacy with things' (J59a,4, *GS* V, p. 423). A sense of estrangement in the city is a crucial aspect of Baudelaire's allegorical vision. Jennings notes that 'in Benjamin's physiognomical portrait, Baudelaire is seen for the first time as the quintessential modern-alienated, spatially displaced, Saturnine' (1987, p. 21). In his attempt to give voice to the 'romance' of the urban landscape, Baudelaire registers and articulates its passion, its agony. Benjamin writes: 'the poetic Passion of the *Fleurs du mal* consists in this: that Baudelaire lays himself open to the deepest possible experience of modern life, and to everything in modern life which is antagonistic to the capacity for experience itself' (*CP*, p. 68). Just as the experience of the commodity involves the commodification of experience, so the experience of the ruin is the ruination of experience.

The site of intoxication and ruination, the city was irresistible, however. For Baudelaire, as for Benjamin, the colour and noise of the street and the hustle and bustle of the modern metropolitan crowd were not only vital components of the text, but were the necessary conditions surrounding its genesis.[9] In Baudelaire's writings, Benjamin notes, the crowd 'has not served as the model for any of his works, but it is imprinted on his creativity as a hidden figure' (*CB*, p. 120). Paris was as indispensable for Baudelaire's literary production as 'Berlin W.W.' was for Benjamin's.[10] Neither at home in it nor content away from it, the city was both enticing and profoundly disturbing to both writers. Benjamin cites Crépet thus: 'what is one to conclude from this? Perhaps simply that Baudelaire was of that family, one of those unfortunates who desire only what they do not have and love only the place where they are not' (quoted in J31,3, *GS* V, p. 362). What Benjamin may have found most significant in the allegorical poetics of Baudelaire was the articulation of his own ambiguous response to the modern metropolis, his own fluctuation between adoration and detestation. The interplay between the city as bestial and the city as beautiful was both the essential theme of, and the very source of inspiration for, Baudelaire's poetry. Its examination constitutes the zenith of the dilemma which Benjamin first articulates in his essay on Naples in 1924. For each in different ways, Paris was both Heaven and Hell, and for each, the only possible response was melancholy.

The crowd

In the early drafts and notes of Benjamin's *Passagenarbeit* the urban population appears in the enigmatic guise of the dreaming collectivity. To rouse the dreaming collectivity from its slumbers is the precondition for the true fulfilment of those longings and desires which the commodity purports to satisfy yet indefinitely postpones. For Benjamin, the task of the historical materialist is to bring about an awakening through the recognition and representation of the forgotten history of the oppressed. This vision of the urban population as a potentially benign but presently dormant power is replaced in the Baudelaire studies by two other formulations which, though equally problematic and undifferentiated, are far more pessimistic in character: those of the crowd and the mass.

Benjamin writes: 'the crowd – no subject was more entitled to the attention of nineteenth-century writers' (*CB*, p. 120). For him, the hallmark of modern metropolitan experience was the encounter with the crowd, the reaction of the individual to the great assemblage of strangers that forms the urban populace. In the great metropolitan centres of Europe, the individual was confronted for the first time by the unknown, unknowable multitude. Benjamin cites Hugo's poem 'La Pente de la rêverie' thus: 'Crowd without name! chaos! of voices, of eyes, of footsteps. Those that one has never seen, those one doesn't know. All the living!' (quoted in *CB*, p. 62). This quantitative change in human numbers and its qualitative impact on human experience drew a variety of responses. Benjamin notes: 'fear, revulsion, and horror were the emotions which the big-city crowd aroused in those who first observed it' (*CB*, p. 131).[11] Benjamin notes that the desire to allay the paranoia engendered by a life among strangers finds particularly clear literary expression in the so-called urban physiologies which began to appear in the early 1840s. These were short articles published in the newspapers and journals of the time which sought to describe the various characters found in the crowd. Supposedly humorous sketches, these texts presented rather crude, facile stereotypes for the reassurance of readers. As such, they were often the products of that self-appointed expert and self-styled great observer of urban life, the *flâneur*, the figure who wove his way through the urban crowd *en route* to the literary market.[12]

The experience of the anonymous crowd was not limited to fleeting encounters in the streets of the city. As Benjamin notes, citing Simmel: ' "before the development of buses, railways, and trams in the nineteenth century, people had never been in a position of having to look at one another for long minutes or even hours without speaking to one another." This new situation was, as Simmel recognized, not a pleasant one' (*CB*, p. 38). The unease occasioned by having to look at strangers for extended periods of time was relieved by depicting them as harmless, benign figures. Benjamin observes that 'in the origins of the physiognomies [correction, physiologies] was the wish, among others, to mini-mize and destroy this disquiet' (M16a,2, *GS* V, p. 560). The crowd as safe haven was part of a particular bourgeois fantasy: the comfortable and comforting assumption not that you were just like everyone else, but that everyone else was really just like you. The physiology was an aspect of the mythology of the crowd-as-consensus. Benjamin writes: 'It was indeed the most obvious thing to give people a friendly picture of one another. Thus the physiologies helped fashion the phantasmagoria of Parisian life in their own way' (*CB*, pp. 38–9).

A second, more successful literary response in the nineteenth century to the anxieties provoked by the crowd again drew upon the dubious literary talents of the *flâneur*. The alleviation of panic was not the goal of this second genre. Instead, it sought precisely the opposite: that is, to play upon and exacerbate fear. Unlike the dull physiologies, Benjamin notes, 'the literature which concerned itself with the disquieting and threatening aspects of urban life was to have a great future' (*CB*, p. 40). This genre was the detective story.[13] In such tales one no longer rubbed shoulders in the crowd with like-minded citizens, but rather was in danger of encountering at any moment the most ruthless and bloodthirsty of villains. Edgar Allen Poe's story 'The Man of the Crowd' constitutes, Benjamin observes, an 'X-ray' of the detective story. He notes that, 'in it, the drapery represented by crime has disappeared. The mere armature has remained: the pursuer, the crowd, and an unknown man who arranges his walk through London in such a way that he always remains in the middle of the crowd' (*CB*, p. 48). The criminal vanishes into the urban multitude. For Benjamin, 'the original social content of the detective story was the obliteration of the individual's traces in the big-city crowd' (*CB*, p. 43).[14]

At the same time, in order to avoid the tedium of the homogeneous crowd, the detective story romantically transformed the city into a place of danger, of intrepid and daring figures, of heroic exploits and deeds of magnificent infamy. Baudelaire writes: 'What are the dangers of the forest and the prairie compared with the daily shocks and conflicts of civilisation? Whether a man grabs his victim on a boulevard or stabs his quarry in unknown woods – does he not remain both here and there the most perfect of all beasts of prey?' (*CB*, p. 39).[15] The detective story sought to generate not a sympathetic portrait of the stranger but a heroic sense of self. Benjamin writes: 'the detective story, regardless of its sober calculations, also participates in fashioning the phantasmagoria of Parisian life. As yet it does not glorify the criminal, though it does glorify his adversaries and, above all, the hunting-grounds where they pursue him' (*CB*, p. 41).

The precarious character of civilization was strictly for harmless consumption. The crowd-as-danger was not concerned with the revolutionary political potential of the new urban masses, or even with the petty crime of the poor. Rather, the focus of attention was the middle-class *apache*, the aristocratic villain, the gentleman criminal who, like the gambler, seeks the challenge and excitement of crime for its own sake, not merely for pecuniary benefit.[16] In the detective story the individual is both enthroned as hero (the detective, the hunter) and denied (he or she vanishes without trace, becomes merely one of the crowd). It seeks above all to transform the crowd-as-*ennui* into the city-as-wilderness, the demise of the individual into a tale of his or her desperate, heroic struggle to survive in a hostile environment.

Fear, loathing, contempt, but also excitement and jubilation;[17] in various measures and admixtures, these characterized the literature of the crowd in the epoch of its birth. Fascinated by the 'incomparable power' (J31a,4, *GS* V, p. 363) of Poe's description of the urban crowd, Benjamin writes: 'the locus *où tout, même l'horreur, tourne aux enchantements* (where everything, even the horror turns into enchantment) could hardly be better exemplified than in Poe's description of the crowd' (*CP*, p. 47). For Benjamin, however, the decisive relationship between individual and crowd finds its most perceptive, because most contradictory, formulation in Baudelaire. Here the crowd becomes not so much the new thematic content of lyric poetry as its fundamental optic.[18] Benjamin notes that, 'As regards Baudelaire, the masses were anything but external to him; indeed, it is easy to trace in his works his defensive reaction to their attraction and their allure. . . . The masses had become so much a part of Baudelaire that it is rare to find a description of them in his works' (*CB*, p. 122). The scurrying, elusive urban crowd is the definitive motif of the modern. It is the ultimate embodiment of the ephemeral, the momentary, the unpredictable. Constantin Guys, Baudelaire's 'painter of modern life', asserts: 'who can yet be *bored in the heart of the multitude*, is a blockhead! a blockhead! and I despise him!' (Baudelaire, 1986, p. 10).[19] The ecstasy of the 'multiplication of numbers' (*CB*, p. 58)[20] is also the thrill of anonymity. In the crowd the modern individual could lose himself,[21] could disappear without trace. The crowd becomes the hiding-place of modernity, the haunt of the bohemian and the fugitive.

As a crowd, the city's inhabitants coalesced into a mobile maze within the metropolitan labyrinth. The city-as-labyrinth was the dreamscape of antiquity, the crowd-as-labyrinth that of the modern epoch. Benjamin states that the crowd is 'the newest means of intoxication for the solitary individual. – In addition, it erases all trace of the individual: it is the latest asylum of the outlaw. – It is, finally, the newest and most impenetrable labyrinth in the maze of the city' (M16,3, *GS* V, p. 559).[22] As the medium for endless *flâneries* and adventures, the crowd was an enticing entity for Baudelaire.[23] Yet at the same time its barbarous composition filled him with disgust. In his work, the diverse responses of the nineteenth century exist in a condition of unresolved tension. Benjamin writes of him thus:

If he succumbed to the force by which he was drawn to them and, as a *flâneur*, was made one of them, he was nevertheless unable to rid himself of a sense of their essentially inhuman make-up. He becomes their accomplice even as he dissociates himself from them. He becomes deeply involved with them, only to relegate them to oblivion with a single glance of contempt. There is something compelling about this ambivalence. (*CB*, p. 128)

Baudelaire writes: 'the lover of universal life enters into the crowd as though it were an immense reservoir of electrical energy' (1986, p. 9). This is a rather appropriate analogy, because 'shock' is the quintessential experience of the crowd and the definitive signature of modernity. Baudelaire, Benjamin observes, 'placed the shock experience at the very centre of his artistic work' (*CB*, p. 117). In the city, one must avoid the host of oncoming pedestrians and negotiate a ceaseless flow of random encounters with unknown others as one threads one's way through the crowd. Motion 'involves the individual in a series of shocks and collisions' (*CB*, p. 132). Jostled, pushed and shoved by the seething urban crowd, the city dweller must remain ever vigilant, constantly on guard and alert. In the midst of the crowd, the individual is bombarded by a plethora of unassimilable stimuli. The city is the site of the inundation and overwhelming of the individual by sudden, unexpected, diverse sense-impressions.

Experience is no longer a continuous development, but is reduced instead to a seemingly random series of half-impressions, of images and thoughts only partially registered, still less understood. Coherent, integrated experience is destroyed within the urban multitudes. Benjamin articulates this process in terms of the transformation of *Erfahrung* into *Erlebnis*. Both these terms mean 'experience', but of very different sorts. *Erfahrung* (derived from the verb *fahren* meaning 'to travel') refers to experience as the accumulation of knowledge. It means experience in the sense of being widely travelled, of having witnessed many things, of having gained wisdom. The experience related by the story-teller is what one may designate *Erfahrung*: coherent, communicable, readily intelligible. *Erlebnis* is concerned with the domain of inner life, with the chaotic contents of psychic life.[24] The shocks of the metropolitan environment are unassimilable by the consciousness of the individual, and are parried or deflected into the realm of the unconscious where they remain embedded. Benjamin writes: 'The greater the share of the shock factor in particular impressions, the more constantly consciousness has to be alert as a screen against stimuli; the more efficiently it is so, the less do these impressions enter experience [*Erfahrung*], tending to remain in the sphere of a certain hour of one's life [*Erlebnis*]' (*CB*, p. 117). *Erlebnis* is concerned with the unprocessed, disordered particles of experience, the haphazard and accidental. *Erlebnis* is the corollary of forgetfulness, or rather constitutes the basis for that form of memory which is more a form of forgetting: the *mémoire involontaire*. For Benjamin, the city is the site of the rise of *Erlebnis* and the concomitant demise of *Erfahrung*. The experience of the modern urban complex is that of the fragmentation of experience itself.

In this vision of urban life Benjamin clearly draws upon the work of Georg Simmel. In his 1903 essay 'The Metropolis and Mental Life', Simmel explores the impact of the city upon the 'inner life' of the individual. Simmel notes: 'the psychological foundation upon which the metropolitan individuality is erected, is the intensification of emotional life due to the swift and continuous shift of external and internal stimuli' (Simmel, 1971, p. 325). The urbanite is unable to manage 'the rapid telescoping of changing images, pronounced differences within what is grasped at a single glance, and the unexpectedness of violent stimuli' (ibid.). He or she can only react mechanically, automatically. Interaction becomes instant reflex.[25]

The experience of the metropolis is based upon the avoidance of negative encounters as life becomes a purely defensive strategy. Simmel writes: 'the metropolitan type – which naturally takes on a thousand individual modifications – creates a protective organ for itself against the profound disruption with which the fluctuations and discontinuities of the external milieu threaten it' (Simmel, 1971, p. 326). The response to the danger of becoming 'saturated' by stimuli is to block them out, to become indifferent to them. Simmel notes that

> There is no psychic phenomenon which is so unconditionally reserved to the city as the *blasé* attitude . . . The essence of the *blasé* attitude is an indifference toward the distinctions between things. Not in the sense that they are not perceived, as in the case of mental dullness, but rather that the meaning and value of the distinctions between things themselves are experienced as meaningless. (Simmel, 1971, p. 329)

To become indifferent, blasé, is to succumb to forgetfulness, to be lulled into torpor. In the city one must come to be unmoved and undisturbed by what one encounters. The individual refrains from exhibiting any interest, any concern. While Saisselin states that 'the city expanded the range of the seeable' (1985, p. 21), for Benjamin it is the home of the unseeing stare, for the metropolis demands that one appear to look without seeing. In the crowded buses and trains of the city the passenger must still find empty spaces into which he or she may safely stare. In the metropolis the avoidance of the gaze and the refusal to return it are paramount.[26] In the crowd, one may see many people, but one notices no one, one looks at no one, one recognizes no one. No distinctions are made. For Simmel, this leads to neurasthenia as the individual cultivates the 'strangest eccentricities' (Simmel, 1971, p. 336) in appearance and manner in order to be different, in the hope of attracting attention. For Benjamin, the crowd, like fashion, becomes the ceaseless parade of the always-the-same. The crowd is the dullness of the nothing-new, the ultimate locus of boredom.

For Baudelaire, and for Benjamin, the crowd is both generative of experience, producing intoxication, yet simultaneously destructive of it, leading to boredom. This shifting, fragile balance is perhaps best illustrated by Benjamin's interpretation of Baudelaire's poem 'À une passante' (To a Passer-by) from the *Tableaux parisiens*. This poem describes a momentary encounter between the poet and an unknown woman in the city. The poet is walking in a street surrounded by the milling crowds of the urban centre. Suddenly he spies an elegant and beautiful woman among the anonymous multitude. Their glances meet momentarily, and mutual attraction is registered. Then, as suddenly as she appeared, the woman vanishes into the crowd once more, presumably never to be seen by the poet again. Benjamin comments: 'What this sonnet communicates is simply this: far from experiencing the crowd as an opposed, antagonistic element, this very crowd brings to the city-dweller the figure that fascinates. The delight of the urban poet is love – not at first sight, but at last sight' (*CB*, p. 125). In the poem the crowd is the source of unexpected pleasure and excitement. In an environment in which the reciprocity of the gaze is denied, fleeting mutual recognition, 'love at last sight', is a unique occurrence, a moment of shock. The exchange of glances becomes thrilling, memorable.

However, as Benjamin also notes, 'the inner form of these verses is revealed in the fact that in them love itself is recognized as being stigmatized by the big-city' (*CB*, p. 46). The crowd brings the object of desire[27] within the poet's field of vision, but she is once more borne away by it. While the beauty of the ephemeral, *modernité*, is stimulating and intoxicating, the object of desire is elusive. The look of 'love at last sight' is alluring and wistful, but it is rooted in denial and frustration. Missac writes: 'the woman, who one loves, has something elusive about her; the passers-by cross paths only in "a flash"; the two meanings of the word "passion" combine in misfortune' (1991, p. 14). The erotic becomes a momentary act of seeing, of voyeurism. The glimpsed figures of the urban crowd may awaken sexual desire, but it remains unfulfilled. For the poet, the city is the site of temptation: it is the home of Tantalus.[28] Benjamin writes of Baudelaire thus: 'His experience of the crowd bore the traces of the "heartache and the thousand natural shocks" which a pedestrian suffers in the bustle of a city and which keep his self-awareness all the more alert' (*CB*, p. 61).

Benjamin successfully identifies a series of fundamental themes in his analysis of the experience of the individual *vis-à-vis* the crowd (loss of identity, shock, disorientation, fear, intoxication, excitement), but fails to integrate these in a thorough, coherent investigation. 'Paris as Heaven', 'Paris as Hell': it is in the motif of the crowd that this dual identity finds its quintessential expression. The image of the crowd is a monad in which Benjamin's contradictory responses to modernity are crystallized. On the one hand, destructive of genuine experience and diversity, the crowd rigorously regiments the individual and denies his or her autonomy. The crowd is the negation of individuality and the self. On the other hand, despite its brutalizing tendencies, the crowd retains a certain allure for the outcast who wishes to remain undetected. The anonymity afforded by the crowd denies, yet surreptitiously facilitates, the possibility of the idiosyncratic. In the crowd one is able to lose oneself. The crowd is the finest setting in which to be alone, to find precisely that solitude which Benjamin found most desirable, to experience the 'loneliness peculiar to the modern city' (Buck-Morss, 1986, p. 128). For Benjamin, Baudelaire's metropolitan lyricism precisely captures that moment in which the rural, pastoral idyll is transformed into the intoxication of the modern, in which 'I wandered lonely as a cloud' becomes 'I wandered lonely in the crowd'.[29] The crowd is the haunt of the melancholic.

Benjamin's ambivalent response to the urban crowd was superseded by a growing pessimism. In his later writings on Baudelaire and Paris, an increasing emphasis is given to the dehumanizing tendencies at work in the crowd: towards conformity, uniformity, anonymity and passivity. The metropolitan crowd emerges in a new light: namely, as a threatening, undifferentiated mass. The mass is the final extinction of the bourgeois individual.[30] The mass is defined not in relation to its place in the mode of production, but rather in its participation in consumption.[31] The mass coalesces around the commodity. Benjamin states that

> The audience of the theater, an army, the inhabitants of a city [form] the masses, which as such do not belong to a particular class. The free market increases these masses rapidly . . . in that every commodity collects around itself the mass of its customers. The totalitarian states have made this mass their model. The *Volksgemeinschaft* drives everything out of individuals that stands in the way of their complete assimilation into a massified clientele. (J81a,1, *GS* V, p. 469, cited by Buck-Morss, 1989, p. 307)

The mass has as its ideology the reactionary denial of class affiliation and conflict. It is disorganized, brutish and blind. The following passage in 'Berlin Chronicle' encapsulates Benjamin's understanding of such an agglomeration:

> Climbing the stairs in this fashion, with nothing before me but boots and calves, and the scraping of hundreds of feet in my ears, I was often seized – I seem to remember – by revulsion at being hemmed in by this multitude. . . . [S]uch a mob of school children is among the most formless and ignoble of all masses, and betrays its bourgeois origin in representing, like every assembly of that class, the most rudimentary organizational form that its individual members can give their reciprocal relationships. (*OWS*, p. 302)

The urban mass likewise has its origin in the bourgeois subject: as individual, indifferent to the plight of others; as customer, bent on the petty acquisition of commodities. The bourgeois and/or *petit bourgeois* background of the urban mass has profound political implications. The mass is the stuff of which Fascism was made.

The concept of the mass appears as the afterlife of the dreaming collectivity and the crowd. Benjamin writes of the urban population, apparently critically rejecting his own earlier formulations, thus: 'In fact this "collective" is nothing but illusory appearance [*Schein*]. This "crowd" on which the *flâneur* feasts his eyes is the mold into which, seventy years later, the *Volksgemeinschaft* was poured' (J66,1, *GS* V, p. 436, cited by Buck-Morss, 1989, p. 307). The truth of the modern urban population is revealed in its final, dehumanized incarnation: as supporters of, and collaborators with, the Nazi movement. Benjamin replaces the rather simplistic affirmation of the radical potential of the dormant urban population which characterized his initial formulation in the *Passagenarbeit* with, some ten years later, an equally one-dimensional denunciation of it. The dreaming collectivity has become the nightmare of the mob. Modernity is the triumph of barbarism, a reversion to mythic domination. Thus Benjamin zigzags, in response to the political conditions of his own time, between whole-hearted affirmation and outright condemnation. The Parisians of the nineteenth century are seen at different times as both the forerunners of the coming communistic utopia and the precursors of Fascist terror, a historical constellation which owes more to Benjamin's increasing despair regarding the political events and contingencies of the 1930s than to the social realities of the Second Empire.

The heroism of modern life[32]

Paris, capital of the nineteenth century, compared itself with the great urban centres of the ancient world: sinful Nineveh, decadent Babylon, and sad Carthage. Above all, it dreamed of itself as the great new imperial capital of the cosmos, as a modern Rome. Just as a self-conscious and pompous classical style dominated architecture, design and sculpture, so it also held sway over Parisian self-perception. But if Louis Napoleon was to play its Caesar, who was to be the new Horatius? In the metropolitan labyrinth, the dream of the ancients had been realized, Benjamin notes; but what of Theseus and Ariadne? The bold Parisian did not have to look far for the new hero of modernity, only into a mirror. As an escape from the *ennui* of modern urban existence, the *tedium vitae* produced by the nothing-new of fashion and the faceless uniformity of the metropolitan crowd, the city was transformed by Poe, Dumas and Sue into a place of adventure. It was dressed up as a locus of unspoken dangers, menacing shadows, villainous figures stalking the city's streets and of evil lurking in every dimly lit alley-way. This metamorphosis of the urban centre, the home of the mundane and routine, into the site of the extraordinary and macabre involved another character: the sober bourgeois citizen became a heroic figure, the individual who risks the hazards of the metropolis single-handed. The urban hero defies the modern fates: he or she does not succumb to the temptations of the commonplace commodity and resists the urge to hurry when all around are scurrying to and from their labours; he or she retains a sense of personal identity and integrity even in the midst of the anonymous, bustling crowd, and refuses to bow down before the modern gods of punctuality and rational calculation. The modern hero is a figure at odds with his or her own epoch, yet addicted to the intoxication and romance of modernity itself.

For Benjamin, the notion of modern life as in any sense 'heroic' is problematic, paradoxical and often ironic. On one level, Benjamin unequivocally rejects it. On another, it becomes a source of valuable insights into the experience and phantasmagoria of modernity, into the modern sensibility. Benjamin recasts the notion, and extends its range and import.[33] For Benjamin, there are three dimensions to the heroism of modern life: the attempt to give form to the modern; its endurance of, and antagonism towards, the modern; and its phantasmagorical character or 'irreality'.

Benjamin, like Baudelaire, rejects the conceit of the bour-geoisie's self-equation with the heroes of the ancient world. For him, the bitingly satirical images of the lithographer Daumier 'provided the critical distance necessary to recognize the preten-sions of the bourgeois cloak of antiquity' (Buck-Morss, 1989, p. 147). Benjamin quotes Baudelaire thus:

> Daumier swoops down brutally on antiquity and mythology and spits on [them]. And the impassioned Achilles, the prudent Ulysses, the wise Penelope, and that great ninny Telemachus, and beautiful Helen who loses Troy, and steaming Sappho, patron of hysterics, and ultimately everyone, has been shown to us in a comic ugliness that recalls those old carcasses of actors of the classic theater who take a pinch of snuff behind the scenes. (b2,3, *GS* V, p. 901, cited by Buck-Morss, 1989, p. 147)

The romantic, melodramatic notion of the city-as-wilderness with its steadfast heroic bourgeois citizen unflinchingly defying metro-politan monstrosities is clearly revealed as nothing other than the pompous self-aggrandizement of the narrow tedium and petty trivialities of bourgeois daily life.[34] The heroism of modernity is nothing other than a fundamental aspect of its self-deception, its phantasmagorical character.

Whereas the Surrealists identified the new gods of the metro-polis in their *mythologie moderne*, Baudelaire discovered its new heroes. For him, modern life does contain a 'heroic' dimension, despite its bombastic pretensions. Although rejecting bourgeois neoclassicism he asserted that a fresh conception of the heroic was necessary for the nascent aesthetic of *modernité*. For Baudelaire, modern heroism resides in the attempt to give voice to the transience of contemporary life. Benjamin notes: 'in the epoch to which he [Baudelaire] belonged, nothing came closer to the "task" of the ancient hero, to the "labours" of a Hercules than the task imposed upon him as his very own; to give shape to modernity' (*CB*, p. 81). To give form to the fluidity of urban experience was the highest goal of the writer. Such a duty involved not a foolish dressing in the worn-out robes of antiquity, but the redemption of the fragmentary and fleeting facets of modern social life so that, at some distant future moment, they themselves might constitute the 'antique'.[35] Baudelaire 'experienced the ancient claim to immortality as his claim to being read as an ancient writer some day' (*CB*, p. 81). For Baudelaire, the poet was the ultimate hero in his struggle to articulate the modern.

This act of representation involves resistance.[36] To give form to the modern, one must combat it,[37] bring it to a standstill. Benjamin notes: 'to interrupt the course of the world – that was Baudelaire's deepest wish' (J50,2, *GS* V, p. 401). Modern heroism still involves an act of hubris. In a letter to his mother of 23 December 1865 cited by Benjamin, Baudelaire writes: 'I would like to set the entire human race against me. I see in this a pleasure that would console me for everything' (J46a,10, *GS* V, p. 395). The heroes of modernity are not merely anachronistic, out of step with their own time, however.[38] For Benjamin, they are characters who most acutely embody the prevailing tendencies of their society and epoch, while denying and resisting them. These figures are monadological in the sense that they contain within them the contradictory forces that shaped the age. The 'true' hero of modernity does not merely give form to his or her epoch or simply endure it, but is both scornful and complicitous. Hence, it is self-deception rather than rage or mere folly that is the hallmark of modern heroism. Symptomatic of, yet paradoxically struggling against, the inexorable unfolding of the socio-economic and political processes of the nineteenth century, the heroism of modern life is a category refined and crucially extended by Benjamin. It is not only the urban poet who deserves the title of hero, but also those on whom he models himself: the *flâneur*, the dandy, the collector, the gambler, the worker, the rag-picker and the prostitute.[39] These are more than just victims of modern society; they are more than mere figures of pathos. For Benjamin, the heroes of modernity are those doomed to endure it, to suffer its consequences while at the same time engaged somehow in subverting it.

The defiance of the modern hero is always a hollow protest. His or her hubris resides precisely in the claim to heroic status. For Benjamin, it is the grandeur of this conceit, the magnificence of the delusion itself, that lends nineteenth-century Parisian life its heroic quality. It is precisely the phantasmagoria of the modern, the 'irreality' of Paris, that paradoxically makes heroism possible. Benjamin notes: 'the index of heroism in Baudelaire: to live at the heart of irreality' (*CP*, p. 43). The heroism of modernity is precisely the attempt, doomed to failure, to escape the ultimate terror of contemporary existence: namely, boredom. The heroism of the modern individual is located in the quest for novelty and excitement in a metropolitan environment that fundamentally frustrates and denies them. It is the great gesture in defiance of the obvious fact that in modernity there is no heroism at all. The heroism of modern life is doubly mythic: it draws on ancient myth, and it does not actually exist. The response to the absence of heroism is paradoxically heroic.

Modern heroism can only ever be a playing at heroism. Benjamin states: 'the hero, who stands fast on the scene of modernity, is in fact above all an actor' (J77a,3, *GS* V, p. 461).[40] Benjamin writes of Baudelaire thus: '*Flâneur*, apache, dandy, and rag-picker were so many roles to him. For the modern hero is no hero; he acts heroes. Heroic modernism turns out to be a *Trauerspiel* in which the hero's part is available' (*CB*, p. 97). It is a theatrical presentation before a mirror, to an audience of one. Even the crowd, with its draped-mirror eyes, pays scant attention to the heroic performer. Playing the part of the hero for one's own amusement soon becomes tedious. The attempt to avoid boredom becomes the shortest, surest route to it. Frisby points out that for Benjamin, 'even the forms of heroism in modern life were to be exposed as forms of modern melancholy and boredom' (1988, p. 263). The modern hero, in seeking to avoid the tedium of the mundane and commonplace, plunges more swiftly and deeper into it. Trapped in repeated suffering or caught in unchanging boredom, the modern hero is a profoundly melancholic figure, a stoic.[41]

Although Benjamin points out that 'Baudelaire's *flâneur* was not a self-portrait of the poet to the extent that this might be assumed' (*CB*, p. 69), it is none the less in this guise, Odysseus[42] on the pavement, that the clearest articulation of modern heroism is to be found. Although the figure of the lone individual wandering in the urban labyrinth is evident in Benjamin's other city sketches, he notes that it was 'Paris [that] created the *flâneur* as a type' (M1,4,

GS V, p. 525). The *flâneur* is the stroller, the pedestrian who finds delight and pleasure in ambling contentedly and unhurriedly through the city. He is at home in the metropolitan environment.[43] Benjamin writes:

> The street becomes a dwelling for the *flâneur*; he is as much at home among the façades of the houses as a citizen in his four walls. To him the shiny, enamelled signs of businesses are at least as good a wall ornament as an oil painting is to a bourgeois in his salon. The walls are the desk against which he presses his notebooks; news-stands are his libraries and the terraces of cafés are the balconies from which he looks down on his household after his work is done. (*CB*, p. 37)

As the *flâneur* turns the boulevard into an interior setting, so the interiorized street, the arcade, is his favourite haunt. Benjamin points out that 'strolling could hardly have assumed the importance it did without the arcades' (*CB*, p. 36). Whether within the arcade or out on the boulevard, the urban setting becomes a landscape for the *flâneur* in which he finds amusement, distraction and novelty. To promenade without purpose is the highest ambition of the *flâneur*. Walking in the city is its own reward. Benjamin observes: 'an intoxication comes over those who wander through the streets for a long time without any particular goal. The activity of walking itself grows in power with each step taken' (M1,3, *GS* V, p. 525). The *flâneur* is the aimless, complacent, haughty bourgeois who wanders through the urban complex in search of nothing more than diversion, to see and to be seen.

The *flâneur* endured the modern, mocked it, fashioned its contours, and deceived both it and himself. For Baudelaire, the *flâneur* is only one guise adopted by the poet. He is the incarnation of the 'painter of modern life', the spectator of contemporary manners and urban scenes. To be at the very heart of the crowd in the centre of the metropolis is essential to the *flâneur*.[44] Baudelaire writes:

> The crowd is his element, as the air is that of birds and water of fishes. His passion and profession are to become one flesh with the crowd. For the perfect *flâneur*, for the passionate spectator, it is an immense joy to set up house in the middle of the multitude, amid the ebb and flow of movement, in the midst of the fugitive and the infinite. (1986, p. 9)

For Baudelaire, the *flâneur* becomes 'one flesh' with the crowd. Benjamin states unequivocally, however, that 'it is hard to accept this view. The man of the crowd is no *flâneur*' (*CB*, p. 128). While the urban crowd is the medium through which the *flâneur* moves, in Benjamin's view, this figure must on no account be equated with the 'man of the crowd', Poe's enigmatic, perpetual seeker of the multitudes. The reason for this rejection of Baudelaire's formulation is clear. For Benjamin, the distinctive heroism of the *flâneur*, whether poet or not, resides precisely in his refusal to become part of the crowd. The *flâneur* is not merely a pedestrian; he is the heroic pedestrian. On the Parisian boulevards, Benjamin notes, 'there was the pedestrian who wedged himself into the crowd, but also the *flâneur* who demanded elbow room and was unwilling to forego the life of a gentleman of leisure' (*CB*, p. 54). The *flâneur* is that character who retains his individuality while all around are losing theirs.[45] The *flâneur* derives pleasure from his location within the crowd, but simultaneously regards the crowd with contempt, as nothing other than a brutal, ignoble mass. However, 'the "crowd" is a veil which conceals the "mass" from the *flâneur*' (J59,2, *GS* V, p. 421) so that, like Baudelaire, the *flâneur* 'becomes their accomplice even as he dissociates himself from them. He becomes deeply involved with them, only to relegate them to oblivion with a single glance of contempt' (*CB*, p. 128). It is this persistent aloofness that is the hallmark of the *flâneur*'s heroic constitution.[46] He is precisely the one who heroically resists incorporation into the milieu in which he moves. Indeed, the disappearance of the *flâneur* into the crowd, the instant in which they become 'one flesh', is the moment of extinction of the *flâneur*.

For Benjamin, the *flâneur* is heroic in his arrogant retention of an aloof independence and a disdainful individuality. The most spectacular and flamboyant incarnation of the *flâneur* is the dandy.[47] Dressed in the latest, finest, most dazzling garments available (and socially permitted), the dandy was the self-styled walking peacock who trod precariously on, and sometimes stepped outrageously over, the limits of bourgeois good taste and sobriety. Benjamin cites Louis Thomas thus: 'the dandy, said Baudelaire, must aspire to be sublime without interruption. He must live and sleep in front of a mirror' (J10,8, *GS* V, p. 319). Paris, the city of mirrors, was not surprisingly, therefore, the home of the nineteenth-century dandy. Benjamin (citing S. F. Lahrs in an 1847 work by August Lewald) notes: 'egotistical – "that is what one becomes in Paris, where one can hardly take a step without noticing one's beloved self. Mirror to mirror" ' (R1a,4, *GS* V, p. 668). In the mirror-filled spaces of the metropolis, one could endlessly admire oneself and feel oneself admired. For the *flâneur*-as-dandy, the city was a stage for the phantasmagorical presentation of an outlandishly costumed self.

Baudelaire observes that dandyism involves 'the joy of astonishing others, and the proud satisfaction of never oneself being astonished' (1986, p. 28). The dandy's blasé attitude did not extend to matters of clothing and appearance. Self-conscious indifference here gave way to a self-styled expertise, for the dandy considered himself to be a knowledgeable figure in the spheres of fashion and taste. He thought of himself as the last expert consumer. His idiosyncratic style of dress marked him out as a personage of discrimination and discernment. The greatest desire of the dandy-as-*flâneur* was to stand out in the crowd. For Benjamin, the dandy is the social type who sought to resist the grey uniformity of the urban multitude through the acquisition of the most fashionable and foppish. In this antagonism to the anonymity of modern mass society, 'dandyism borders on the spiritual and the stoical' (Baudelaire, 1986, p. 28). The dandy was the quintessential conspicuous consumer, the clearest embodiment of Simmel's notion of fashion as social distinction. The dandy heroically failed to perceive that fashion itself was the great nothing-new, the thinly disguised always-the-same of commodity production and fetishization, the very source of the uniformity he so despised. For Baudelaire, 'dandyism is the last spark of heroism amid decadence' (D5,1, *GS* V, p. 167). Its passing is a source of melancholy. Benjamin cites Baudelaire thus: 'dandyism is a setting sun; like a declining star, it is superb, without heat and full of melancholy' (J6a,4, *GS* V, p. 312). The last great customer, the dandy was soon to be supplanted unceremoniously by the mass consumer.[48]

As a dandy, the *flâneur* might distinguish himself from the crowd by his appearance. Alternatively, or additionally, he might choose to do so through his activity, or rather, through his lack of activity, for the business of the *flâneur* was 'doing nothing'. The *flâneur* asserted his individuality through unconventional attire, and through an unusual occupation: idleness. He sought to convey the (ingenuous) impression of the man of leisure. It was in a calm, unhurried, and (hence) dignified manner that the *flâneur* paraded through the streets of the city.[49] He was pedestrian in both senses of the word: on foot and slow. Benjamin comments: 'His leisurely appearance as a personality is his protest against the division of labour. It is also his protest against their industriousness. Around 1840 it was briefly fashionable to take turtles for a walk in the arcades' (*CB*, p. 54). The extravagant performance of the dandy and the conspicuous idling of the dawdling *flâneur* converge in this peculiar image. The dandy resists uniformity of dress, the idler uniformity of motion. Both casually flaunt precious commodities: expensive clothing on the one hand and time on the other. The *flâneur* ambles, saunters and strolls, but must not hurry. He is fundamentally out of step with the rhythms of modern life. Herein lies his heroism. Benjamin writes of the *flâneur* thus: 'his composure would be nothing other than an unconscious protest against the tempo of the production process' (J60a,6, *GS* V, p. 426). The idler has not been coerced into compliance with the dehumanizing pace of machine-time in the industrial age. Sloth is heroic. Benjamin notes: 'Marx speaks of the "victory . . . of industry over heroic laziness" ' (m1a,1, *GS* V, p. 962).

The *flâneur* as a modern hero, though, is a sham. He plays the part of the disinterested, unhurried aristocrat, but this is only a deception, a dramatic performance. Just as the *flâneur*-as-dandy is secretly complicitous with the ever-the-same of fashion, so the indolence of the *flâneur*-as-idler is only a hollow protest. Despite his dawdling, the idler reaches his goal with time to spare. Benjamin writes: 'The labyrinth is the correct route for those who still always arrive at their destination early enough. For the *flâneur* this goal was the market' (J61,8, *GS* V, p. 427). The *flâneur* goes to the market in the guise of a curious onlooker, but in reality is there to sell his goods. Benjamin states: 'As *flâneurs*, the intelligentsia came into the marketplace. As they thought, to observe it – but in reality it was already to find a buyer' (*CB*, pp. 170–1). The *flâneur* gave form to the modern epoch, but not necessarily as a poet. He was the writer of the *feuilleton* section of newspapers, the sketcher of modern manners, the journalistic prototype of the contemporary society columnist. The *flâneur* was the heroic gossip. He was, in addition, the author of the physiologies. Benjamin points out that 'the physiologies were the first booty that the *flâneur* brought home from the market' (J82a,3, *GS* V, p. 470). Dawdling allowed the *flâneur* to sharpen his powers of observation, to go ' "botanising" on the asphalt' (*CB*, p. 36).[50] He was the self-appointed physiognomist, preoccupied with appearances.[51] Indeed, his own display of idleness was a thin veneer, a flimsy façade designed to convince the purchaser of these literary trifles of the length of time 'socially necessary' to produce them. Benjamin writes of the *flâneur* thus:

> On the boulevards he spent his hours of idleness which he displayed before people as part of his working hours. He behaved as if he had learned from Marx that the value of a commodity is determined by

the working time socially necessary to produce it. In view of the protracted periods of idleness which in the eyes of the public were necessary for the realization of his own labour-power, its value became almost fantastic. (*CB*, p. 29)

When 'time is money', it may be beneficial to take a long time. The *flâneur* did not reject or resist the equation of time and money, the commodification of time, but recognized it and exploited it to the full. The idler could afford to take his time, because this slowness was a calculated scheme for pecuniary gain. He thereby transformed laziness into a paid occupation.

The *flâneur*-as-idler is thus doubly phantasmagoric: in what he writes (the physiologies) and what he does (the pretence of aristocratic idleness and the reality of bourgeois commercial interest). Indeed, for Benjamin, the *flâneur* becomes the strolling embodiment of the commodity. As the finely dressed dandy, as the apparently nonchalant but actually ever-vigilant physiologist, the *flâneur* 'took the concept of consumption itself for a walk' (M17a,2, *GS* V, p. 562). For Benjamin 'the sandwichman is the last incarnation of the *flâneur*' (M19,2, *GS* V, p. 565).[52] The eventual fate of the *flâneur*, the truth of this character, is to be found in the pathetic figure who wanders around the city, seemingly without a destination, but with a placard attached to him advertising commodities for sale. The degenerate and thus quintessential *flâneur*, the afterlife of the dandy, is a walking commodity who attracts the gaze and attention of passers-by, only now as pauper not peacock.

Whether as dandy or idler, the city of Paris was not so much the home of the heroic bourgeois *flâneur* as his fantastical theatre. Benjamin notes: 'to the *flâneur*, his city – though he was born in it, like Baudelaire – is no home. It constitutes for him a stage' (J66a,6 *GS* V, p. 437). It was to become an increasingly crowded, congested stage. The *flâneur* carelessly snubbed the crowd, secretly pandered to its miserable literary tastes, and was finally overwhelmed by it. In the streets of the modern metropolis the *flâneur* finally loses himself. The hustle and bustle of the crowd were both necessary to the *flâneur* and the source of his eventual demise. They were essential as a backdrop to the life of leisure, as a contrast highlighting the dawdling tempo of the *flâneur's* gentle perambulations. Eventually, though, the jostling crowd denied the *flâneur* the required elbow-room, and the self-styled aristocrat of the pavement was left to fight his way inelegantly through the hated masses. Although the city forms the 'sacred ground of the *flânerie'* (M2a,1, *GS* V, p. 530), the urban complex gave birth to precisely those forces that were soon to destroy the *flâneur*: the crowd and forms of mass production, standardization and commodification. The *flâneur* sought not so much to resist these tendencies as to deceive them, and he failed splendidly. He is only a mock-hero. The dandy is no more than a sheep in wolf's clothing. The idler desires nothing more than the avoidance of *ennui*. Benjamin notes: 'the idler becomes fatigued less quickly than the man who amuses himself' (m4,1, *GS* V, p. 967). The dawdling *flâneur* becomes a measure of the listlessness of modern life. In the dream capital of the nineteenth century, 'the *flânerie* is the rhythm of this slumber' (e°2, *GS* V, p. 1054). As the snobbish somnambulist, the *flâneur* is a true hero of modernity because he is no hero at all, only a player at heroism, an idle dreamer destined for a rude awakening.

The gambler is another heroic bourgeois figure, and is an important character in Benjamin's writings on Paris.[53] In refusing to equate labour, time and money, the gambler appears to resist the discipline of capitalist production. Indeed, the gambler denies the financial importance of gambling itself, purporting instead to relish the game for its own sake. The gambler impatiently embraces and unflinchingly endures the unexpected joys and catastrophic blows of fate. For Benjamin, the stoic gambler encapsulates the disintegration of experience in the modern age, the element of 'shock' that characterizes modern urban life.

Gambling is a manifestation of the dread of boredom. Benjamin writes: 'The more that life becomes administratively regulated, the more people must learn waiting. Games of chance have the great charm of liberating people from waiting' (D10a,2, *GS* V, p. 178). Gambling brings with it the possibility of instant wealth. The exhilaration of gambling stems, in part at least, from the prospect of accumulating money without the need for sustained, regulated, disciplined toil. For Benjamin, gambling as a means of financial procurement severs those connections that capitalism establishes between ascetic labour and monetary accumulation. Gambling is a telescoping of time, its fantastical contraction. Benjamin notes: 'To the phantasmagoria of space, to which the *flâneur* was addicted, there corresponded the phantasmagoria of time, to which the gambler dedicated himself. Gambling transformed time into a narcotic' (*CB*, p. 174). The equation of work, time and money is momentarily denied in the activity of gambling. Gratification is immediate rather than deferred, and thus waiting is brought to a swift, premature end. This is doubtless one reason for the moral stigma attached to it. Gambling is the pursuit of the impatient and the lazy.[54] It is fundamentally immoral.

For Benjamin, it is precisely this that gives it a heroic aspect. Gambling is the economic basis of idling, the disdainful refusal to submit oneself to the rigours of labour and the debasement of the market. To have abundance without toil is the utopian promise extended by gambling. It denies scarcity and the need for rational calculation. Gambling purports to contain elements that are profoundly antagonistic to the central tenets of modern industrial capitalism.[55] The heroism of the gambler as a modern type resides in the manner in which fate and danger replace industry and boredom. But as such, it is only a façade. The gambler as financial speculator does not resist capitalist prescriptions, but rather fundamentally embodies them. Benjamin cites Paul Lafargue thus: 'the whole of modern economic development has the tendency to transform capitalism more and more into a vast international casino, in which the bourgeoisie win and lose as a consequence of events which remain unknown to them' (O4,1, *GS* V, p. 621). Capitalism formalizes the activity of the gambler and his desire to make money simply from money through the institution of the stock-market. The gambler becomes the quintessential capitalist figure in the Second Empire.

The nineteenth century saw the transformation of gambling from an aristocratic privilege into a respectable bourgeois pastime (see *CB*, p. 135). The problem for the bourgeois gambler was how to play in an aristocratic manner with only middle-class financial resources; that is, how to make money but appear to be seeking only modest distraction. Dostoyevsky, in his famous novella entitled *The Gambler* writes:

> There are two types of gambling, one that is gentlemanly and another that is vulgar and mercenary, the gambling of the disreputable. The distinction is strictly drawn – and yet how essentially base the distinction is! A gentleman, for example, may stake five or ten louis d'or, rarely more; he may, however, stake as much as a thousand francs if he is very rich, but only for the sake of gambling itself, for nothing more than amusement, strictly in order to watch the process of winning or losing; he must not by any means be interested in the winnings themselves. (1966, pp. 29–30)

The aristocratic gambler plays 'not out of any plebeian desire to win' (Dostoyevsky, 1966, p. 30), but solely for the sake of amusement. The gentleman (or lady) gambler is intrigued but unperturbed by the spin of the roulette wheel or the turn of the cards.[56] Dostoyevsky adds: 'a real gentleman . . . even if he loses everything he owns, must show no emotion. Money must be so far beneath a gentleman that it is hardly worth troubling about' (ibid.). Dostoyevsky's story is ironically concerned with all the calamities, disasters and frustrations caused exactly by (or by the lack of) that which is 'hardly worth troubling about'.

The bourgeois gambler is doubly mythic: he or she aspires to the ethos of the aristocracy, to be a 'gentleman' or a 'lady'; yet, even for the aristocrat, this is only a superficial veneer. Just as the *flâneur* must hold on to his sense of self in the crowd, the gambler must retain his nerve. Both are seekers of intoxication, of exhilaration in the urban complex. Both aspire to an aristocratic bearing, yet neither can afford it. The casino exists for the gambler just as the market does for the *flâneur*: on one level, it is the place for disinterested observation, for amusement; on another, it is the site of economic gain. Both the gambler and the *flâneur* must appear to be engaged merely in casual recreation, while in actuality they are seeking to secure a precarious economic existence.

Wolin points out that 'for Benjamin, the figure of the gambler becomes a parable for the disintegration of coherent experience in modern life' (1982, p. 233). The buffeting received by the *flâneur* in the crowd is matched by the blows of fate which strike the gambler. Benjamin observes that 'betting is a means of giving events a shock-like character' (O13,5, *GS* V, p. 640). He adds: 'the ideal of shock-like experiences [*Erlebnisses*] is the catastrophe. This becomes very clear in gambling: through ever larger stakes [*Misen*], by which the loss might be recovered, the gambler is bound for absolute ruin' (O14,4, *GS* V, p. 642). The experience of the gambler, like that of the individual in the modern metropolis, is fundamentally characterized by shock, dissonance and fragmentation. As a figure marked by catastrophe, the gambler is subject to both the experience of ruin and the ruination of experience. According to Benjamin, the modern individual 'has been cheated out of his/her experience' (*CB*, p. 137). The gambler meets this deception with the stoic resignation of one for whom experience has become nothing more than endurance, with the composure of one cunningly and desperately playing the part of the hero in a world without heroism.

The gentleman gambler, like the dandy, must be astonished by nothing, but rather, through a display of stoicism, must astound everyone. He or she must maintain a haughty, and ingenuous, indifference to the unfolding of events. The impassive subjection to the will of fate, the endurance of suffering at the whim of (mis)fortune is paramount. Benjamin writes: 'in the bordello and the casino there is the same most sinful pleasure: to situate fate within desire' (O1,1, *GS* V, p. 612).[57] Benjamin links the centrality of fate for the fortune-hunter with the activity of the fortune-teller. He asks: 'Were Tarot cards earlier than playing cards? Do the playing cards represent a deterioration from the techniques of fortune telling? To know the future in advance is also decisive in card games' (O13a,2, *GS* V, p. 640). The gambler desperately seeks to discover the unknowable, to predict the unforeseeable, to bring about the uncontrollable. He or she may attempt to do this through the physiognomic deciphering of the character of opponents, through deceptive performances, and/or through the use of a 'system': 'the gambler is a highly superstitious being. The regulars of the gambling den always have a magic formula' (O4,1, *GS* V, p. 621). Armed only with a few lucky numbers and a 'magic formula', the gambler heroically confronts fate. Just as the city is transformed into a place of danger by the *flâneur*, so is the casino by the gambler. The phantasmagoric character of gambling is encapsulated by Anatole France: 'it is terrible, it gives when it pleases misery and shame: that is why one adores it. The attraction of danger is at the source of all great passions . . . It gives, it takes away . . . It is silent, blind and deaf. It is omnipotent. It is a god' (quoted in O4a, *GS* V, p. 622).

In spite of the gambler's 'magic formula', the outcome of the spin of the roulette wheel bears no relation to that of the previous spin. Each game is independent of those preceding it and those following it. The world is repeatedly encountered 'for the first time'. The role of memory is negated. The hallmark of the gambler is amnesia. Benjamin describes the gamblers in a lithograph by Senefelder thus: 'no matter how agitated they may be, they are capable only of a reflex action. They behave like the pedestrians in Poe's story. They live out their lives as automatons and resemble Bergson's fictitious characters who have completely liquidated their memories' (*CB*, p. 135). Forgetfulness brings with it repetition. The play of the gambler, like that of the child, is rooted in a desire for 'once more'. The image of the spinning roulette wheel, like that of the child seated on the merry-go-round, is an allegory of the nothing-new. Silent before the blind powers of fate and doomed to repetition, the gambler is the embodiment of the experience of myth.

For Benjamin, the industrial worker is also a figure of repetition and the demise of experience in the modern epoch. He compares the gambler and the worker thus: 'Since each operation at the machine is just as screened off from the preceding operation as a *coup* in a game of chance is from the one that preceded it, the drudgery of the labourer is, in its own way, a counterpart to the drudgery of the gambler. The work of both is equally devoid of substance' (*CB*, pp. 134–5).[58] The rise of the production line brought with it the acute division of labour into a series of discrete, precisely measurable, endlessly repeatable units. For Benjamin, the factory worker, like the gambler at the gaming table, performs a set of disconnected and continually re-enacted movements. Benjamin notes: The manipulation of the worker at the machine has no connection with the preceding operation for the very reason that it is its exact repetition' (*CB*, p. 134). The birthplace of the commodity is the site of unchanging drudgery. The worker takes on a heroic countenance here as the bearer of unending, pointless toil. Benjamin cites Engels thus: 'The dismal routine of a ceaseless agony of labour, in which the identical mechanical process is undergone again and again, is like the task of Sisyphus: the burden of work falls back repeatedly, like the rock, upon the exhausted workers' (D2a,4, *GS* V, p. 162).[59] The worker endures the repetition inherent in the production of the always-the-same.

Within the production techniques of modern capitalism the worker is a slave to the machinery he or she is tending. Benjamin cites Marx thus: 'It is no longer the case that the worker employs the means of production, but rather the means of production use the worker. Instead of being consumed as a material element in his productive activity, they devour him as the driving force of their own life process' (G12a,3, *GS* V, p. 260). Strictly monitored by the time-and-motion supervisor, the factory worker is transformed into a machine. Wolin notes that the modern assembly-line worker 'repeatedly performs the same monotonous, partial function. He must force his actions to conform to the autonomous rhythms of the machine. His activity thus degenerates to that of a mindless automaton' (1982, p. 232).[60] The suffering of the worker is rooted in the dehumanizing tendencies and repetitious character of commodity production. This dehumanization finds its highest expression, though, in another heroic, proletarian figure in the metropolis: the prostitute.

Wolff writes: 'the literature of modernity . . . has been impoverished by ignoring the lives of women. The dandy, the *flâneur*, the hero, the stranger – all figures invoked to epitomise the experience of modern life – are invariably male figures' (1990,

p. 41). When women do appear in this literature, it is in the guise
of certain stock characters, the most frequent being the prostitute.[61] Benjamin notes that Baudelaire was preoccupied with the
question of 'how the face of prostitution altered with the growth
of the great cities. For so much is certain: Baudelaire gives
expression to this change, it is one of the chief objects of his
poetry' (*CP*, p. 53). Benjamin's own writings on prostitution are
extremely mixed. The 'One-Way Street' fragments include a
distasteful, crass series of comparisons between books and
prostitutes (see *OWS*, p. 68). One may recall that in 'Berlin
Chronicle' Benjamin refers to the 'almost unequalled fascination of
publicly accosting a whore in the street' (*OWS*, p. 301). While
Benjamin critically observes that 'Baudelaire never wrote a poem
about prostitution from the prostitute's point of view' (J66a,7, *GS*
V, p. 438), he himself, as Buck-Morss points out (1986, p. 120),
never wrote anything from the prostitute's standpoint either. In
Benjamin's writings on Paris, more insight is evident than in his
Berlin writings, though Benjamin does not discuss prostitution in
relation to patriarchy. Instead, he focuses upon capitalist socio-
economic relations. The figure of the prostitute is significant in
two respects: as the counterpart of the worker and as the
embodiment of the commodity. Capitalism involves the denigration of the female body and the dehumanization of women.

Buck-Morss notes that in Benjamin's analysis 'the prostitute is
the ur-form of the wage-laborer, selling herself in order to survive'
(1989, p. 184). Work and prostitution are intimately and inextricably connected for Benjamin. He writes: 'the closer that work
comes to prostitution, the more inviting it becomes – as is the case
in the argot of the prostitute – to represent prostitution as labour'
(J75,1, *GS* V, p. 455). In modern capitalist society, work and
prostitution become interchangeable categories. Benjamin notes
that 'Prostitution can legitimately claim to be "work", in the
moment in which work itself becomes prostitution' (J67,5, *GS* V,
p. 439). He cites Marx thus: 'the factory workers in France call the
prostitution of their wives and daughters the "nth" [xte] working
hour, which is literally true' (O10,1, *GS* V, p. 633). Selling one's
labour power is different from selling oneself, however. The
prostitute does not produce an article for sale, but rather is herself
for sale; hence she resembles not so much the worker as the
commodity.

Just as the body of the worker becomes 'mechanized' in modern
society, so that of the prostitute is commodified: it becomes an
object to be bought, something available for consumption. Desire

for the prostitute is the corollary of commodity fetishism, the lust for the inorganic.[62] For Benjamin, the prostitute appears as a central figure in the poetry of Baudelaire precisely as the incarnation of the commodity.[63] In Baudelaire the prostitute is nothing other than an allegorical figure representing the commodity.[64] The prostitute is, according to Buck-Morss, the commodity made flesh and flesh made into a commodity. As such, the prostitute is the figure of the denigration of the human body and of nature itself through the process of commodification.[65] The body of the prostitute becomes a monadological figure or emblem of commodification as ruination.

As a commodity, the prostitute frequented the arcades. Indeed, as we have seen, one of the principal reasons cited by Benjamin for the decline of the commodity palaces was the prohibition of prostitutes. Expelled from the home of the commodity, the prostitute took the other commodities with her. It is the prostitute rather than the *flâneur* who really 'takes the commodity for a walk', who endures the ultimate humiliation of becoming a walking commodity, for, unlike the sandwichman, she has nothing to advertise or sell but herself.[66] Wilson compares the *flâneur* and the prostitute thus: 'the prostitute could be said to be the female *flâneur*. There were, of course, important differences, but both shared an intimate knowledge of the dark recesses of urban life. They understood, better than anyone, the pitiless way in which the city offered an intensity of joy that was never somehow fulfilled' (1991, p. 55). The differences here are more significant than any similarities, however. The bourgeois *flâneur* was an observer, a voyeur who might choose to peer into the 'dark recesses' of the city, but was not forced to inhabit them. The prostitute is not free to look, but, as a commodity, becomes the object of the male gaze.

As a commodity, the prostitute takes on the character of a mass-produced artefact. Benjamin writes: 'in the prostitution of the metropolis, the woman herself becomes an article that is mass-produced' (*CP*, p. 40). The prostitute is a model not only of the reification of the human body within capitalism, but also of the cessation of individual identity.[67] The vast number of prostitutes in the modern metropolis constitute an important element in the dehumanized urban mass. Benjamin writes: 'In the form in which prostitution appeared in the big cities, the woman appears not only as a commodity but in the fullest sense as a mass article . . . later, the uniformed girls of the revue underline this' (J66,8, *GS* V, p. 437).[68] The prostitute becomes a heroic figure in her incorporation of the horrors of capitalist exploitation and the corruption of bourgeois sexual life. The prostitute, valued as a commodity, reviled as a human being, is a figure of martyrdom. Benjamin notes: 'types: martyr, tyrant – prostitute, speculator' (M°5, *GS* V, p. 1023).

Despite Benjamin's preoccupation with the tradition of the oppressed and his avowedly historical materialist perspective, the figures of the worker and the prostitute play far less prominent roles in his conceptualization of modern heroism than one might expect. On one level, this stems from his ironical usage of the term 'hero': the bourgeois gambler, *flâneur* and dandy are only rather ridiculous mock-heroes after all, and they serve merely to suggest the phantasmagorical character of the modern metropolis. Modern heroism in this sense is only bourgeois delusion. On another level, however, it is indicative of Benjamin's own problematic, tortuous reception of the Marxist tradition itself. One might argue that a crucial problem in Benjamin's analysis is his failure to develop the significance of proletarian activity in the city. In the *Passagenarbeit* the shift of emphasis away from the sphere of production and towards that of consumption results in the centrality of the consumer: the bourgeois subject. The worker and the prostitute are almost relegated to the role of historical extras. When they do appear in his writings on Paris, they are portrayed as the embodiments of suffering under the conditions of modern capitalism. They are victims of the horror of urban existence. It is far from clear how the worker and the prostitute are anything other than self-sacrificial figures doomed to endure modernity silently. The prostitute as the figure of greatest suffering in the city is also perhaps the one most poorly developed in Benjamin's analysis. He does not voice her anguish, but rather speaks for her. He thus replicates precisely what demands his critical engagement: the reduction of the marginal figures of the metropolitan landscape to a state of bitter silence.

There is a third figure of defiant destitution in the metropolis who takes on a heroic visage in the Paris writings: the rag-picker. Benjamin writes

> When the new industrial processes had given refuse a certain value, rag-pickers appeared in the cities in large numbers. They worked for middlemen and constituted a sort of cottage industry located in the streets. The rag-picker fascinated his epoch. The eyes of the first investigators of pauperism were fixed on him with the mute question as to where the limit of human misery lay. (*CB*, p. 19)

For Benjamin, the rag-picker 'is the most provocative figure of human poverty. He is a *Lumpenproletariat* in a double sense: he is dressed in and preoccupied with rags [*Lumpen*]' (J68,4, *GS* V, p. 441). The rag-picker is a social outcast who derives his or her precarious subsistence precisely from that which is cast out. He or she is, as Wohlfarth (1986a, p. 147) notes, both the 'bottom of the barrel' and the 'scraper of it'. The rag-picker, as a despised figure of suffering in the city, is the counterpart of the urban prostitute. Both are demeaned by their socio-economic circumstances and by a degrading activity. But the heroism of the rag-picker, unlike that of the prostitute, does not stem from martyrdom.

Benjamin's account of the labour of the *chiffonnier* is derived from Baudelaire:

> Here we have a man whose task it is to gather the day's rubbish in the capital. Everything that the big-city has thrown out, everything it lost, everything it despised, everything it broke, he catalogues, he collects. He examines the archives of debauchery, the stock-pile of waste. He sorts through, making an intelligent selection; like a miser gathering his treasure, he brings together the rubbish that, chewed over by the divinity of Industry, becomes useful and pleasurable artefacts. (J68,4, *GS* V, p. 441)

The rag-picker assembles the urban detritus; he or she is a collector of what no one else desires. The rag-picker rescues from complete destruction the broken, the obsolete and the despised, refunctioning them and making them useful once more. Frisby notes: 'it is the rag-picker who makes use of the scraps, the fragments, since he is aware of their history. The fragments can be used again, they can be reassembled in a context that renders their mosaic intelligible' (1988, p. 186). The rag-picker inhabits and recycles the ruins of modernity. He or she is an urban 'archaeologist' who unearths the old-fashioned commodities that in turn reveal the truth about new ones: namely, that they are the same old rubbish.

Wilson writes of the rag-pickers: 'of all the bizarre kinds of work that the growing urban scene produced at this time, none was more symbolic than theirs' (1991, p. 54). The rag-picker is a heroic figure for Benjamin because he or she is a model for redemptive practice. Missac points out that for Benjamin, 'the activity of the rag-picker represents a form of allegory for the work of the historian' (1991, p. 85). The clearest evidence of such a view is Benjamin's description of Kracauer:

A rag-picker early in the dawn, who with his stick spikes the snatches of speech and scraps of conversation in order to throw them into his cart, sullenly and obstinately, a little tipsy, but not without now and then scornfully letting one or other of these discarded cotton rags – 'humanity', 'inwardness', 'depth' – flutter in the morning breeze. A rag-picker, early – in the dawn of the day of the revolution. (Cited by Frisby, 1988, p. 109)

The historical materialist, like the rag-picker, is concerned with the salvation of objects and people from the oblivion of forgetting, with collection and recollection. The rag-picker not only embodies the deprivations of modernity, but fundamentally resists the fragmentation of experience in the urban complex and the growth of modern amnesia. The rag-picker is the quintessential figure who 'excavates and remembers'.

Benjamin states: 'Baudelaire patterned his image of the artist after an image of the hero' (*CB*, p. 67). The heroism of the poet resides in his or her quest to give form to the modern, to represent the transient and fleeting character of urban existence. In addition, the urban poet was heroic for Baudelaire because in him or her the *flâneur*, gambler, prostitute and rag-picker combine. The great observer of modern life, it is the poet who struggles through the crowded street, now dawdling, now hurrying, to the market-place. It is the poet who surrenders to chance encounters, and is then marked by the shock experiences, of the metropolitan setting. The poet sells him or herself to the highest bidder, and thus prostitutes his or her art and turns it into a commodity.[69] Like the rag-picker, the poet saves the fleeting images, the linguistic scraps, which he or she finds in the city. The leavings of modern society are the stuff of which modern poetry is made: 'The poets find the refuse of society on their street and derive their heroic subject from this very refuse' (*CB*, p. 79). Benjamin adds: 'rag-picker or poet – the refuse concerns both' (*CB*, p. 80).

The poet is the ultimate hero of the modern city, for he or she incorporates all the others or, rather, plays at being them.[70] The man-of-letters is the great actor on the urban stage. In adopting numerous guises, in playing the parts of all the other 'heroes of modernity', the poet becomes the greatest hero of them all. *Flâneur*, prostitute and rag-picker all come to stand for him or her just as he or she 'stands in for' them. The counterpart in Baudelaire to the commodity as allegorical object is therefore the poet as allegorical figure. The poet as hero – this was a most satisfactory conclusion for Baudelaire. Benjamin takes this a step further. For him, it is Baudelaire's arrogant yet deeply ironical assertion of his own heroic stature, his hubris, his self-deception that actually, and paradoxically, make the poet 'heroic'. Baudelaire recognized the hollow sham of modern heroism, yet eagerly embraced it. Benjamin observes: 'Baudelaire battled the crowd – with the impotent rage of someone fighting the rain or the wind' (*CB*, p. 154). It is this 'impotent rage', this futile, ridiculous conflict that marks him out as the first great urban poet. Baudelaire is not simply marked by modernity; he struggles absurdly yet magnificently with it. Recognizing, yet heedless of, his own folly, Baudelaire is finally unmasked as a melancholy but proud Don Quixote in the modern metropolis.

Conclusion

Overview

Benjamin writes: 'no face is surrealistic in the same degree as the true face of the city' (*OWS*, p. 230). The metropolitan countenance is deceptive and deceitful. The historical materialist, like the poet, must adopt as many guises and disguises as the multi-faceted city itself: physiognomist, archaeologist, rag-picker, (re)collector, child. Benjamin writes: 'The wisest thing – so the fairytale taught humankind in olden times, and teaches children to this day – is to meet the forces of the mythical world with cunning and with high spirits' (*ILL*, p. 102). To disenchant modernity through enchantment demands a shrewd and intimate knowledge of its chicanery and machinations. It requires stealth;[1] it requires hope. Benjamin's ever more complex writings on the theme of the modern city bear witness to his fundamental preoccupation with the development of such a penetrating, thoroughgoing and ultimately redemptive critique of the phantasmagoria of modernity. Benjamin's cityscapes seek to explore the relationships between architecture and action, experience and identity, metropolis and myth, ruination and remembrance. Within these various writings a number of innovative historiographic and textual principles unfold which seek to facilitate the critical representation of transient, elusive urban phenomena, to retrieve lost things and recall forgotten times. While Benjamin's cityscapes may teeter agonizingly on the threshold of despair, they do not succumb to it. His gaze is sorrowful and melancholy, but the ruination of things is for the joyful purpose of their liberation and salvation. Like the hiding child, forgotten objects burst forth from their place of concealment to deliver themselves up to the redeemer.

Benjamin's writings on the city engage with, and elaborate, a number of recurrent themes, motifs and methodological concerns. The principal task of this final chapter is to elucidate their intricate correspondences. In so doing, I wish to return to the six dimensions of Benjamin's cityscapes presented in the Introduction: namely, the physiognomical, phenomenological, mythical, historical, political and textual. I begin with a consideration of the gaze of the physiognomer, the shifting perspective of the figure who comes to decipher the urban landscape and, as a destructive character, to reduce it to rubble. Then I will look at Benjamin's differentiated understanding of the experience of the individual in the modern urban setting. Both individual and collective life in the metropolitan environment are marked by discontinuity, forgetfulness and repetition. After that, I will explore the subtle, complex constellation formed by myth, history and politics. Mythic consciousness and forms of activity pervade the modern metropolitan setting. Liberation from mythic compulsion and repetition is to be achieved through critical modes of historical understanding which nourish present political practice. Yet the mythic also contains, in inverted form, utopian elements which must be salvaged. This dual character of myth and Benjamin's attempt to unravel it form the basis of his ambivalent reading of modernity, his vision of the city as both Heaven and Hell. Benjamin's concern with textual innovations closely corresponds to this historical undertaking. I will argue that, in their reading and writing of the city, their attempt to marry immanent and redemptive criticism, Benjamin's texts seek to adopt and simultaneously to resist the tendencies they identify. These writings come to embody those features which Benjamin perceives as distinctive and characteristic of the modern metropolis. The cityscapes themselves become 'city-like'. It is here, in his attempt to give critical form to the modern, to read and write the city, that Benjamin himself takes on the ambiguities and paradoxes which define Baudelaire's hero of modernity.

Physiognomy

The city is a space to be read. This is the basis of the physiognomical dimension in Benjamin's cityscapes. The metropolis is a multi-faceted entity, a picture puzzle that eludes any unequivocal decipherment. There is no single picture, no over-arching perspective, that can capture the fluidity and diversity of this environment. Insights into the character and experience of the city are to be gleaned, therefore, only from fleeting images and sudden moments of illumination, from the fragments stumbled upon in this complex and ever shifting social matrix. Benjamin's cityscapes bear witness both to this heterogeneity and transience of urban life and to the consequent impossibility of systematic interpretation and analysis. Benjamin eschews any form of totalizing critique of the modern city in favour of a series of more sensitive, provisional readings, which themselves remain open to revision and renewal. There is a plethora of metaphors, images and perspectives at play in Benjamin's work. He compares the city to a theatre, a labyrinth, a prison, a monument, a ruin. The city has many faces: all beguiling, all false. The architecture of modernity is the most pronounced manifestation of its mythic, dream-like character. The city is never what it appears to be.

For Benjamin, it is the gaze of the physiognomist which brings to light the true character of the city. Physiognomic reading is no superficial activity, no cursory glance. It must go beneath the surface of things, penetrate to their core. Benjamin is concerned with revealing what is hidden: the horror that beauty may conceal and the beautiful that lies buried in the ugly. Physiognomical reading brushes architecture against the grain.[2] Physiognomical reading is an act of critical unmasking. The physiognomist must adopt a plethora of shifting perspectives in order to gain such insight. Static contemplation of distance, auratic perception, merely conspires with the deceptive façades of metropolitan architecture. What is required is not distance but proximity, a closeness to things, enlargement. These are key elements for Benjamin in the generation of an alternative, critical vision, but something more is needed.

The physiognomical gaze is not merely microscopic or micro-logical; it is also destructive. The physiognomist must reveal the truth that is hidden within, and so concealed by, the appearance of things. There must be a stripping away or crumbling of the exterior, an act of demolition. The physiognomical gaze hastens the demise of its object, accelerates its natural history. It is a way of seeing which involves the ruination of a thing so as to look deeply within it. The act of true reading is possible only at the point of the death of the object. The physiognomist's gaze is a look of 'love at last sight'.

The physiognomist transposes the object into its afterlife, the time when its truth content becomes manifest. Reading against the grain is thus fundamentally destructive of myth. Monuments to progress and civilization are deciphered as glorifications of the nothing-new of barbarism and misery. The newest, latest, most fashionable is revealed as the nothing-new, the ruinous and outmoded. Physiognomical vision reveals the 'immortal' as the transient, the 'timeless' as the temporary, the most modern as the already archaic. Physiognomical reading is an act of disenchantment. Ruinous in effect, melancholic in character, physiognomical reading ultimately corresponds to the allegorical gaze. It is under the mournful eyes of the allegorist that the modern city is transformed into a series of signs to be deciphered, a text to be read. Konersmann notes: 'the allegorical world is readable; the redemption of phenomena begins with their recognition as text' (1991, p. 78). Physiognomical reading is a fundamental constituent of Benjamin's historiographic practice.

Phenomenology

The city is a monad, a fragment within which the totality of modern life may be discerned. While the phantasmagoria of modernity finds its most palpable expression in the architecture of the city, the individual and collective experiences of the metropolis are also imbued with mythic forms. The experience of the urban environment, which for Benjamin constitutes the definitive modern experience, is characterized by particular forms of mythic consciousness and activity. Benjamin does not offer a purely one-dimensional rejection of such experience, however. It is the immanent critique of the experience of modernity that leads to its negation. The city is the site of a manifold transformation in the character of experience encompassing a number of interconnected tendencies, among them the processes of intensification, stultification, fragmentation, diminution, fetishization and sequestration.

Benjamin's understanding of the intensification of experience in the urban complex draws upon key themes in the writings of Baudelaire and Simmel. It was Baudelaire, and later the Surrealists, who recognized that the metropolis constitutes a site of intoxication. As home to the unexpected, to novelty and distraction, the city for them is a space to be explored with joyous abandon. It offers the excitement of the anonymous crowd, the exhilaration of freedom and the ecstasy of losing oneself. It is a place of shock. For Baudelaire, the city was the only place which promised an escape from tedium, the great terror of modernity. Although for Benjamin, too, the city is occasionally a site affording the pleasures of losing oneself, of the intoxication of the *flânerie*, he also recognizes the danger in surrendering to these delights. To be carried drowsily along by the narcotics of chance and fate is nothing other than a capitulation to the forces of myth. There must be an awakening from the reveries of modernity.

For Benjamin, as for Simmel, the city is the home of boredom rather than excitement. The stimuli in the metropolis overwhelm the individual consciousness. The urban psyche adopts a series of defensive strategies in which the faculties are dulled. The intensification of social life brings with it the blasé personality, not heightened awareness but rather an indifference towards things and others. The blasé individual, craving stimulation and simultaneously unresponsive to it, embarks on a spiralling and inevitably fruitless quest for novelty. Over-stimulation leads, on the one hand, paradoxically to boredom, to the misery of the always-the-same; on the other, it brings with it the frenetic, neurasthenic personality searching for the something-new.

The intoxication of modernity is itself part of the mythic character of the metropolis, and finds its final embodiment in the unchanging parade of commodities and fashions, in repetition and compulsion. Forgetting, reification and fetishization are the key experiences of the city, and these are rooted in the commodity form. The commodity, its origins forgotten, appears as a magical thing, an object of devotion. The erotic impulse is transposed on to the world of objects in the form of fetishism and conspicuous consumption. The defining characteristic of metropolitan life is the desire for the commodity and the concomitant commodification of desire. The erotic impulse finds satisfaction only in the voyeuristic and the inorganic. For the bourgeois male the commodity becomes flesh (fetishization) and the flesh becomes a commodity (prostitution). The fetishized commodity is bound up with the confinement of sexuality to the interior. In the modern metropolis, the eroticized object is perpetually on display in the department store window, while sexuality is hidden away in the dead space of the private domicile. Its shadowy recesses are caches for the fantasies of the bourgeois citizen. The clutter of objects expels the natural history of the body and even death from the mundane perceptual realm. The fetishization of the inorganic and interiorization of life result in the sequestration of experience and its diminution.

The fragmentation of experience is intimately linked to these processes of intensification and sequestration. In the metropolis the coherent experience characteristic of traditional life is fundamentally dislocated and broken. Shock is the key metropolitan experience. With its swirling, buffeting crowds, its swift and compelling tempo, its rude encounters and intrusive distractions, the modern city gives rise to the disintegration of *Erfahrung* and its replacement by *Erlebnis*. From an integrated whole, experience is transformed into a plethora of disparate, disconnected impressions. This change is intimately bound up with transformations in the character and possibilities of memory. For Benjamin, the metropolis is a locus of forgetting, the site of the dissolution of remembering into dull amnesia. Conscious memory, the ability to relate one's tale, suffers the same fate as its counterpart, experience as *Erfahrung*. There is no place in the modern city for the possessor of wisdom, the story-teller.

Benjamin does not lament such transformations. His enterprise is not a nostalgic one. There are positive moments which must be recovered. These same mythic forces and tendencies which bring monotony and misery may paradoxically serve to overcome the atrophied experience of modernity. The fetish is a wish-image in which is buried the genuine utopian desire for a life free from necessity and compulsion. In the metropolis the visual becomes paramount, and perception is altered. The ease of contemplation and distance is supplanted by the rapid glance, the fleeting image. Shock, the hallmark of metropolitan experience, becomes for Benjamin a central methodological principle in the form of Surrealist montage. Shock is a category of awakening. It disrupts the cosy comfort of bourgeois life, a life wallowing in the complacent conviction of its own immortality. The discontinuous and disparate must be gathered together and preserved by the Critical Theorist, not to create new coherent stories, new overarching narratives, but so that they may be assembled in startling juxtapositions which engender surprise and recognition. The fragmentary, broken character of urban experience gives the lie to forms of representation and historical practices which emphasize only continuity and progress. The calm, measured narrative unfolded by the story-teller is to be replaced by the frantic, immediate language of the journalist-as-rag-picker.

The city is a space of forgetting, but for the true physiognomist it may yet come to form a mnemonic device. Under the physiognomical gaze, the metropolis may prompt the sudden, spontaneous, fortuitous recall of half-forgotten moments. The *mémoire involontaire*, with its transience and elusiveness, is an element of the shock character of modern urban life. As the momentary, evanescent mutual recognition of present and past, the *mémoire involontaire* forms the fundamental model for Benjamin's elaboration of the dialectical image. It is precisely this historiographic concept, the present remembrance and redemption of the forgotten past, that may lead to the dissolution of myth and freedom from its compulsions. In his preoccupation with the visual, the imagistic, his methodological refunctioning of montage, shock, fragmentation and the *mémoire involontaire*, Benjamin incorporates the key experiences of modernity in his texts in order to bring about their recognition and negation. This is how Benjamin's critical undertaking seeks to disenchant the metropolis through enchantment.

Mythology

For Benjamin, as for Horkheimer and Adorno, modernity, the supposed epoch of enlightenment and progress, is revealed as nothing other than the pre-eminent time of myth. Human subjection to the omnipotent forces of nature, to compulsion and fate, has been reversed. The mythic character of modern society derives from the rapacious, frenzied exploitation of nature by human beings and, as its corollary, the domination of one human being by another. The Enlightenment has failed to bring about the government of reason, and has led only to new forms of misery and oppression. Unchanging suffering is masked by the ideology of history-as-progress. In complacently proclaiming itself free of the burden of myth, the modern lapses ever more deeply into it. Modernity is barbarism disguised as the height of civilization. Whereas the Critical Theory developed by Horkheimer and Adorno offers an unremittingly bleak evaluation of the consequences and possibilities of this reversion to mythic domination and irrationalism, Benjamin is at pains to identify the positive moments lodged within the modern. Benjamin's analysis does not succumb to a pessimistic resignation before the barbarism of modernity, but posits an intricate, highly differentiated vision of myth. His goal is the liquidation of myth in order to free these moments, to permit their realization. Benjamin is concerned with an immanent critique of mythic forms, with destruction from within. Although Adorno admonished Benjamin for his supposed abandonment of the category of Hell in the Paris writings, perhaps Benjamin's achievement was precisely his refusal to surrender the utopian moments of the past and present, his stubborn retention of the category of Heaven.

The outlines of Benjamin's project may be discerned in his subtle though often perplexing use of mythological references and figures. These serve a variety of functions. Benjamin uses the figures of mythology as an ironic indictment of the pomposity and pretensions of the modern bourgeoisie. The clearest example of this is his rearticulation of Baudelaire's conceit of the heroism of modern life, a notion which permits a witheringly satirical view of mid-nineteenth-century neoclassicism. Benjamin also adapts and extends the significance of this conception. The heroes of modernity are figures who come to embody the modern, to represent particular facets of the experience of the metropolis. They are marked by the city, yet resist its processes and tendencies. The figures of the *flâneur* and the dandy, for example, come to stand for the demise of the bourgeois subject, the twilight of the aristocratic customer-as-connoisseur. As figures out of step with their time, they are its true representatives. On the one hand, the heroes of modernity stand for the experiences and delusions of modernity. On the other, they are roles for the poet, allegories of the modern artist. The prostitute, the *flâneur* and the other heroes of modernity are figures of ruination, allegorical characters. In elaborating the notion of the heroism of modern life, Benjamin's texts perform a critical inversion. The suffering of the hero is no longer rooted in fate, but rather in specific historical forms and circumstances. The hero, the timeless figure of myth, is given particular historical co-ordinates. The mythic is transposed into the allegorical, which is the very dissolution of myth.

For Horkheimer and Adorno, the prototypical figure of modernity is Odysseus. In Benjamin's writings on the city, however, the most important mythic figures are Theseus and Orpheus. These are not prototypes of the bourgeois subject, but rather provide models for the activity of the Critical Theorist. Theseus enters the labyrinth, that dream-architecture of the ancients which has been realized in the modern metropolitan cityscape, in order to destroy the beast that inhabits its spaces. He enters with high hopes, because he will cunningly mark his way, leave traces behind, so that he does not forget the route back. Orpheus too visits the realms of darkness. He enters Hades, Hell, in his quest to rescue his beloved, the dead Eurydice. For Benjamin, the Critical Theorist must enter the labyrinth, the domain of Hell, the mythic itself. The task is to liquidate what is monstrous within it and reclaim and redeem what is beautiful.

One is not to remain there; instead, one must remember one's way back, so as to emerge once more into the light. To destroy the mythic, one must have known it at close quarters. Benjamin writes: 'If one wishes to destroy something, one must not only know it; if the job is to be done well, one must have felt it' (*GS* III, p. 265). To overcome myth, one needs more than a passing acquaintance with it. One must be surrounded by it, yet not disheartened.

Myth contains both positive and negative moments. The fetishized commodity is not merely the modern form of repetition and compulsion; it is also a wish-image, the distorted expression of genuine longing. This revelation of the differentiated character of myth (and of modernity as the time of myth) derives from the dialectical gaze of the physiognomist. The mythic is the unredeemed. The mythic is not to be celebrated, but rather must be ruined, reduced to rubble to free its positive potential. To do this, however, one must find the destructive, or rather *self*-destructive, moment hidden within the myths of modernity. Myth is not one-dimensional, but dialectical in character. The mythic paradoxically contains the seeds of its own overcoming, the end of myth. The impoverished, attenuated experience of modernity contains within it the textual and historiographic principles which will lead to the transcendence of such an existence.

The clearest articulation of this is found in Benjamin's conception of mythic consciousness as dreaming. Dreaming is an activity which leads to awakening. He notes: 'in the dream context we seek a teleological moment. This moment is the waiting. The dream secretly awaits the awakening' (K1a,2, *GS* V, p. 492). Indeed, the moment of awakening is itself lodged in the dream as a secret, destructive element. Benjamin appropriately articulates this with respect to a classical (and urban) analogy: 'The coming awakening stands like the Greek wooden horse in the Troy of the dream' (K2,4, *GS* V, p. 495). Awakening is the afterlife of dreaming, the revolutionary moment of recognition and liberation in which the contents of the dream are to be refunctioned and realized. Benjamin notes: 'The utilization of dream elements upon awakening is the canon of dialectics. It is an example for the thinker and an exigency for the historian' (N4,4, Smith ed., 1989, p. 53).

For Horkheimer and Adorno, the dialectic of enlightenment has not led to the flowering of reason in the modern epoch, but has instead brought the negation of critical thought. For Benjamin, the modern metropolis is home to the *dialectic of myth*, to its contradictory impulses and ambiguities. The city is the setting for the highest form and eventual extinction of myth. One must not simply let myth unfold, one must unravel it. Benjamin sets himself the critical task of carefully disentangling the contradictory impulses at work within mythic consciousness. This immanent critique is the attempt to disenchant modernity through enchantment, the inspiration to compose a dialectical fairy-tale.[3]

History

As the principal home of the myths of modernity, the metropolis must be subjected to penetrating historical analysis in order that such a phantasmagoria be unmasked and overcome. Hence Benjamin's writings on the city are intimately bound up with the development of a critical and redemptive historical method. Benjamin seeks to dissolve myth in the space of history. As a precondition, history itself must be purged of its mythic elements. Myth is then to be scrutinized by the withering gaze of the historical materialist, the true historian.

The modern metropolis is the site for the creation of a false history. In the monuments and museums of the city the past becomes phantasmagorical. The history generated by modernity is itself part of the mythical character of the epoch. Petrified in the architecture of the metropolis, mythic history finds expression in what Benjamin terms 'historicism'. The hallmarks of this are historical empathy, closure and the doctrine of progress. For Benjamin the tasks of the historian correspond to those of the physiognomist;[4] critical historical reading involves the ruination of false history. History is discontinuous and broken; it is catastrophic in character. Progress is nothing other than persistent suffering. The concept of progress forms the ideological basis of the technological domination of the natural world and the concomitant exploitation of other human beings. Under capitalism, technology avariciously pillages nature and enslaves humanity. It is this history of suffering humanity that is the basis of the historical materialist vision of the past. Historical empathy, with its emphasis on continuity, can only ever be empathy with the victorious, the dominant, the powerful. In his notes for the 'Theses on the Concept of History' Benjamin writes: 'The continuum of history is that of the oppressor. While the notion of the continuum razes everything to the ground, the idea of the discontinuum is the basis of genuine tradition' (*GS* I, p. 1236). The representation of the past as discontinuous both reveals its catastrophic, non-cumulative character, and keeps faith with the tradition of the oppressed. Benjamin notes: 'The history of the oppressed is a discontinuity – the task of history is to make the tradition of the oppressed its own' (ibid.).[5] Like the labour of the physiognomist, the historical enterprise possesses a constructive as well as a destructive moment.[6] Benjamin states: 'In true historical writing the redemptive impulse is just as strong as the destructive one' (*GS* I, p. 1242). Historical writing involves the redemption of the buried fragments that historicism has ignored. For Benjamin, the past is open, contestable, unfinished. Benjamin's act of historical redemption is concerned with the archaeology of an alternative vision of the past. The goal of the historian is to redeem the experiences of those whose passage is not marked or commemorated in the modern metropolis, to excavate and remember the sufferings and hopes of the forgotten dead.

This alternative counter-history demands innovative historiographic methods. Benjamin's cityscapes may be read as experiments in developing precisely such principles and forms of representation. The city, the locus of false history, of forgetting, also offers models for a critical historiography, for remembering. How to capture and give form to the fleeting, the ephemeral, and the endangered? This is the abiding question addressed both by Benjamin's historiographic texts and his cityscapes. The experiences of the urban environment provide the answer. It is, after all, in the metropolis that one becomes accustomed to, and esteems, the transient. The *Denkbild*, the thought-image, is precisely the attempt to give form to the immediate and the momentary impression. It is a historical snapshot, a frozen moment. The Berlin writings are experiments which seek to articulate a counter-history of modernity. On the one hand, the space and edifices of the city create a mythic past. On the other, they prompt the elusive images and sensations of the *mémoire involontaire* which bear witness to the silent sufferings of the unremembered dead. The *mémoire involontaire* is of profound importance for Benjamin. It is born from the shock experience that characterizes the modern metropolis. Benjamin writes: 'It is to this immolation of our deepest self in shock that our memory owes its most indelible images' (*OWS*, p. 343). Spontaneous and elusive, the *mémoire involontaire* is prompted by the sudden, fleeting encounters to which the individual is subject in the urban crowd. It is the quintessential form of modern remembrance, from whose fragments Benjamin seeks to fashion his reminiscences of Berlin.

The dialectical image, Benjamin's key historiographic principle, is a conception inspired by the *mémoire involontaire*. It is the sudden moment in which past and present recognize each other, in which redemption occurs. Benjamin describes this encounter thus:

> The true picture of the past flits by. The past can be seized only as an image which flashes up at the instant when it can be recognized and is never seen again. 'The truth will not run away from us': in the historical outlook of historicism these words of Gottfried Keller mark the exact point where historical materialism cuts through historicism. For every image of the past that is not recognized by the present as one of its own concerns threatens to disappear irretrievably. (*ILL*, p. 257)

This is an urban image. Such an understanding of the dialectical image as ephemeral recognition echoes a passage that was to stand at the centre of Benjamin's writings on Baudelaire: the poem 'To a Passer-By'. It is here that the full significance of this sonnet for Benjamin becomes evident. The poem does not simply give form to the shock encounter and the joy of *modernité*. It is an allegory of modern remembrance, of the *mémoire involontaire*, in which the object of memory appears suddenly and unbidden, only to vanish elusively once more.[7] Indeed, in its expression of the fleeting moment of recognition in the metropolis, 'À une passante' constitutes nothing less than an allegory of the dialectical image. The woman, like the endangered past, appears without warning; there is mutual attraction, and then she disappears without trace, never to be seen again. The historian, like the poet, must preserve this moment, must redeem its promise. Benjamin's dialectical image, the gaze of the true historian, is also the mournful 'love at last sight'.[8]

Politics

In Benjamin's cityscapes a distinctive, highly idiosyncratic approach unfolds which critically engages with the Marxist tradition. The 'Theses on the Concept of History' involve not only a critique of 'historicism' but also a desire to rid historical materialism of its own false conceptions. For Benjamin, 'orthodox Marxism' is not free of mythic elements; for it too participates, albeit with a different emphasis, in the conceptions of history-as-continuum, history-as-progress. In its exclusive focus upon the development of the means of production and the category of labour, orthodox Marxism may also be lulled into instrumentalism and the glorification of the technological domination of nature by humankind. Benjamin presents a different conception, one which restores what he regards as the true character of political revolution. He contends: 'In the notion of the classless society Marx secularized the idea of Messianic time' (*GS* I, p. 1231). History is not an unfolding, progressive sequence, but rather comprises unchanging suffering. Proletarian revolution is not the culmination of historical development, but a moment of rupture, the cessation of history as catastrophe.

The restoration of the Messianic character of revolutionary activity is bound up with another theological motif: the notion of redemption. For Benjamin, the past does not 'weigh like a nightmare upon the brain of the living',[9] but is to be redeemed. Past suffering is neither rejected nor regarded as finished. Instead, it forms the fundamental spur for revolutionary activity in the present. Horkheimer recognized the theological character of such a formulation. Such a notion, he contended, must be rooted ultimately in the conception of the Day of Judgement, in the idea that there will come a moment when all past sins will be revealed and finally called to account. For Benjamin, the mythic features of 'historicism' are to be dissolved through historical materialism. In turn, those of the Marxist vision of history are to be undone within the domain of theology. Only with the secret aid of theology can historical materialism be successful, for only then can it be shorn of its own mythic accretions.[10] As a result, it is precisely where Benjamin is informed by, yet strays from, the Marxist perspective, where his ideas are imbued with theological motifs, where his texts are most paradoxical and puzzling, that his work has its greatest critical power.

This innovative undertaking is not without its own flaws, however. In light of his concern with the redemption of the forgotten tradition of the oppressed, Benjamin's own emphasis upon the marginal figures of the urban complex proves to be not only unorthodox, but also problematic. In his reformulation of the concept of the heroism of modern life, for example, he presents an odd assortment of characters from a variety of political orientations and socio-economic backgrounds. While the redemption of the sufferings of such figures as the prostitute, the rag-picker and the beggar clearly corresponds to the imperatives of Benjamin's critical historical enterprise, his preoccupation with the bourgeois figures of the metropolitan landscape – the *flâneur*, the dandy, and the gambler – is somewhat perplexing. In using such urban types as allegorical figures, who come to stand for social processes and for one another, the crucial class distinctions between them may be lost. The miseries endured by the prostitute are not to be seen as comparable to those of the bohemian poet who must sell his poems, his 'soul', in the literary market-place. One is entitled to ask whether Benjamin gives voice to the experience of the prostitute or that of her customers. The rag-picker's precarious, squalid existence is likewise not to be confused with that of the man-of-letters. Prostitute and rag-picker – these may be poor metaphors for the poet. Benjamin is not always as sensitive to such discrepancies as one would like. His attention is sometimes perhaps too easily caught by the more outlandish, eccentric individuals of the metropolis. One may wonder, moreover, whether the conceptualization of the collectivity as a slumbering, dreaming entity does justice to the active political engagement and struggles of the oppressed classes of the modern epoch. As Benjamin himself came to realize, remembrance of the sorrows and frustrations of a bourgeois child, with its individualistic, contemplative emphasis, may prove a tenuous model for redemption of the forgotten dead.

Text

Benjamin writes: 'Through its street names, the city is a linguistic cosmos' (P3,5, *GS* V, p. 650). The physiognomical gaze transforms the urban setting into a hieroglyph, a rebus, to be deciphered. The archaeology of the metropolis involves the discovery and interpretation of its hidden inscriptions and traces. The city is a secret text to be read.[11] Benjamin notes that 'The historical method is a philological one based on the Book of Life. Hofmannsthal states, "Read what was never written". The reader called to mind here is the true historian' (*GS* I, p. 1238).

In Benjamin's work the city is transformed into a text. The counterpart to this metamorphosis is that the text itself becomes 'urban'. The city is also a space to be written: this is the basis of the constructive moment in Benjamin's cityscapes. Benjamin pioneers new forms of representation, forms which do justice to, and are therefore able to capture, the character of modern urban life. To write the city,[12] to give it form – this is the key to understanding Benjamin's textual practices and innovations. His writings come to take on precisely those features which he identifies as characteristic of the modern metropolis. He seeks not only to 'read' but also to 'write' a city, to incorporate the experience of modern metropolitan life into the text, to give it literary form.[13] In the 'Arcades Project', not only does one encounter the city-as-text but, more important, the text-as-city.

The *Passagenarbeit* constitutes nothing less than a vast text-as-city, text-as-labyrinth. Its formal properties mimic the very set of urban experiences to which it gives voice. It is animated by the rhythms of the city that it endeavours to record. The 'Arcades Project', like the modern metropolis, is a sprawling entity marked by discontinuity, dislocation and fragmentation. There is no possibility of any overarching perspective, no definitive view of the whole. There can be no grand narrative of the metropolis. The *Passagenarbeit* denies the repose of contemplation, and offers instead only those fleeting, momentary images which appear suddenly, as if from nowhere, and then, like the beloved in the crowd, are swept along and vanish in the tumult. In the Paris texts, as in the city itself, order and coherence give way to random bombardment by a plethora of diverse stimuli. The text becomes the site of shock and ambiguity, of the heterogeneous and paradoxical. It is home to discarded, obsolete objects, the comical fashions of yester-year. It is inhabited by a range of diverse, eccentric figures. Within its spaces one may bump into the sauntering *flâneur*, the bored gambler, the wretched prostitute, the pitiful rag-picker. One does not know what one will encounter as one innocently turns the next corner or page. The *Passagenarbeit* always contains the element of surprise, the exhilaration of the unexpected and ephemeral that comprises the intoxication of the modern. Within its pages, the experience of shock is elevated to the status of a historical materialist principle. Benjamin writes: 'Quotations in my work are like wayside robbers who leap out armed and relieve the stroller of his convictions' (*OWS*, p. 95). In the Paris texts, the quotation is an urban pickpocket who escapes and hides in the anonymous crowd. Benjamin himself seeks to disappear without trace, to leave no sign of his passing, and the hapless reader, left to his or her own devices, undergoes what can only be described as 'textual shock'.

The reader becomes the great observer of modernity in the text-as-city. This is an entity, a space in which the sense of sight is paramount, where vision dominates.[14] The image and the task of depiction are essential elements in Benjamin's metropolitan texts. Buck-Morss stresses that the 'Arcades Project' is to be understood as an experiment in the 'dialectics of seeing'.[15] Afraid to leave his precious arcades, Benjamin has instead invited the reader to stroll through the labyrinthine structures of the 'Arcades Project'.[16] Missac writes:

> Readers who are tempted by such a role will not sit down at their desks, pen in hand, but rather saunter through the texts which Benjamin has written or copied out for them and gradually – depending on inspiration – assemble them. In a novel and certainly very modern approach, the diverse architectures of a future book therefore develop, not in contemplation, but 'while walking'. (1991, p. 193)

It is not, then, as a curious *flâneur* in search of amusement that the contemporary reader is invited to meander through the *Passagen-arbeit*, but as a rag-picker. In the image of the rag-picker Benjamin prefigures what it is to write a text in the modern epoch: the slow piecing together of words and phrases, insights and instances, into a montage or mosaic of modernity. Moreover, he fundamentally anticipates what it will be like to gaze upon and (re)read such a text. It is ultimately the task of the reader to rescue the fragments of the text, to redeem and refunction them in the struggles of the present. The reader is the physiognomist of the text-as-city. Reading is the salvation of the text, which complements rag-picking as the redemption of the thing. Benjamin predicts the afterlife, the ever-changing manifestation of the truth content of his own activity as a writer.

Broken and disjointed, the *Passagenarbeit* embodies the collapse of the capacity for sustained, meaningful experience. Its form and content are derived from precisely those elements which bring about the depersonalization and dehumanization of life in the modern metropolis. Benjamin's texts are symptomatic of, yet resistant to, modernity. The *Passagenarbeit* incorporates the experiences of modern life in order to negate them. Writing the city breaks its spell. In order to give form to the modern, one must allow oneself to be deeply marked by it. Benjamin notes: 'It is likely that no-one ever masters anything in which he has not known impotence; and if you agree, you will also see that this impotence comes not at the beginning of or before the struggle with the subject, but in the heart of it' (*OWS*, p. 294). To express the modern, to give it voice, yet to subvert and resist its tendencies – these are Benjamin's goals. Benjamin seeks to marry an 'appropriate' critique to an 'appropriating' one. His work is not, as Adorno claimed, at the crossroads of 'magic and positivism' (*AP*, p. 129); rather, it is situated at the intersection of immanence and redemption. From forgetfulness, remembrance is to be won; the fleeting and ephemeral are to be preserved, the despised extolled, and the esteemed scorned. The movement between extremes and the discovery of the one within the other – these are the bases of the dialectic in Benjamin's work.[17] The city is Heaven, the city is Hell. Benjamin loved and loathed it. It is in this tension that Benjamin reveals himself as a walking contradiction, an elusive, paradoxical figure propelled by the intoxication of the modern while condemning its miseries. Imbued with the modern, yet brushing it against the grain, Benjamin witnesses the phantasmagoria of the city with the ambivalent gaze of the hero of modernity, a gaze full of melancholy and longing, the look of love at last sight.

Notes

Introduction

1. Louise Hoffman perceptively states that for Benjamin 'the city was a magical place where the wonderful and the terrible existed simultaneously' (1983, p. 147).
2. Cited in Timms and Kelley, eds, 1985, p. 181. Fritz Radt, in a letter to Jula Cohn of 13 July 1925, writes of Benjamin: 'for him Berlin is the only city in Germany in which one can live' (Puttnies and Smith, eds, 1991, p. 32). McCole emphasizes that it was not the German capital's social milieu that attracted Benjamin but the urban complex itself. He notes: 'it was not Berlin's intellectual culture but its cityscapes that fascinated him' (1993, p. 73).
3. McCole states that 'a fascination with the search for the true face of the city . . . became a central motif in his work after the mid 1920s' (1993, p. 207).
4. Buck-Morss points out that these programmes 'drew on the common experience of the city much as the novels of Aragon and Breton had drawn on their readers' common experience of Paris, as the context as well as the content of the story' (1989, p. 34).
5. See e.g. Benjamin's reviews of Hessel's *Heimliches Berlin* (1927; GS III, pp. 82–4) and *Spazieren in Berlin* (1929; GS III, pp. 194–9). Benjamin also reviewed Alexys Siderov's *Moscau* (1928; GS III, pp. 142–3) and Jakob Job's *Neapel. Reisebilder und Skizzen* (1928; GS III, pp. 132–5).
6. The annotated bibliography of secondary literature between 1983 and 1992 compiled by Markner and Weber, eds, 1993, lists a total of 2,132 items. There are 40 references in connection with the theme of the city (see p. 308).
7. Brodersen, 1990, pp. 158–61, and Buck-Morss, 1989, pp. 26–32, do consider these texts, however.

8. Some of the most interesting of these are: Witte, pp. 17–26, and Lindner, pp. 27–48, in Bolz and Witte, eds, 1984, and also Szondi in Smith ed., 1988, pp. 18–32.
9. E.g., there were special editions of *New German Critique*, 39 (Fall 1986), and the *Philosophical Forum*, 15, nos 1–2 (Fall–Winter 1983–4).
10. Even in Buck-Morss's 1989 study, the closest to a systematic treatment of Benjamin's city writings, only four or five pages are devoted to a consideration of the *Denkbilder*.
11. The monad is an important notion in Benjamin's work as a whole and in his city writings in particular. The term, derived from Leibniz (see Tiedemann, 1973, p. 62, and Konersmann, 1991, pp. 163–6), originates with a pantheistic conception of the world. According to such a view, God (the infinite, the totality) is present within every single element (the finite, the particular) of his creation. The whole thus resides within each of its fragments. Benjamin extends this theological conception to the task of profane illumination. For him, traces of the general (the social totality) are discernible within the particular (the mundane and trivial). Tacussel notes: 'in this perspective, every object is the fragment of the historic context surrounding it, each detail participates in a figuration of the universal which endows it with meaning' (1986, p. 48). Each individual instance may be read as symptomatic of the whole. Benjamin writes: 'the smallest authentic fragment of everyday life says more than a painting' (*UB*, p. 94). For a discussion of Benjamin's notion of the monad see Roberts, 1982, pp. 115–19.
12. Konersmann notes: 'as a physiognomist Benjamin mistrusted the classifications of systematizing thinkers. He turned his attention to the detail and the particular, to those mundane occurrences which, according to Lichtenberg, contained "the moral universal" [*das moralische Universale*] just as well as "the great things" ("*in den grossen*")' (1991, p. 52).
13. The following is an example of such an approach: 'how a convivial evening has passed can be seen by someone remaining behind from the disposition of plates and cups, glasses and food, at a glance' (*OWS*, p. 83). The social theorist becomes a detective seeking to reconstruct activities and patterns of life from the minute clues that have been left behind.
14. Benjamin writes: 'collectors are physiognomists of the object world' (O°7, *GS* V, p. 1027).
15. In his concern to articulate mundane experiences of the modern urban complex as forms of fragmentation, and his insistence upon doing so with reference to the plight of those that more traditional, conventional analyses have overlooked and ignored, Benjamin clearly shares elements with the wider modernist movement of his time.
16. For a detailed discussion of Benjamin's understanding of myth see Menninghaus in Smith ed., 1988, pp. 292–325.
17. The 'Enlightenment behaves toward things as a dictator toward men. He knows them only in so far as he can manipulate them' (Adorno and Horkheimer, 1986, p. 9).
18. The life of the modern urbanite is largely unburdened by any 'awareness of the ever-vigilant elemental forces'. In the protective interior spaces of the urban complex, the city dweller forgets the surrounding natural world. Benjamin notes: 'is there anyone who has not once been stunned

emerging from the *Métro* into the open air, to step into brilliant sunlight? And yet the sun shone a few minutes earlier, when he went down, just as brightly. So quickly has he forgotten the weather of the upper world' (*OWS*, p. 100). When the city dweller is confronted by the forgotten elemental forces of nature, the fragility of the urban shell is exposed, and shock results. Benjamin writes: 'the most remarkable of all the street images from my early childhood . . . is – it must have been around 1900 – a completely deserted stretch of road upon which ponderous torrents of water continually thundered down. I had been caught up in a local flood disaster, but in other ways too, the idea of extraordinary events is inseparable from that day. . . . This situation left behind an alarm signal; my strength must have been failing, and in the midst of the asphalt streets of the city I felt exposed to the powers of Nature; in a primeval forest I should not have felt more abandoned than here on Kurfürstenstrasse, between the columns of water' (*OWS*, p. 299).

19. Benjamin prefigures Adorno and Horkheimer in this respect also. For them, Odysseus's encounter with the sirens is an illuminating episode. While his crew, their ears stopped with wax, row the ship to safety, Odysseus has himself tied securely to the ship's mast. He alone is permitted to hear the alluring song of the sirens, but is unable to respond. Desire and longing are awakened, but are granted no outlet, allowed no release. While the rowers continue their labour in ignorance, Odysseus endures masochistic denial. For Horkheimer and Adorno he thus becomes the prototype for the modern bourgeois.

20. In his essay of 1917–18 'On the Program of the Coming Philosophy', Benjamin criticizes the impoverished, mechanical conception of experience offered by Kant. He writes: 'this experience, which in a significant sense could be called a *world-view*, was the same as that of the Enlightenment. In its most essential characteristics, however, it is not at all different from the experience of the other centuries of the modern era. It was an experience or a view of the world of the lowest order. The very fact that Kant was able to commence his immense work under the constellation of the Enlightenment indicates that his work was undertaken on the basis of an experience virtually reduced to a nadir, to a minimum of significance' (Smith ed., 1989, p. 2).

21. *Konvolut* N of the *Passagenarbeit* in conjunction with some of his reflections in *CP* (a series of late notes on Baudelaire) came to form the basis for Benjamin's now famous 'Theses on the Concept of History'.

22. As a consequence, each of my analyses of the cityscapes contains a consideration of the precise status and formal character of the text in question.

23. Missac notes that for Benjamin, 'every writer must be prepared to become a photographer; a task Benjamin himself partially undertook, when he . . . resolved to say nothing more, but to show' (1991, p. 126).

24. Benjamin was not the first to note this relationship between city and moving image. Fuld notes (citing H. Kienzl's 'Theater und Kinomatograph', *Der Strom*, 1911–12): 'as early as 1910 discussions of film recognised how the structure of moving pictures was deeply rooted in the experience of the metropolis: "the psychology of the cinematic triumph is metropolitan psychology. This is not only because the big city forms the natural focus for all the emanations of social life, but,

moreover, because the metropolitan soul is precisely that of cinematography: inquisitive, unfathomable, hunted, reeling ecstatically from one fleeting impression to another" ' (1990, p. 250).

25. The connections between Benjamin and Simmel are important here. Bloch was perhaps the first to remark upon their shared rejection of approaches which seek to grasp totalities. The detail, the concrete, concern them both (see Bloch's letter to Benjamin of 18 Dec. 1934 regarding 'One-Way Street' in Puttnies and Smith, eds, 1991, p. 123). Adorno later writes: 'his endeavour to lead philosophy out of the "frozen desert of abstraction" and transform thoughts into concrete, historical images had an affinity with Simmel, the opponent of systematizing thought" (1990, p. 39). See also Brodersen, 1990, p. 56. Benjamin's response to this fragmentation is characteristically both positive and negative. On the one hand, he advocates the stripping away of grand theoretical schemes; narrative must be abandoned in favour of more immediate, concrete textual practices. On the other, he laments the demise of story-telling and the diminishing capacity to tell one's tale in a coherent fashion.

26. Konersmann describes this process succinctly: 'Benjamin's quotations are fragments isolated from their original context. Newly arranged, these elements come together in a mutually illuminating montage. The traditional context is destroyed in order to release unforeseen images' (1991, p. 54).

27. Frisby points out that with Benjamin, as with Simmel and Kracauer, 'the search for a social theory of modernity is fused with . . . a concern for the aims and sometimes techniques of modernism' (1988, p. 51).

28. McCole perceptively notes that 'the hallmark of his work lies in its paradoxical, antinomial coherence' (1993, p. ix).

29. Elizabeth Wilson writes: 'even if the labyrinth does have a centre, one image of the discovery of the city, or of exploring the city, is not so much finally reaching this centre, as of an endlessly circular journey, and of the retracing of the same pathways over time' (1991, p. 3).

Chapter 1   Urban Images: From Ruins to Revolutions

1. Written between May 1924 and April 1925, and submitted on 12 May 1925. In July 1925 Benjamin was urged to withdraw his application because Professor Hans Cornelius found the work bewildering and incomprehensible. With this rejection, the possibility of Benjamin pursuing a career within the German academic establishment ended.

2. See Scholem, 1982, pp. 120–1. Benjamin's father had been seriously ill and had had his right leg amputated. In addition, Benjamin's relationship with his wife Dora was deeply troubled at this time.

3. Lacis was to suggest key elements of the *Denkbilder*: the concept of 'porosity' in 'Naples' and the link between the Revolution and technological transformation in 'Moscow'. Benjamin's 'One-Way Street' was dedicated to her. In addition, it was through Lacis that Benjamin met Bertolt Brecht.

4. This was not the only text which resulted from his Neapolitan experiences. Reworking some of the essay material, Benjamin later gave

radio talks entitled 'Naples' and 'Pompeii and Herculaneum' (see *GS* VII, pp. 206–20).

5. It is doubtless because of this apparent absence of political content that she devotes less than two pages of her nearly 500-page study to 'Naples'.

6. The political significance of reportage was an important point of debate at the International Congress of Writers for the Defence of Culture which opened on 21 June 1935 in Paris and which Benjamin, Brecht and Bloch attended. Egon Erwin Kisch presented a paper entitled 'Reportage als Kunstform und Kampfform'. Schiller et al. note: 'reportage as an "aesthetically discredited" form of literature was a point of departure for Kisch . . . because in the hands of "writers of truth" [Reed, Holitscher and Tretjakow] it became a "combative form" [*Kampfform*]' (1981, p. 217).

7. The term 'porosity' was coined by Lacis (see Buck-Morss, 1989, p. 26). Brodersen notes that Bloch also used this term in an article for the *Weltbühne* in 1926 entitled 'Italien und die Porosität' (see Brodersen, 1990, p. 151).

8. Porosity is, Benjamin notes, 'the inexhaustible law of the life of this city, reappearing everywhere' (*OWS*, p. 171).

9. This notion of the city as landscape is important in suggesting the necessity of experience and practice for navigation in it, a theme to which Benjamin returns in his writings on Berlin and Paris.

10. In his radio broadcast on Naples, Benjamin puts this in a more prosaic manner: 'one would probably have to spend a year as a Neapolitan postman in order to become fully acquainted with the city . . . And even then the postman would never completely know Naples' (*GS* VII, pp. 213–14).

11. This idea resurfaces in a very different form in Benjamin's writings on Paris. The *flâneur* also makes his home in the city street. He does so not by reassembling the domestic in the street, however, but rather by transforming the boulevard into an interior. This is the basis of his love of the arcade, the ultimate street-as-interior.

12. This outward orientation of the Neapolitan individual and the openness of the family group are matched, however, by the inner-directedness and closure of the community as a whole. 'Porosity' does not extend to relationships between local inhabitant and stranger, native and tourist. Neapolitans exhibit a marked antipathy towards visitors to their city. The innocent tourist is the target of the swindler and the trickster, whose theatrical performances are also an important element of the porosity of the city.

13. The admixture of sacred and profane is a consistent theme in Benjamin's writings on Italy; e.g., in the fragment 'Not for Sale' from 'One-Way Street', he describes a mechanical representation of the Passion. The way in which the profane adopts the guise of the sacred becomes important in Benjamin's city writings. It is the basis of the notion of commodity fetishism, which in turn underpins his analyses of Berlin and Paris.

14. This prefigures similar equations of holy and profane time, e.g., in 'A Berlin Childhood Around 1900', where Sedan Day presents itself as a Sunday (*GS* IV, p. 242).

15. In his radio broadcast on Naples Benjamin notes: 'I have told you a little about the mundane and something about the festival, and the most remarkable thing is how they merge, how each day the street has a touch

of the festive . . . and also how Sunday has something of the workaday about it' (*GS* VII, p. 213).

16. Benjamin notes: 'confession alone, not the police, is a match for the self-administration of the criminal world, the *camorra*' (*OWS*, p. 167).

17. Reading this passage, one is reminded of the similarly bizarre opening to Michel Foucault's *Discipline and Punish*. His study begins with a description of the equally public but incomparably horrific torture and execution of the regicide Damiens in France in 1757. For both Benjamin and Foucault, such extraordinary events are symptomatic of, and thus critically reveal, prevailing cultural patterns and forms of perception.

18. Benjamin notes: 'should it disappear from the face of the earth, its last foothold would perhaps not be Rome, but Naples' (*OWS*, p. 167).

19. See M9a,3, *GS* V, p. 547.

20. Kracauer notes the importance of the cityscape as a space for improvisation. He writes: 'the worth of cities is determined by the number of places they contain which permit improvisation' (1987, p. 51). He later notes: 'the image in which ordinary people come to represent themselves is an improvised mosaic' (1987, p. 93). This is a particularly intriguing formulation for two reasons. Firstly, it posits an identity of two apparently antithetical notions: improvisation (spontaneous, fluid) and the mosaic (meticulously structured). Secondly, Benjamin's goal in his cityscapes is precisely to give voice to the experiences of 'ordinary people'.

21. In his essays on Berlin, the city forms a 'theatre of purchases' (*OWS*, p. 327). In the *Passagenarbeit*, Paris constitutes a stage for the dramatic parading of the dandy and the play-acting of the so-called heroes of modern life.

22. This incident is also reported in Benjamin's radio broadcast on Naples (see *GS* VII, p. 207).

23. Benjamin notes of the Neopolitans: 'they prefer to lie in the sun with five *lire* rather than earn fifteen' (*GS* VII, pp. 208–9).

24. In the restaurants of the city, e.g., the art of eating macaroni with the hand is demonstrated 'for remuneration' (*OWS*, p. 171).

25. In his essay on Moscow, Benjamin observes that in the new Soviet capital 'begging is not as aggressive as it is in the South [of Europe], where the importunity of the ragamuffin still betrays some remnant of vitality. Here it is a corporation of the dying' (*OWS*, p. 184).

26. The Neapolitan, in his or her expressive use of the body, has, like the child, retained some features of what Benjamin terms (in his 1933 essay) the 'mimetic faculty'. This refers to the 'gift of producing similarities' (*OWS*, p. 160), the capacity of human beings to mimic (and originally thereby worship or gain power over) natural phenomena through bodily movement, sound and dance. The Neapolitan preoccupation with gesture, with corporeal communication, is a part of that of which 'the observable world of modern man contains only minimal residues' (*OWS*, p. 161): the domain of sensuous similarities.

27. Benjamin was not alone in this respect. In the immediate post-Revolutionary phase a number of Western scholars, academics and *literati* of a variety of political persuasions trekked eastwards to examine at first hand the state of Soviet society, among them Bertrand Russell, André Gide, H. G. Wells and, somewhat later, Lion Feuchtwanger. Although

Russell and Gide both returned disappointed with, and critical of, what they found, many of these visitors saw nothing but the confirmation of their original prejudices. The conservative Wells, who regarded Marxism as 'sheer nonsense' (1921, p. 83), found nothing but misery and chaos. He writes of his visit in September 1920 thus: 'our dominant impression of things Russian is an impression of a vast irreparable breakdown' (1921, p. 17). The Marxist writer Feuchtwanger went to Moscow in January 1937, and his report is full of unqualified admiration for the wonders of the new Soviet state. He notes, that 'everywhere in that great city of Moscow there was an atmosphere of harmony and contentment, even of happiness' (1937, p. 4). With regard to Stalin, Feuchtwanger writes myopically: 'hundreds of anecdotes are told about him, proving how much he has the lot of each individual at heart' (1937, p. 75).

28. His other texts arising directly from his journey to Moscow include 'Debate with Meyerhold' (published 11 Feb. 1927), 'The Political Organisation of Russian Authors' (11 Mar. 1927), 'The Situation of Russian Film Art' (11 Mar. 1927), and 'Russian Toys' (10 Jan. 1930).

29. See *OWS*, p. 207.

30. The factory visited by Benjamin on 23 Jan. 1927 is a good example of this. Here traditional, manual manufacturing practices occur incongruously alongside modern, mechanized processes. Benjamin writes: 'its structure is certainly less the result of "vertical" organisation than evidence of a primitive level of industrial specialisation. Within a few metres of each other in the very same room, you can observe the identical operations being performed by hand and by machine. To the right, a machine rolls long strands of twine onto small spools, to the left a worker cranks a large wooden wheel by hand: the identical process in both cases. The majority of the employees are peasant women and few of them belong to the Party. They do not wear uniforms, they do not even wear aprons, but sit at their places as if they were doing domestic chores' (*MOD*, p. 61).

31. This notion of the 'always-the-same' dressed up as the 'ever-changing' becomes a key theme in Benjamin's analysis of nineteenth-century Paris.

32. See *OWS*, p. 189.

33. Of the suburbs of the city, Benjamin writes: 'the "prairie of architecture", as Reich had called Moscow, is even more of a wilderness in these streets than in the centre of town' (*MOD*, p. 48).

34. As we will see in the next chapter, Benjamin begins 'Berlin Childhood' by drawing a distinction between the experience of the person who, familiar with the city, comes to lose him or herself in the metropolitan landscape and the stranger who merely becomes lost (see *GS* IV, p. 237).

35. Benjamin also observes that 'Moscow swarms with children everywhere' (*OWS*, p. 182).

36. Benjamin notes that, 'like every other city, Moscow builds up with names a little world within itself' (*OWS*, p. 203). This notion of the urban setting as a secret text and a space of naming is important in Benjamin's cityscapes. In the *Passagenarbeit* he notes that the city 'through its street names is a linguistic cosmos' (P3,5, *GS* V, p. 650).

37. Whereas in Naples guidebooks are of no use for the tourist, in Moscow 'maps and plans are victorious' (*OWS*, p. 179).

38. In his famous 1935 essay 'The Work of Art in the Age of Mechanical Reproduction', Benjamin argues for the progressive political potential

inherent in film and cinema. Cinema constitutes an immediate, challeng-
ing, engaging mass art form in which the demands of bourgeois
aesthetics for the contemplation of the distant, singular and hence
'auratic' artwork are radically overthrown.
39. I prefer McCole's translation of this passage to Zohn's; cf. *ILL*, p. 238.
40. Benjamin notes: 'the camera introduces us to unconscious optics as does
    psychoanalysis to unconscious impulses' (*ILL*, p. 239).
41. Benjamin notes: 'politics in the organisation of such crowds of children is
    not tendentious, but as natural a subject, as obvious a visual aid as the
    toy shop or doll's-house for middle-class children. . . . Amid all the
    images of childhood destitution that is still far from having been
    overcome, an attentive observer will perceive one thing: how the
    liberated pride of the proletariat is matched by the emancipated bearing
    of the children' (*OWS*, p. 183). An 'attentive observer' might also contrast
    this 'emancipated bearing of the children' with their rigid organization by
    the Party. Benjamin observes that 'even among them [the children of
    Moscow] there is a Communist hierarchy' (*OWS*, p. 182). He writes: 'the
    kosomoltsky, as the eldest, are at the top. They have their clubs in every
    town and are really trained as the next generation of the Party. The
    younger children become – at six – "pioneers". They too are united in
    clubs and wear a red tie as a proud distinction. *Oktiabr* ("Octoberists"),
    lastly – or "Wolves" – is the name given to little babies from the moment
    they are able to point to a picture of Lenin' (ibid.).

Chapter 2   Urban Memories: Labyrinth and Childhood

1. See Wolin, 1982, pp. 1–13, and Scholem, 1982, pp. 3–18, for details of
   Benjamin's formative years. Brodersen, 1990, pp. 33–89, provides a
   detailed account of Benjamin's relationship to the Youth Movement.
   McCole, 1993, pp. 35–70, presents a thorough and thoughtful discussion
   of the importance of the Movement in shaping Benjamin's subsequent
   intellectual concerns and strategies.
2. The pleasure of returning to a familiar city is noted by Benjamin: 'there is
   perhaps no greater stroke of luck in seeing a city again than to have lived
   and studied there for a long time, to have been away still longer, and
   then, after many disappointing travels, to awaken there one morning
   almost by surprise' (*GS* VII, p. 280).
3. In a letter to Scholem immediately after his arrival in Paris (20 Mar. 1933)
   Benjamin writes of the prevailing conditions in Germany thus: 'a sense of
   the situation there is better conveyed by the totality of the cultural state of
   affairs than by the particulars of individual acts of terror. It is difficult to
   obtain absolutely reliable information about the latter. Without doubt
   there are countless cases of people being dragged from their bed in the
   middle of the night, and tortured or murdered. The fate of the prisoners
   may be of even greater significance, but harder to probe into. Horrifying
   rumours are circulating about this' (*COR*, p. 405).
4. In the Foreword to the last version of the 'Berlin Childhood', Benjamin
   notes that the Berlin texts had an immunizing effect for the exile. He
   writes: 'I remained in this situation and purposely recalled those images
   which the homesickness of the exile preserves most strongly – those of

childhood. In this way, the feeling of longing could exert as little control over the mind as an innoculation does over a healthy body' (*GS* VII, p. 385). This passage is also found in a letter to Ferdinand Lion of 13 May 1938 (Berlin Archive, folder 36, p. 117).

5. For a discussion of these various broadcasts see Schiller-Lerg, 1984, and Mehlman, 1993, esp. pp. 58–67.

6. See Scholem, 1982, pp. 178 and 186–7.

7. Fritz Heinle and his fiancée Rika Seligson committed suicide in response to the outbreak of war in 1914. These deaths had a profound impact on Benjamin. Scholem notes: 'as was evident from Benjamin's every reference to Heinle, death had moved his friend into the realm of the sacrosanct' (Scholem, 1982, p. 17). Benjamin composed a number of sonnets as a tribute to the young poet (see *GS* VII, pp. 27–67).

8. Stüssi comments: 'the "Berlin Childhood" is not an autobiography which shows life as a significant continuity, as "progress". It is a collection of fragments, which should all end in the same entity' (1977, p. 245).

9. In his letter of 21 Jan. 1951 to Scholem, Belmore, one of these friends, notes: 'people hardly feature in these sketches, neither friend nor relatives; one might assume that Walter was an only child' (Puttnies and Smith, eds, 1991, p. 116).

10. In association with Franz Hessel, Benjamin had worked on German translations of three volumes of Proust's *À la recherche du temps perdu* in the late 1920s. Benjamin's essay 'Image of Proust' appeared in the *Literarische Welt* in 1929.

11. McCole notes that the Berlin texts 'disperse personal history into the discontinuous series of urban sites where the child's first, enigmatic encounters with the adult world took place' (1993, p. 207). Brodersen points out how Benjamin's gaze 'is riveted on places and things – on streets, stations and squares, on rooms and apartments, on objects of mundane life' (1990, p. 13).

12. This point is made by numerous commentators. Wolin writes: 'these collections of reminiscences are far from being autobiographical in the traditional sense; they in no way pretend to yield a portrait of the artist as a young man. . . . The true subject of these ostensibly biographical works, then, is not Benjamin's youthful development per se, but, quite literally, a Berlin childhood in general' (1982, p. 2). Fuld notes of Benjamin: 'his "Berlin Childhood" was not supposed to be autobiographical, inseparable from himself, but rather it was to emerge from something transitory yet typical. He doesn't present himself to the reader, but rather offers the experience of a childhood in Berlin, one that would never be lived in such a manner again' (1990, p. 9). Appropriately, the *Berliner Kindheit um Neunzehnhundert* is not included among Benjamin's 'autobiographical writings' in vol. VI of the *Gesammelte Schriften*. This tension between the personal and the general is not resolved in the Berlin writings. Benjamin notes his reluctance to use the first person singular when he announces the following rule: 'never use the word "I" except in letters' (*OWS*, p. 304). In the 'Chronicle' and 'Childhood' essays Benjamin does use 'I' for the most part, but it should be remembered that some sections of these studies appear in other, earlier versions (especially in 'One-Way Street') in which the third person is used.

13. Menninghaus later adds: 'the "Berlin Chronicle", "One-Way Street" and the "Berlin Childhood Around 1900" constitute Benjamin's Berlin *Passagen-Werk*; they literally mark his own "passage" ' (1986, p. 43).

14. As will become clear, the *mémoire involontaire*, in modified form, did indeed come to constitute the basis of Benjamin's dialectical image, the constellation formed as the present recognizes and redeems a moment in the past.

15. In support of his argument, Szondi cites Benjamin's review of Hessel's *Spazieren in Berlin* (1929). Here Benjamin writes: 'the superficial induce-ment, the exotic, the picturesque has an effect only on the foreigner. To portray a city a native must have other, deeper motives – motives of one who travels into the past instead of into the distance. A native's book about his city will always be related to memoirs; the writer has not spent his childhood there in vain' (Smith ed., 1988, p. 19, and *GS* III, p. 194).

16. The incongruous language here is a particularly clear example of Benjamin's contradictory perception of the urban setting. The city is a site of 'melancholy' and 'mourning' on the one hand, yet is 'radiant' and 'glorious' on the other.

17. Szondi also seems a little confused regarding the relationship between the various city writings. The Berlin texts, he argues, stand in the closest relation to the *Passagenarbeit*: 'the path that [Benjamin] entered on in Paris in search of Paris was thus the same one that . . . he urged upon whoever undertakes to write about his native city: a journey into the past' (Smith ed., 1988, p. 31). The 'Chronicle' and 'Childhood' share the same 'motives' as the *Denkbilder*. It is rather peculiar that Szondi should then assert that the Paris material 'has nothing in common with the earlier city portraits' (Smith ed., 1988, p. 31).

18. McCole notes: 'many of the texts in "One-Way Street" and "Berlin Childhood Around 1900" play on children's experience of the world through its tactile proximity' (1993, p. 246).

19. In 'One-Way Street', the passages on the child which were reformulated for incorporation in the 'Berlin Childhood' are tellingly entitled 'Enlarge-ments'.

20. This process of distortion may be seen as closely related to the 'estrangement effect' (*Verfremdungseffekt*) pioneered by Brecht's 'epic theatre'. The quiet contemplation of the drama by the spectator is disturbed as the dramatic action itself is subject to interruption. Benjamin regarded such an approach as an important critical and didactic principle. See Benjamin's 'What is Epic Theatre?' (*UB*, pp. 1–22).

21. The child's linguistic confusion is a recurrent theme in the Berlin writings. See also the sections entitled 'Markthalle Magdeburger Platz', 'Blumeshof 12' and 'Die Mummerehlen'.

22. Benjamin notes: 'the way in this labyrinth [the Tiergarten] . . . led over the Bendler Bridge, whose gentle slopes became the first hillsides for me' (*GS* IV, p. 9).

23. Proust also mentions the 'anaesthetic effect of habit' (1983, p. 11). He later writes: 'in the broad daylight of our habitual memory the images of the past turn gradually pale and fade out of sight, nothing remains of them, we shall never recapture it' (1983, p. 692).

24. For her, as for Scholem and Szondi, 'Childhood' is not so much an essay as a 'prose-poem'. Scholem sees the text as 'guided by a poetically

philosophical conception (1982, p. 191). Szondi regards the cityscapes as a whole as 'poetic writings' (Smith ed., 1988, p. 26).

25. Szondi notes that 'the labyrinth is thus in space what memory . . . is in time' (Smith ed., 1988, p. 22).
26. In his *Trauerspiel* study, Benjamin advocates the treatise as the highest form of philosophical reflection. He writes: 'the absence of an uninterrupted purposeful structure is its primary characteristic. Tirelessly the process of thinking makes new beginnings, returning in a roundabout way to its original object' (*OGTD*, p. 28).
27. Stüssi notes that 'the labyrinth is not only the object of representation, but rather describes simultaneously the method [*Weg*] of representation' (1977, p. 44).
28. Stüssi argues that there is an important distinction between Proust and Benjamin: whereas for Proust memory leads in a circle, for Benjamin recollection leads into the open, it is incomplete because oriented towards the future (1977, p. 52).
29. In *Elective Affinities* Goethe writes – it is part of an extract from Ottilie's journal – 'nothing is so fleeting but it leaves some trace of itself behind' (Goethe, 1971, p. 227).
30. The idea that the past does not have a final, irrevocable character but is instead open, subject to transformation in the present, is fundamental to Benjamin's concepts of history and redemption. In a letter of 16 Mar. 1937, Horkheimer responded critically to such a conceptualization of the past as open. Horkheimer writes: 'past injustice has occurred and is done with. The murdered are really murdered. . . . If one really takes incompleteness seriously, one has to believe in the Last Judgement' (Smith ed., 1989, p. 61). Benjamin replies: 'what the science has "established", recollection can modify. Recollection can make the incomplete (happiness) into something complete and the finished (suffering) into something incomplete' (Smith ed., 1989, p. 61).
31. One might also regard the child, one's former self, as an 'enslaved ancestor' in need of redemption by the adult.
32. Benjamin is concerned with those who have 'lost' in the struggles of the past: 'a constant and important question for me is what is one to understand by the expression: to lose a war, to lose a trial' (Berlin Archive, folder 36, p. 135).
33. The squares of Moscow were empty in 1926–7, for the new Soviet order had not yet had time to decide on, and give concrete form to, its own version of history. The monuments to the Tsarist regime had been torn down or, in the case of churches and cathedrals, were now emptied and abandoned. The 'old' form of the past had been obliterated, but the 'new', the 'significant history' of the Revolution had yet to be determined. The spaces vacated by Peter the Great and Catherine the Great awaited refilling by Marx and Lenin. The cult of Lenin was still at its incipient stage. Citing a British trade union delegation document, Benjamin notes that ' "when the memory of Lenin has found its place in history, this great Russian revolutionary reformer will even be pronounced a saint" ' (*OWS*, p. 208). Benjamin notes the sale of icons of Lenin in the Moscow markets (see *OWS*, p. 182).
34. One is reminded here of Marx's famous formulation of the recurrence of historical events in 'The Eighteenth Brumaire of Louis Bonaparte': 'Hegel

remarks somewhere that all facts and personages of great importance in world history occur, as it were, twice. He forgot to add: the first time as tragedy, the second as farce' (McLellan, ed., 1977, p. 300).

35. This notion of the 'afterlife' of the object, that its truth is manifest in the moment of ruination, is the key inspiration for Benjamin's analysis of the Parisian arcades, which lingered in the twentieth century only as ruins. As such, it is usually seen as an insight derived from Surrealism; but Benjamin's concept pre-dates his encounter with this movement. The initial inspiration is perhaps to be found in Benjamin's understanding of immanence and reflection in the work of Friedrich Schlegel and Novalis, which he explored in his thesis 'Der Begriff der Kunstkritik in der deutschen Romantik' (see esp. the section 'Das Kunstwerk', *GS* I, pp. 72–87). For Benjamin, early Romantic criticism was premissed on a concern with the unfolding of the truth content of the work of art from within. Criticism is, in a sense, the continued life of the work of art. McCole (1993, pp. 89–106) provides an insightful reading of Benjamin's notion of immanent critique. The notion of the 'afterlife' of a text is a key element in Benjamin's 1921 essay 'Task of the Translator', where translation, rather than criticism, becomes a medium of renewal (see esp. *ILL*, p. 73–6).

36. The German/Prussian victory at the Battle of Sedan on 1 Sept. 1870 became an annual public celebration.

37. Benjamin's inspiration in this regard is not Proust but Daudet. Benjamin describes his project in 'Berlin Chronicle' thus: 'I . . . have the encouragement provided by an illustrious precursor, the Frenchman Léon Daudet, exemplary at least in the title of his work which exactly encompasses the best that I might achieve here: Paris Vécu. "Lived Berlin" does not sound so good but is as real' (*OWS*, p. 295). Benjamin reviewed Daudet's book in his radio broadcast for the Frankfurter Rundfunk Bücherstunde of 24 Jan. 1930, and noted that 'a topographical rather than a chronological design lay at its heart' (*GS* VII, p. 280). Daudet sought 'to turn his own biography into a monument of Paris' (ibid.). Bollenbeck's criticism of Fuld's biography of Benjamin on the grounds that 'biographies should not erect monuments' (1980, p. 148) is hence somewhat misplaced.

38. Benjamin notes that 'the private citizen, who in the office took reality into account, required of the interior that it support him in his illusions' (*CB*, p. 167). Saisselin notes: 'the bourgeois interior, in contrast to the spaces in which others worked for him, became the space of private fantasies. Here, as Benjamin put it, he gathered objects from remote places and the past to create the space of his dreams and secret longings; here, too, his psyche betrayed him through the objects he gathered' (1985, p. 29).

39. This is an important statement, for it clearly establishes a thematic link between the *Denkbilder* and the subsequent Berlin texts. One of the key features of Neapolitan social life, it may be recalled, was the visibility of the body (the deformed beggar) and the richness of bodily gesture (the theatrical performance of the street auctioneer). A fundamental aspect of what Benjamin found 'noteworthy and important' was the manner in which life spills out on to the street. In Moscow, there is no private space even for 'private affairs', and personal life migrates to the office and the club.

40. In 'Moscow' Benjamin condemns the middle-class apartment as a place where 'nothing human can flourish', owing to the triumphant advance of the fetishized commodity (see *OWS*, p. 188).
41. McCole notes: 'venturing into the tangled world of the nineteenth century interior led one back into this "thicket of primeval history" with its unmastered, indeed unrecognised mythic compulsions' (1993, p. 218).
42. One is reminded of Proust's description of the home of M. and Mme Verdurin: 'the house was gradually filled with a collection of foot-warmers, cushions, clocks, screens, barometers and vases, a constant repetition and a boundless incongruity of useless but indestructible objects' (Proust, 1983, p. 223). In his writings on Baudelaire, Benjamin states: 'since the days of Louis Philippe the bourgeoisie has endeavoured to compensate itself for the inconsequential nature of private life in the big city. It seeks such compensation within its four walls. Even if a bourgeois is unable to give his earthly being permanence, it seems to be a matter of honour with him to preserve the traces of his articles and requisites of daily use in perpetuity' (*CB*, p. 46).
43. For Benjamin, one of the crucial characteristics of the Baroque stage was the omnipresence of the corpse. The dramatic intensity of the *Trauerspiel* resided precisely in its presentation of the ruination of the body, the natural history of the human subject.
44. Benjamin seems here to be prefiguring Foucault's analysis of the rise of modern institutions. Foucault's central argument in his analyses of the rise of 'carceral' society is that the development of the prison, asylum and clinic should not be seen simply as the product of scientific 'progress' and humanitarianism, but stemming instead from sets of contingencies regarding the perception of space, time and the body. The prison, e.g., becomes the pervasive mode of punishment in the nineteenth century not in response to horror at the barbarism of public execution but in conjunction with new forms of temporal and spatial order. These include the movement from the punishment of the body to the rehabilitation of the soul, the rise of the concept of factory time and time-as-punishment, spatial isolation first in the penal institution itself and second in the 'silent and solitary' prison cell. Public spectacle becomes private contrition.
45. For Benjamin, the absence of the corpse in the 'perceptual world of the living' brings about the demise of the capacity to communicate wisdom and experience. The coherence of one's life and the ability to relate it as a narrative depend, Benjamin claims, upon the proximity and visibility of the dead. The absence of the corpse is the fundamental impediment to the possibility of telling one's tale. Benjamin writes: 'death is the sanction of everything that the storyteller can tell. He has borrowed his authority from death. In other words, it is natural history to which his stories refer back' (*ILL*, p. 94).
46. Benjamin writes: 'it is not exactly common for a child to grow up close to a city so harmoniously and happily that it is then a pleasure for the mature man to recall this childhood in memory' (*GS* VII, p. 93).
47. It is, one may recall, in 'solitary games' that the child 'grows up at closest quarters to the city' (*OWS*, p. 293).
48. Street names also prove a source of disappointment to the child. Benjamin writes: 'how much the name Hofjägerallee promised and how little it contained' (*GS* IV, p. 237).

49. The fantasy of the child is to turn the interior into a metropolis, and as such, is exactly the reverse of that of the bourgeois adult, whose dream, Benjamin notes in his *Passagenarbeit*, is to transform the city into an enclosed, domesticated space (see d2, *GS* V, p. 1052) free from disturbance by the elements (see D4,2, *GS* V, p. 166).

50. This may seem somewhat trivial, but, of course, Benjamin's most significant insights are drawn from things and events which appear to be of no consequence. His levity should not distract the reader from an important point. The child, in his or her act of transgression and theft, does indeed prefigure precisely the liberation of objects from their normal location in the world that is the redemption of things. The passage calls to mind Benjamin's account of the art gallery in Moscow where 'children and workers' have begun to 'take possession of bourgeois culture' instead of having 'the appearance of planning a burglary' as they tour the museum (*OWS*, p. 183).

51. The notion of hiding is an important motif in Benjamin's writings. In Naples a grain of Sunday is hidden in every weekday, and in Moscow the Russian village plays hide-and-seek in the city. The Berlin texts are an exercise in urban archaeology, the uncovering of the buried past experiences of the modern subject. For Benjamin, the truth of an object is never present: it is always hidden within. Truth is revealed as the deceptive exterior of the object decays with the passage of time.

52. Benjamin writes of the hiding child: 'without waiting for the moment of discovery, he grabs the hunter with a shout of self-deliverance' (*OWS*, p. 74). This image of self-revelation finds a recent parallel in a short story by the Argentinian Jorge Luis Borges (1899–1986). In 'The House of Asterion', Borges inverts the Theseus myth. In Borges' story, the Minotaur, though still a monstrous, lethal figure, becomes child-like. The Minotaur kills those who enter the labyrinth not out of malice but accidentally, through over-zealous play. According to this version, the Minotaur is a lonely prisoner of the labyrinth who wishes only to have, yet sadly destroys, its playmates. It rushes to greet Theseus, not to devour him but to welcome him as a new companion, and is slain. While I do not wish to overstate the similarities between Borges' Minotaur and Benjamin's child, a number of connections are apparent: both are figures of disorder; both are playful characters imprisoned within the labyrinth; both are lonely seekers of playmates; both rush forth to embrace the world of culture (Theseus, the bourgeois father) with a joy that is short-lived. The urban child as Minotaur may seem a far-fetched interpretation of Benjamin's position, but he does indeed seem concerned with many of the themes of the Theseus myth: the city is a labyrinth in which one finds and loses one's way, in which one must learn to retrace one's steps, and which, Benjamin notes at the beginning of 'Berlin Chronicle', is 'not without its Ariadne' (*OWS*, p. 293).

53. The mimetic faculty is a historical one, subject to change. Benjamin notes that 'the direction of this change seems definable as the increasing decay of the mimetic faculty. For clearly the observable world of modern man contains only minimal residues of the magical correspondences and analogies that were familiar to ancient peoples' (*OWS*, p. 161). The sphere of non-sensuous correspondences (of written language, of script) has become pre-eminent.

54. It is in the zoo that the anonymous members of the animal kingdom come to be given their names. With its classification of genus, species and subspecies, the zoo presumes to outdo Adam in naming all the creatures of the earth. Zoology is the triumph of the order of science over the chaos of nature, and the zoo is the ultimate site of imprisonment in the city. The animals in the zoo are imprisoned in three ways: within their individual cages; within the city, the principal site of culture; and within the linguistic categories and classifications of scientific discourse. The terror of the wilderness and of contamination by nature is kept securely and safely behind bars. The zoo is the setting in which the modern individual asserts his or her distinction and separation from animals. The latter are solely objects of the gaze, unable to touch the onlooker. There is proximity but no point of contact, no contiguity. In this sense, animals in the zoo are 'auratic', distant despite being close. This notion of distance is important, because it connects the zoo with the museum. The zoo denies the intimate link between human beings and the natural world in the same way that the museum severs past and present. The zoo is to nature what the museum is to history: the site of its classification and arrangement, its mythical organization and fantastical presentation.
55. Fuld notes: 'his earliest acquaintance with the city was only under the aspect of money and commodities: when his mother took him shopping. He saw how "paternal money paved a way for us between counters and shop assistants, mirrors and the glances of my mother" ' (1990, p. 18). Here again one encounters Benjamin's notion of lack of knowledge as insightful. The child, unfamiliar with the multi-faceted city, perceives the centre of the urban complex simply as a 'theatre of purchases', a place of commodity consumption. This not-knowing, however, is actually extremely perceptive: the city really is a space of commodity fetishism and consumerism.
56. The figure of the bourgeois collector is important in Benjamin's work. He writes: 'the collector was the true inhabitant of the interior. He made the glorification of things his concern. To him fell the task of Sisyphus which consisted in stripping things of their commodity character by means of his possession of them. But he conferred upon them only a fancier's value, rather than a use-value. The collector dreamed he was in a world which was not only far-off in distance and in time, but which also was a better one, in which to be sure people were just as poorly provided with what they needed as in the world of everyday, but in which things were free from the bondage of being useful' (*CB*, pp. 168–9).
57. Although it may resemble the zoo or the museum in miniature, this collection is actually antithetical to these institutions. To impose order upon such a peculiar agglomeration would be to destroy the child's collection. It forms, Stüssi notes, 'a chaotic counter-order' (1977, p. 207) to the tediousness of the bourgeois interior. The child's disorganized mass of artefacts stands in direct contrast to the stagnant, rigid systematization of the museum. The collector is a subversive figure. Arendt notes: 'tradition puts the past in order, not just chronologically but first of all systematically in that it separates the positive from the negative, the orthodox from the heretical, and that which is obligatory and relevant from the mass of irrelevant or merely interesting opinions and data. The collector's passion, on the other hand, is not only

unsystematic but borders on the chaotic, not so much because it is a passion as because it is not primarily kindled by the quality of the object – something that is classifiable – but is inflamed by its "genuineness", its uniqueness, something that denies classification' (Introduction to *ILL*, p. 44). Benjamin fundamentally rejects any fixed and final division of objects or of the past into 'relevant' and 'irrelevant'.

58. Arendt notes: 'collecting is the redemption of things which is to complement the redemption of man' (*ILL*, p. 42).

59. In his writings on Paris, Benjamin outlines his notion of the 'dreaming collectivity'. This peculiar concept refers to the dormant utopian desires of the contemporary generation that Benjamin seeks to awaken and bring to realization. As we will see in the next chapter, Benjamin argues that these desires find distorted actualization in the phantasmagoria of the modern metropolis, and in particular in the city's architecture, the 'dream-houses' of the arcades, the museum, the exhibition hall, and the railway station.

60. Benjamin's critique of the bourgeois revulsion for the poor and the destitute, and the consequent desire of the middle classes to make them invisible, is reminiscent of Engels. Engels cites the following from a letter to the *Manchester Guardian* by 'A Lady': 'for some time past our main streets are haunted by swarms of beggars, who try to awaken the pity of the passers-by in a most shameless and annoying manner, by exposing their tattered clothing, sickly aspect, and disgusting wounds and deformities. I should think that when one not only pays the poor-rate, but also contributes largely to the charitable institutions, one had done enough to earn the right to be spared such disagreeable and impertinent molestation' (Engels, 1987, p. 277).

Chapter 3   Dialectical Images:
Paris and the Phantasmagoria of Modernity

1. Adorno, in a letter of 10 Nov. 1938, writes: 'Gretel once said in jest that you are an inhabitant of the cave-like depths of your arcades and that you shrink from finishing your study because you are afraid of having to leave what you have built' (*AP*, p. 131). This may refer to a letter of 7 Mar. 1938 in which Gretel Adorno writes: 'my only fear is that you are so at home in the arcades that you will not want to leave their palatial splendour, and that only when you have closed this door will there be any chance of another subject interesting you' (Berlin Archive, folder 28, pp. 29–30).

2. 'In the spirit of allegory', Benjamin notes, the *Trauerspiel* 'is conceived from the outset as a ruin, a fragment' (*OGTD*, p. 235).

3. Ben Brewster, e.g., notes that 'Benjamin's fascination with Paris dates back to 1913, when, at his father's instigation, he made his first visit to the city' (Brewster, 1968, p. 73). French writers were also an early preoccupation for Benjamin. In the 1920s he translated Charles Baudelaire's *Tableaux parisiens* and *Les Fleurs du mal* and sections of Proust. While Aragon may have been the inspiration for the central theme of the work, Benjamin also refers to the opening description of the dismal interior of the arcade which forms the main setting for Emile Zola's *Thérèse Raquin* (see a°,4, *GS* V, p. 1046).

4. See McCole, 1993, pp. 213–20. McCole points out that it is in 'Dreamkitsch' that the themes of dream consciousness and dream images find their initial articulation. He writes: 'the ideas first formulated in "Dreamkitsch" supplied the germ for Benjamin's "Arcades Project" ' (1993, p. 213).

5. See *GS* V, pp. 1041–3.

6. Hence Wolin's claim that 'Walter Benjamin intended the *Passagenwerk* or "Arcades Project" to be the culmination of his life-work' (1986, p. 201) is a little misleading. In mid-1928 Benjamin clearly had no such grandiose view of the character of this study.

7. 'Surrealism: The Last Snapshot of the European Intelligentsia' (in *OWS*, pp. 225–39).

8. *OWS*, pp. 240–57.

9. Horkheimer writes (18 Sept. 1935): 'I can only offer my verdict very briefly: your work promises to be simply wonderful' (*GS* V, p. 1143).

10. It was perhaps Gretel Adorno who made the most pointed remark regarding the *exposé*, however. She wrote: 'in it one would never have suspected the hand of Walter Benjamin' (letter of 28 Aug. 1935, *GS* V, p. 1140).

11. Benjamin regarded this essay as intimately bound up with the Paris study. In a letter to Werner Kraft of 27 Dec. 1935 he notes that the essay 'stands materially in no relation to the major study, whose plan I have mentioned, but in the closest methodologically' (*GS* V, p. 1151). This is a rather surprising comment, since one might have expected the reverse of this formulation. The relationship between art and technology in the nineteenth century is a central theme of the Paris materials. The fate of art in the modern epoch is examined in relation not only to Baudelaire's poetry and aesthetic essays but also to Daumier's lithography, the rise of newspapers and journalism, the development of photography, the *art nouveau* movement, etc. The methodological connections, by contrast, are far more obscure.

12. In a letter to Horkheimer of 17 Dec. 1936 Benjamin writes of this visit thus: 'the last evening was devoted to my Paris book. It had, however, figured in our other discussions, and Wiesengrund's suggestion that you entrust me with a study of Jung also resulted from these. I believe it is a propitious suggestion: nevertheless I must tell you – as I admitted to Wiesengrund, by the way – that I have so far read very little of Jung's work – Wiesengrund is to show me the important literature by Jung and his school' (*GS* V, p. 1156).

13. Mentioned in his letter of 1 Mar. 1937 to Adorno (see *GS* V, pp. 1156–7).

14. In his letter to Scholem of 8 July 1938 Benjamin writes of the Baudelaire study thus: 'in this sense I can say that a very precise model of the "Arcades Project" would be furnished if the "Baudelaire" were to succeed' (*GER*, p. 231).

15. On 20 July 1938, in a letter to Gretel Adorno, Benjamin notes: 'An additional factor is that some of the fundamental categories of the *Arcades project* are developed here for the first time. Of these categories, that of the new and the immutable occupies first place. . . . Furthermore, motifs that had formerly appeared to me only as spheres of thought, more or less isolated from one another, are brought into conjunction with each

other for the first time in this work – and this may give you the best idea of what it is: allegory, *Jugendstil*, and aura' (*COR*, p. 570).

16. See *COR*, pp. 555–8.
17. Adorno writes (letter of 29 Feb. 1940): 'with what enthusiasm did I read your Baudelaire. . . . That is equally true of Max [Horkheimer]. I believe it is hardly an exaggeration to call this the most accomplished piece of work you have published since the Baroque book and the Kraus study' (*AB*, p. 415).
18. Ivornel, e.g., points out with some justification that this leads to 'petrifying as an *oeuvre* (*Werk*) what Benjamin himself designated more fluidly and openly as his *Passagenarbeit*' (1986, p. 62).
19. Viz., *Passagen* (1927), *Erste Notizen/Pariser Passagen I* (1927–30), *Pariser Passagen II* (1928/9), and *Saturnring* (1928–29).
20. Benjamin notes in his *Trauerspiel* study: 'it is common practice in the literature of the baroque to pile up fragments ceaselessly, without any strict idea of a goal, and in the unremitting expectation of a miracle' (*OGTD*, p. 178).
21. In a letter from New York of 7 Mar. 1938, Gretel Adorno writes: 'not only that I like it here better than in London, I am quite convinced that you would feel the same. For me the most bemusing thing is that by no means everything is as new or advanced as one might think. On the contrary, everywhere there is the contrast between the most modern and the shabby. There is no need to seek out the Surrealistic, you fall over them every step of the way. In the early evening the tower blocks are imposing, but later, when the offices are closed and the lights become sparse, they remind one of poorly lit European back tenements' (Berlin Archive, folder 28, pp. 29–30).
22. Buck-Morss regards Adorno's argument as somewhat misplaced. She asserts that 'class differentiations were never lacking in Benjamin's theory of the collective unconscious, which even in his earliest formulations he considered an extension of Marx's theory of the superstructure' (1989, p. 281). Buck-Morss is correct in noting that the 'dream theory' is related to Benjamin's account of cultural forms as the 'expression' of prevailing material circumstances, but the problem of precisely who the dreamer of the nineteenth century is remains. What is the class character of the collective and its dream? Buck-Morss's answer to this question is clear-cut: the subject and content of the dream are 'clearly of bourgeois origins' (1989, p. 284). She insists unhesitatingly that 'the collective dream manifested the ideology of the dominant class' (1989, p. 281). This complicates, rather than resolves, the problem, though. For if the collective dream of the nineteenth century were merely that of the bourgeoisie, why does Benjamin argue that the goal of the historical materialist is to arouse this collectivity from its slumbers in order to realize the dream? Surely Benjamin is not arguing that the revolutionary task is to fulfil the dreams of the middle classes?
23. In his notes for the 'Theses on the Concept of History', Benjamin compares eternal recurrence with the punishment of the school child: 'the fundamental conception of myth is the world as punishment – the punishment which first creates the prisoner. Eternal recurrence is the punishment of having to stay behind projected onto the cosmos: humanity must write its lines innumerable times' (*GS* I, p. 1234). In the

Passagenarbeit he notes: ' "eternal recurrence" is the fundamental form of primordial, mythic consciousness' (D10,3, *GS* V, p. 177).

24. Benjamin also recognizes that this notion of the unchanging may also become mythic. The bourgeoisie endeavour to transform the transitory and historical – viz., the conditions of their own domination – into the eternal and enduring. They desire to make themselves and the objects and monuments associated with their power, immortal. Benjamin quotes Brecht thus: 'the dominant have a great aversion to stark transformation. They desire that everything remain as it is, ideally for a thousand years. Ideally, the moon remains stationary and the sun also moves no further. Then no-one would get hungry any more and want to eat in the evening. If they have fired, then the opponent should not be allowed to shoot back, their shot ought to be the last' (B4a,1, *GS* V, p. 121). The bourgeoisie wish to render their domination timeless and endless. If history is a process of continual change, as the doctrine of progress would have it, it is in the interests of the powerful of the epoch to in some sense bring history to an end. The bourgeois demand to be the be-all and end-all of the world.

25. It was not only bourgeois ideology and 'historicism' that conspired in such a vision. For Benjamin, orthodox Marxism also participated in the affirmation of historical change as technological development. In his notes for the 'Theses', Benjamin writes: 'the structure of Marx's fundamental ideas is as follows: through a series of class conflicts in the course of historical development, humanity achieves the classless society. But perhaps the classless society is not to be conceptualised as the endpoint of historical development' (*GS* I, p. 1232). The revolutionary moment and the end of oppression are not to be seen as part of a historical continuity, but rather as interruptions within such a process. Benjamin notes: 'Marx said revolutions are the locomotives of world history. But perhaps it is quite different. Perhaps revolutions are the grab for the emergency brakes by the generations of humanity travelling in this train' (ibid.). For Benjamin, 'the concept of the classless society must be given its true messianic countenance once more, for this is in the interests of proletarian revolutionary politics' (ibid.).

26. See Konersmann, 1991, pp. 90–7, for an insightful critique of Benjamin's interpretation of Ranke.

27. See *GS* I, pp. 1240–1.

28. For Benjamin, the fairy-tale has a fundamentally anti-mythic character. Whereas myths recount human subjection to the immutable forces of nature, the fairy-tale emphasizes the circumvention of fate through wit and cunning. In his essay on Franz Kafka, Benjamin states: 'reason and cunning have inserted tricks into myths; their forces cease to be invincible. Fairy tales are the traditional stories about victory over these forces, and fairy tales for dialecticians are what Kafka wrote when he went to work on legends' (*ILL*, p. 117). In 'The Storyteller', Benjamin notes that 'the fairy tale tells us of the earliest arrangements that mankind made to shake off the nightmare which the myth had placed upon his chest' (*ILL*, p. 102). Nature may appear as beneficent in this when, e.g., animals come to the aid of human characters. This 'shows that nature not only is subservient to the myth, but much prefers to be aligned with

humanity' (ibid.). Adorno notes that for Benjamin 'the fairy-tale appears as the outwitting of myth or as its fracturing' (Adorno, 1990, p. 111).

29. The fairy-tale that is most pertinent to the 'Arcades Project' is perhaps the one recounted by Benjamin in his radio broadcast 'Berliner Spielzeug-wanderung I': viz., Godin's 'Schwester Tinchen'. Tinchen enters the magical realm of a sorcerer who has kidnapped her four brothers. She knows that if she is distracted from her task, she too will fall under his spell. The sorcerer surrounds her with wondrous toys and playmates in the hope that her resolution will fail. Each time she is tempted to abandon her quest, however, a bluebird, which sits on her shoulder, reminds her of her goal (see *GS* VII, pp. 98–101). One can almost read this as an allegory of the *Passagenarbeit*. For a discussion of this point, see Mehlman, 1993, pp. 67–71.

30. This concept of dreaming is thus the clearest articulation of Benjamin's differentiated understanding of the character of myth. In his concern with myth as possessing both negative and positive poles, Benjamin seeks to avoid a one-dimensional, totalizing, purely pessimistic version of modern society. Paris is not simply the locus of false ideas, the site of Hell. For Benjamin, Paris is both Heaven and Hell. He writes: 'two mirrors reflect each other, thus Satan plays his favourite trick and opens up in this manner (as a partner does in the eyes of the lover) the perspective into infinity. Be it now divine, be it devilish, Paris has a passion for mirror-like perspectives' (R1,6, *GS* V, p. 667). For Benjamin, Paris is above all the 'mirror-city' (*Spiegelstadt*), both sacred and satanic. Hence Adorno's complaint regarding the 1935 *exposé*, that it included 'the abandonment of the category of Hell' (*AP*, p. 111) is characteristically both astute and misplaced.

31. Breton was 'the first to perceive the revolutionary energies that appear in the "outmoded", in the first iron constructions, the first factory buildings, the earliest photos, the objects that have begun to be extinct, grand pianos, the dresses of five years ago, fashionable restaurants when the vogue has begun to ebb from them. The relation of these things to revolution – no one can have a more exact concept of it than these authors' (*OWS*, p. 229).

32. Apollinaire in his 1912 poem *Zone* writes of Paris: 'here even the cars seem old-fashioned' (cited in Timms and Kelley, eds, 1985, p. 84).

33. Benjamin states: 'the dream – that is the ground in which the finds are made that break objects away from the prehistory of the nineteenth century' (C2a,11, *GS* V, p. 140).

34. Eagleton describes Benjamin as 'the *bricoleur* whose texts violently yoke the most heterogeneous materials together while appearing blandly undisturbed by their boldness' (Eagleton, 1981, p. 56).

35. Wolin states that Benjamin sought to devise 'a presentation of knowledge that retained as few affinities with traditional philosophical conceptualisation as possible. Hence the "image-oriented" approach to truth, whose basic principle was very much akin to the Surrealist principle of montage: renunciation of conventional philosophical narrative in favour of an approach that called for an *unmediated* juxtaposition of insights' (Wolin, 1986, p. 204).

36. One is reminded here of Benjamin's attempt to eschew theory in favour of the utmost concreteness that informed his work on Moscow. This link

is important, because although the Paris writings are not *Denkbilder*, they may perhaps be understood as an assemblage of such.

37. Benjamin notes: 'When thinking reaches a standstill in a constellation saturated with tensions, the dialectical image appears. This image is the caesura in the movement of thought' (N10a,3, Smith ed., 1989, p. 67). Djuna Barnes captures the spirit of such a conceptualization in her 1936 novel *Nightwood* when she writes: 'an image is a stop the mind makes between uncertainties' (Barnes, 1985, p. 160).

38. Benjamin writes: 'In order for a part of the past to be touched by actuality, there must be no continuity between them' (N7,7, Smith ed., 1989, p. 60).

39. Benjamin cites Adorno's letter of 5 Aug. 1935 thus: 'Dialectical images are constellations of alienated things and thorough-going meaning, pausing a moment in the undifferentiation of death and meaning' (N5,2, Smith ed., 1989, pp. 54–5). Such images have an 'elective affinity' for the Parisian arcades, which themselves stand on the threshold of extinction.

40. Benjamin notes Paul-Ernest de Rattier's comment: 'Paris will be the world, and the Universe will be Paris' (E7a,4, *GS* V, p. 198).

41. The significance of Jacques Offenbach's operettas within the fantastical world of nineteenth-century Paris was to be explored by Siegfried Kracauer in his 1937 study *Jacques Offenbach und das Paris seiner Zeit*.

42. See D4,2, *GS* V, p. 166.

43. Thorstein Veblen, who coined the phrase 'conspicuous consumption' in his 1899 study *Theory of the Leisure Class*, emphasizes the metropolitan origin of such activity. Whereas in small communities the social rank of individuals would be widely known, the greatly expanded social milieu of urban life necessitated the unequivocal display of wealth, merit and status for the purpose of recognition. See Veblen, 1992, esp. pp. xiii and 71–2.

44. It was not until the mid-1930s that Benjamin began to read Marx systematically.

45. In his letter to Scholem of 20 May 1935 (*GER*, p. 159), Benjamin points out that commodity fetishism was to be to the 'Arcades Project' what the *Trauerspiel* had been to the book on the Baroque written some ten years earlier. In a letter to Gretel Adorno of March 1939 Benjamin notes: 'I have busied myself, as well as possible in the limited time, [with] one of the basic concepts of the "Arcades", placing at its core the culture of the commodity-producing society as phantasmagoria' (*GS* V, p. 1172).

46. Benjamin states that 'living means leaving traces' (*CB*, p. 169).

47. Eagleton points out that 'the business of erasing, preserving or rewriting traces is always one of political struggle' (1981, p. 34).

48. Aragon writes: 'now that we have coaxed the lightning to curl round our feet like a kitten and, fearless as eagles, have counted the freckles on the face of the sun, to whom shall we now pay supreme homage? Other blind forces are born to us, other major fears, and thus we end up prostrating ourselves before the machines that are our daughters' (Aragon, 1987, p. 132). This notion of human subjection before the machine becomes a key theme in the critique of technology developed by Adorno and Horkheimer. Horkheimer notes: 'the more devices we invent for dominating nature, the more we must serve them if we are to survive' (1974b, p. 97).

49. For Benjamin, the twin tendencies of nineteenth-century social life, the eroticization of the commodity and the attempt to hide the sexual within the safe confines of the bourgeois interior, find their ultimate union in the form of *art nouveau* (*Jugendstil*).

50. Benjamin here prefigures important themes developed by Critical Theory. For Marcuse, 'a whole dimension of human activity and passivity has been de-eroticised in modern capitalism' (Marcuse, 1964, p. 73). Marcuse emphasizes that one-dimensional society involves the 'systematic inclusion of libidinal components into the realm of commodity production and exchange' (1964, p. 75). Adorno and Horkheimer note that 'the mass production of the sexual automatically achieves its repression' (1986, p. 140).

51. Saisselin writes: 'if Benjamin is right in following Baudelaire and Guys in their opinion about the relation of the city and *ennui*, then it becomes possible to see in the city and its products, its commodities and luxuries, its articles *de nouveauté* and its shop windows, a way to construct a new aesthetics, closely linked to capitalism, built on the need to dissipate *ennui*' (1985, p. 27). But Benjamin is *not* following Baudelaire and Guys. The latter regard the pleasures of the modern metropolis as the means to avoid boredom, whereas Benjamin presents them as its source.

52. See B1a,4, *GS* V, p. 113.

53. Benjamin notes enigmatically: 'arcades: houses, passageways that have no exterior. Like the dream' (F°9, *GS* V, p. 1006).

54. See also A°6, *GS* V, p. 993.

55. Benjamin points out that 'in the first half of the previous century, the theatre was happily transferred to the arcade' (C°3, *GS* V, p. 997).

56. Benjamin notes that in Paris 'there was a Passage du Désir' (A6a,4, *GS* V, p. 98).

57. Asclepius was a Greek hero and god of healing, identified with the ritual act of sleeping.

58. See O°47, *GS* V, p. 1031.

59. This edifice was the ultimate monument to modern progress. Benjamin writes: 'this heroic epoch of technology found its monument in the incomparable Eiffel Tower' (*GS* V, p. 1062).

60. Saisselin notes that 'the two spaces in fact correspond to the internal contradictions of bourgeois aesthetics' (1985, p. 47): contemplation of the singular artwork and fetishization of the commodity.

Chapter 4   Urban Allegories: Paris, Baudelaire and the Experience of Modernity

1. The poetry and prose of Baudelaire had an enduring fascination for Benjamin. Between 1914 and 1924 Benjamin worked intermittently on translations of Baudelaire's *Tableaux parisiens* and other sections from *Les Fleurs du mal*. Benjamin's 1921 essay 'The Task of the Translator' was conceived as a preface to these translations, which he hoped to print in the first edition of his own proposed, but never published, journal entitled *Angelus Novus*.

2. Jennings argues that in Benjamin's texts 'Baudelaire at last appears in his proper context, as a big-city poet attempting to define the modern experience of big-city life' (1987, p. 22).
3. Baudelaire reiterated the point in his review of the 'Salon of 1846'. He remarks that the modern metropolitan environment 'is rich in poetic and marvellous subjects. We are enveloped and steeped as though in an atmosphere of the marvellous; but we do not notice it' (Baudelaire, 1965, p. 119).
4. Baudelaire notes that the contemporary observer 'marvels at the . . . amazing harmony of life in capital cities, a harmony so providentially maintained amid the turmoil of human freedom' (Baudelaire, 1986, p. 11).
5. Benjamin's approach did not find favour with some of his colleagues. In his critical response to Benjamin's 1938 draft 'The Paris of the Second Empire in Baudelaire', Adorno wrote: 'unless I am very much mistaken, your dialectic lacks one thing: mediation. Throughout your text there is a tendency to relate the pragmatic contents of Baudelaire's work directly to adjacent features in the social history of his time, preferably economic features' (*AP*, p. 128). Adorno rejects Benjamin's attempt to avoid theoretical mediation, and condemns what he regards as the rather crude materialist approach which results. Adorno illustrates his complaint with reference to Benjamin's blunt equation of Baudelaire's poems on the theme of wine (he cites 'L'âme du vin' as an example) with prevailing duties payable on wine.
6. The arcade is in a sense doubly empty: at the height of its prestige it contained only the commodity, a hollow entity; in the present, it is devoid of customers, an abandoned shell.
7. Citing Baudelaire, Benjamin notes: 'the original interest with allegory is not linguistic but optical. "Images, my great, my primitive passion" ' (J59,4, *GS* V, p. 422).
8. Benjamin also notes: 'That which is affected by the allegorical intention is distinguished from the context of life' (J56,1, *GS* V, p. 414).
9. Benjamin quotes a letter written by Charles Dickens while in Lausanne in 1846 in which he longs for the inspiration of the metropolis: 'the effort and labour to write, day by day, without this magic lantern are monstrous. . . . My characters seem to want to stand still if they do not have the crowd surrounding them' (quoted in M4a,4, *GS* V, pp. 536–7). Baudelaire's poetry, like Dickens's novels, is animated by the urban environment.
10. Louise Hoffman perceptively notes that for Benjamin, as for Baudelaire, 'the milieu of large cities . . . was necessary to him socially and intellectually; yet he remained an outsider, even a victim in these capitals' (1983, p. 146). Urban life, she adds, was 'essential to Benjamin, yet also barely tolerable' (1983, p. 149).
11. Friedrich Engels's description of the urban crowd in *The Condition of the Working Class in England* is cited by Benjamin (*CB*, p. 121) as an example of such a negative reaction. Engels writes: 'they crowd by one another as though they had nothing in common, nothing to do with one another, and their only agreement is the tacit one, that each keep to his own side of the pavement . . . while it occurs to no man to honour another with so much as a glance. The brutal indifference, the unfeeling isolation of each

in his private interest, becomes the more repellent and offensive, the more these individuals are crowded together, within a limited space' (1987, p. 69).

12. Saisselin notes of the physiologies: 'this physiognomic genre supposed . . . a new aesthetic observer. This observer was no longer the man of taste in contemplation before a picture of a landscape. . . . He was the *flâneur* of the modern city' (1985, p. 23). Benjamin points out that the physiologies 'investigated types that might be encountered by a person taking a look at the marketplace' (*CB*, p. 35).

13. The connection in Benjamin between the rise of the crowd and the birth of the detective story is an important and usually underplayed one. Buck-Morss perceptively notes that in the Paris texts 'ur-history turns into a detective story' (1989, p. 211). Frisby, in Tester, ed., 1994, pp. 81–110 (esp. pp. 90–3) discusses the connections between the detective and the *flâneur*. Living as the leaving behind of traces, their eradication in the urban multitude, the crowd as the hiding-place *par excellence* of modernity, the avoidance of being seen, of surveillance, of giving oneself away, and the critical importance of recovering traces and clues left by previous generations – all these suggest that it was not only the collector and the archaeologist but also the detective that formed a model of redemptive practice for Benjamin. In her letter to Benjamin of 5 Jan. 1935, Elisabeth Hauptmann writes: 'detective story writers discover and delineate the smallest visible traces left by people: cigar ash, a half open window or trodden grass, and draw their conclusions from them. Those who leave traces are naturally those who are involved in the operations (business, crime). (Whoever wishes to avoid such operations must know this and leave no trace)' (Berlin Archive, folder 11, p. 18).

14. Benjamin quotes part of Brecht's *Handbook for City-Dwellers* (precisely the poetry which he regarded as conveying the definitive experience of the urban subject) in relation to the detective story thus: 'Regarding the crime novel: "Whoever does not give his signature, whoever leaves no image behind, Whoever was not there, whoever said nothing, How can they be caught! Erase the traces!" ' (in M16,2, *GS* V, p. 559).

15. Alexander Dumas's novel *Les Mohicans de Paris* (1859) is noted by Benjamin in light of this. Drawing directly on J. Fenimore Cooper's tale of adventure and daring in the New World, Dumas's story was concerned with 'the possibility of giving scope to the experiences of the hunter in the urban environment' (M11a,6, *GS* V, p. 551).

16. Examples would include Wilkie Collins's villain Count Fosco in *The Woman in White* and, of course, Sir Arthur Conan Doyle's Professor Moriarty in his Sherlock Holmes stories.

17. Benjamin notes Hugo's celebration of 'the crowd as hero in a modern epic. . . . Hugo placed himself in the crowd as a *citoyen*' (*CB*, p. 66).

18. See *CB*, p. 60. Benjamin asserts that 'the mass was the agitated veil; through it Baudelaire saw Paris' (*CB*, p. 123).

19. See also D5,3 *GS* V, p. 168.

20. See also J34a,3, *GS* V, p. 369.

21. Janet Wolff points out that, with the exception of figures like Georges Sand, who dressed as a boy to roam the Parisian streets in 1831 (1990, p. 41), such experiences were not available to women. She writes: 'the experience of anonymity in the city, the fleeting impersonal contact

described by social commentators such as Georg Simmel, the possibility of unmolested strolling and observation first seen by Baudelaire, and then analysed by Walter Benjamin were entirely the experience of men' (1990, p. 58). Sand gives the following account: 'no-one paid attention to me, and no-one guessed at my disguise. . . . No-one knew me, no-one looked at me, no-one found fault with me; I was an atom lost in that immense crowd' (cited by Wolff, 1990, p. 41).

22. This is given cryptic form in *CP*, where Benjamin notes: 'the modern stands in opposition to the antique, the new stands in opposition to the always-the-same. (The modern: the masses; the antique: the city of Paris)' (*CP*, p. 49).

23. The modern labyrinth of the crowd as the newest space in which one might come to lose oneself was no less a temptation for Benjamin himself. Commenting on Engels, Benjamin half scornfully states: 'The charm of his description lies in the intersecting of unshakable critical integrity with an old-fashioned attitude. The writer came from a Germany that was still provincial; he may never have faced the temptation to lose himself in a stream of people' (*CB*, p. 122).

24. For an account of the history of the term *Erlebnis* see Gadamer, 1975, pp. 55–63.

25. Benjamin writes of Poe: 'His pedestrians act as if they had adapted themselves to the machines and could express themselves only automatically. . . . The shock experience which the passer-by has in the crowd corresponds to what the worker "experiences" at his machine' (*CB*, pp. 133–4; see also J60a,6, *GS* V, pp. 425–6).

26. Benjamin notes that in Paris 'even the eyes of passers-by are draped mirrors' (c°,1, *GS* V, p. 1049), which thus fail to return the gaze cast upon them.

27. Wolff notes critically: 'none of the women meet the poet as his equal. They are subjects of his gaze, objects of his "botanising" ' (1990, p. 42).

28. The fetishized commodity and fashion are perhaps the highest expression of this elusive, unsatisfied desire in the city.

29. Benjamin notes: 'Baudelaire loved solitude but he wanted it in a crowd' (*CB*, p. 50).

30. Benjamin notes: 'Hegel on September 3rd 1827 from Paris to his wife: "I walk through the streets, the people appear to be exactly the same as in Berlin – all dressed the same, even the same faces – the same view, but in a populous [*volkreichen*] mass" ' (M19,6, *GS* V, p. 565).

31. In the department store, Benjamin observes that 'the customers perceive themselves as a mass' (A12,5, *GS* V, p. 108).

32. An earlier version of the first half of this section appeared in *Telos*, 91 (Spring 1992), 108–16, under the title 'The Heroic Pedestrian or the Pedestrian Hero? Walter Benjamin and the *Flâneur*'.

33. The notion of heroism also permeates the very language Benjamin uses in his numerous descriptions of urban life. The Tiergarten did not lack its Ariadne or, presumably, its Theseus (Benjamin himself perhaps). In the *Passagenarbeit*, Benjamin describes the descent into the Parisian *Métro* as that into Hades (C11,2, *GS* V, pp. 135–6). Indeed, he wishes to stress that the endurance of the modern is in some sense heroic. Yet in so doing, he treads a thin line between exposing the phantasmagoric and actually contributing to it himself. It is sometimes far from clear where the heroic

in Benjamin becomes mock-heroic, where the affirmation of the struggle against the pernicious forces of consumer capitalism becomes derision at the pompous delusions of modern individuals. The attempt to disenchant the world through enchantment, to demythify modernity precisely by drawing upon figures from mythology and antiquity, is a tortuous undertaking in which the Critical Theorist may take on the dubious characteristics of modern heroism: raging against modernity while unwittingly and unavoidably reasserting it.

34. Benjamin cites Edmond Jaloux's pompous and absurd lamentations on the perils of crossing the street. The hapless pedestrian: 'is unable to do it today without taking a thousand precautions, without examining the horizon, without asking advice from the prefect of police, without mingling with a stupefied and jostling herd. . . . If he attempts to collect the fantastic thoughts that come to him and which are bound to be excited by the images of the street, he is deafened by the klaxons, dumbstruck by the loud gossipers' (quoted in M9a,3, *GS* V, p. 547).

35. Benjamin points out that 'in Baudelaire, the modern is nothing other than the "newest antiquity" ' (J59a,4, *GS* V, p. 423).

36. Jennings underplays this point when he writes: 'Benjamin reveals Baudelaire as a hero – not for his resistance to the deprivation of life under industrial capitalism but for his willingness to be marked by modern life in its contradiction and paradox' (1987, pp. 22–3).

37. One of the most important images of the poet presented by Baudelaire is that of the fencer duelling with the forces of modernity (see *CB*, p. 68).

38. Benjamin notes that Baudelaire 'found nothing to like about his time' (*CB*, p. 97).

39. Buck-Morss notes: 'as Ur-forms of contemporary life, Benjamin went to the margins, historical figures whose existence was precarious in their own time' (1986, p. 101).

40. Benjamin observes that 'the poet . . . is the stand-in for the ancient hero' (*CB*, p. 80).

41. Benjamin cites Baudelaire thus: 'lost in this mean world, jostled by the crowd, I am like a weary man whose eye, looking backwards, into the depths of the years, sees nothing but disillusion and bitterness, and before him, nothing but a tempest which contains nothing new, neither instruction nor pain' (quoted in *CB*, pp. 153–4, also J47a,2, *GS* V, p. 396).

42. Bolz and van Reijen write: 'the *flâneur*, who looks at the commodities in the arcade and thereby becomes a commodity himself, appears as the reincarnation of Odysseus, who, as Homer himself and then later Horkheimer and Adorno in the *Dialectic of Enlightenment*, point out, had a problematic relationship to his own identity' (Bolz and van Reijen, 1991, pp. 12–13).

43. The *flâneur* is male. Wolff points out that the nineteenth-century *flâneuse* is a 'non-existent role' as 'women could not stroll alone in the city' (1990, p. 41).

44. Frisby notes: 'it is the *flâneur* who passes through the labyrinthine world of the arcade, who seeks a way through the labyrinth of the city and through its "newest labyrinth", the masses' (1988, p. 228).

45. Although Frisby states that to 'lose oneself' is 'intimately bound up with the art of the *flâneur*' (1988, p. 229), this is somewhat deceptive. To

surrender oneself to the intoxication of the crowd is one thing; to lose one's sense of self is another.

46. Benjamin writes, paradoxically drawing on Baudelaire, 'individuality as such receives a heroic contour as the mass comes to dominate the scene. That is the origin of the conception of the heroic in Baudelaire' (J81a,1, *GS* V, p. 468).

47. Benjamin's interest in the dandy was also a long-standing one. Fuld points out that when in September 1926 Thankmar von Münchhausen asked Benjamin to suggest titles for translation for Inselverlag 'his list included old works like d'Aureilly's book on dandyism' (1990, p. 179).

48. Benjamin notes: 'Concerning the theory of dandyism. Clothing is the last trade in which the customer is treated individually. . . . The role of the client becomes an increasingly heroic one' (J79,3, *GS* V, p. 464).

49. Saisselin, citing Jules Janin's *The American in Paris* or Heath's *Picturesque Annual for 1843*, notes that 'Paris is the principal city of loungers; it is laid out, built, arranged, expressly for lounging' (1985, p. 23).

50. See also J82a,3, *GS* V, p. 470.

51. Benjamin notes: 'the phantasmagoria of the *flâneur*: to read from people's faces their occupation, origin, and character' (M6,6, *GS* V, p. 540). The *flâneur* 'made his study from the physiognomical appearance of people' (M6a,4, *GS* V, p. 541).

52. See also M17a,2, *GS* V, p. 562.

53. In a letter to Benjamin of 29 Feb. 1940 Adorno writes: 'the theory of gambling, if you will pardon the metaphor, is the first ripe fruit from the coffin (*Totenbaum*) of the Arcades' (Berlin Archive, folder 30, p. 26).

54. It should be remembered that in his essay on Naples, Benjamin emphasizes the importance of both indolence and the *lotto*. Luck, chance and fate were perceived as the bringers and destroyers of fortunes.

55. Tacussel observes that the *flâneur* and the gambler are 'urban personalities, regulating their social existence on a temporal rhythmicity and an experience of space in dissonance with the ideals that mobilised nascent industrial Europe' (1986, p. 49).

56. Benjamin cites Baudelaire thus: 'life has only one true charm and that is the charm of gambling. But what if we are indifferent to winning or losing?' (J85,6, *GS* V, p. 475).

57. See also g°1, *GS* V, p. 1056.

58. This is a rather superficial comparison, however. It would seem rather naïve to equate the compulsion that drives the gambler and the shocks encountered at the casino with the enforced labour of the worker and his or her degradation. The gulf in socio-economic status between these different social types is obvious. There is a clear distinction between addiction and coercion. In linking such categories in this way, Benjamin unintentionally does violence precisely to that integrity of suffering labour to which his work claims to bear witness.

59. The brutality and misery experienced by the industrial worker is expressed by Benjamin in terms of another classical image. He writes: 'What the man working for wages achieves in his daily work is no less than what in ancient times helped a gladiator win applause and fame' (*CB*, p. 75). This image of the gladiator is interesting in two respects. First, it contrasts with the gentlemanly image of the poet as fencer presented by Baudelaire. Second, it invokes the figure of Spartacus who

led a slave rebellion against Rome in 73–71 BC, and whose name was adopted as a pen-name by Karl Liebknecht. The Spartacist group established in 1916 formed the basis of the German Communist Party of 1919 led by Liebknecht and Rosa Luxemburg.

60. In his 1957 essay 'The Concept of Man' Horkheimer writes: 'machinery requires for its operation no less than its invention, the kind of mentality that concentrates on the present and can dispense with memory and straying imagination' (1974a, p. 22). He adds: 'men are acting more and more like machines' (1974a, p. 26).

61. Wilson observes that 'woman is present in cities as temptress, as whore, as fallen woman, as lesbian, but also as virtuous womanhood in danger, as heroic womanhood who triumphs over temptation and tribulation' (1991, p. 6). She adds: 'prostitutes and prostitution recur continually in the literature of urban life, until it almost seems as though to be a woman – an individual, not part of a family or kin group – in the city, is to become a prostitute – a public woman' (1991, p. 8).

62. Benjamin states: 'The love for prostitutes is the apotheosis of empathy with the commodity' (J85,2, *GS* V, p. 475, also O11a,4, p. 637).

63. Buck-Morss notes: 'Baudelaire sought, "in a heroic way", to present the commodity itself in human form' (1989, p. 184).

64. Benjamin notes: 'The commodity form comes to light as the social content of the allegorical vision in Baudelaire. Form and content combine in the whore as in their synthesis' (J59,10, *GS* V, p. 422). The prostitute is 'seller and commodity in one' (*CB*, p. 171).

65. Benjamin notes that 'it is in the prostitute that the commodity form of nature is embodied' (J65a,6, *GS* V, p. 435).

66. If the *flâneur* is the Odysseus of the boulevard, 'the whores who inhabit the arcades figure as the contemporary embodiment of the Sirens, in that they put the venality of lust on display' (Bolz and van Reijen, 1991, p. 13).

67. Missac writes: 'the prostitute is no longer a harmful phantom, nor just a "type" who systematically corresponds to the *flâneur*, but is the product of reification in mass civilisation' (1991, p. 15).

68. The dehumanizing tendencies of the strictly synchronized, uniformed dance troupes of the revue were explored in Siegfried Kracauer's 1927 essay 'The Mass Ornament' (see Bronner and Kellner, eds, 1989, pp. 145–54).

69. Wilson notes: 'Baudelaire indeed believed that poets resembled prostitutes. They had something to sell – their writings. Since this expressed their soul, their truest self, in selling it they were in some sense prostituting themselves' (1991, p. 55). Benjamin notes that Baudelaire 'frequently compared such a man, and first of all himself, with a prostitute' (*CB*, p. 34).

70. Buck-Morss notes: 'Baudelaire was "his own impresario", displaying himself in different identities – now *flâneur*, now whore, now rag-picker, now dandy' (1989, p. 187).

Conclusion

1. Benjamin writes: 'With cunning, not without it, do we break free from the realm of dreams' (G1,7, *GS* V, p. 234).

2. In his review of Werner Hegemann's historical study of the Berlin tenement blocks, Benjamin emphasizes both the critical and the positive moments of physiognomical reading. Hegemann, Benjamin claims, 'has no sense of historical physiognomy' precisely because 'he doesn't understand that the tenement house, though terrible as a dwelling, has created streets in the windows of which not only grief and crime but also the morning and evening sun have reflected in tragic magnitude as nowhere else, and that the childhood of the city-dweller has drawn the same lasting substance from stairway and asphalt as the farm boy has from the stable and field. A historical representation has to include all this' (*GS* III, p. 265).
3. Adorno notes that 'the reconciliation of myth is the theme of Benjamin's philosophy' (1990, p. 15).
4. Benjamin writes: 'To write history means giving dates their physiognomy' (N11,2, Smith ed., 1989, p. 67).
5. A later formulation develops this theme: 'The task of history is not only to make the tradition of the oppressed its own, but also to create it' (*GS* I, p. 1246).
6. Benjamin writes: ' "Reconstruction" by means of empathy is one-sided. "Construction" presupposes "destruction" ' (N7,6, Smith ed., 1989, p. 60).
7. Proust himself uses the image of the chance encounter with an unknown woman in the street to express the elusiveness of memory. M. Swann tries to recall Vinteuil's piano sonata, but the melody escapes him. Proust writes: 'but when he returned home he felt the need of it: he was like a man into whose life a woman he has seen for a moment passing by has brought the image of a new beauty which deepens his own sensibility, although he does not even know her name or whether he will ever see her again' (1983, p. 229). Later, when Swann hears the sonata at the Verdurins': 'it had so individual, so incomprehensible a charm, that Swann felt as though he had met, in a friend's drawing room, a woman whom he had seen and admired in the street and had despaired of ever seeing again' (1983, p. 231).
8. Taina Rajanti (1991, pp. 22–4) suggests a correspondence between the poet in 'To a Passer-by', startled and 'paralysed' by the sudden apparition in the crowd, and another witness of catastrophe who stands with staring eyes and gaping mouth, the figure of the 'angel of history' described in the ninth of Benjamin's 'Theses on the Concept of History' and inspired by Paul Klee's image of the *Angelus Novus*. See *ILL*, pp. 259–60.
9. Marx, in 'The Eighteenth Brumaire of Louis Bonaparte' (McLellan ed., 1977, p. 300).
10. In the first of his 'Theses' Benjamin stresses that historical materialism 'can easily be a match for anyone if it enlists the services of theology' (*ILL*, p. 255).
11. Wilson writes: 'the city itself is a "text" – that is to say that it is something to be read and interpreted. It is an artefact, a work of art, created by the human mind and imagination, and contains many layers of meaning' (1991, p. 10).
12. Sieburth perceptively notes this transformation of the urban complex into a locus of signs when he writes: 'Names endow the city with the features

of a face or text; to write a city is therefore to mime its nomenclature, to engage in onomastic inventory' (Smith ed., 1989, p. 15).

13. Baudelaire is Benjamin's model in this respect. The following account of Baudelaire is a self-description by Benjamin: 'His prosody is comparable to the map of a big-city in which it is possible to move about inconspicuously, shielded by the blocks of houses, gateways, courtyards' (*CB*, p. 98).

14. Benjamin notes that 'Interpersonal relationships in big cities are distinguished by a marked preponderance of the activity of the eye over the activity of the ear' (*CB*, p. 38).

15. It is more than an interplay of perspective, however, for Benjamin's purpose is imbued with a theological moment. The invitation to wander the space of the text-as-city, to inspect it, echoes a central motif of Judaic mysticism: the need to bear witness. Benjamin's cityscapes are not optical puzzles, but acts of witness, of remembering what is seen so that testimony may be given. Scholem cites a passage from the *Zohar* which concludes: 'come and see: this is the way of the Torah' (1969, p. 55).

16. Sieburth notes that 'Benjamin . . . describes his Arcade [*sic*] not as a work but as an on-going event, a peripatetic meditation or *flânerie* in which everything chanced upon en route becomes a potential direction his thoughts might take' (Smith ed., 1989, p. 27).

17. In his review of Hegemann, Benjamin writes: 'as dialectical materialism says: to indicate thesis and antithesis is good, but engagement is only possible if one recognizes the point at which one becomes the other, since the positive disintegrates in the negative and the negative in the positive. The enlightenment philosopher thinks in opposites. To expect dialectics of him is perhaps unwarranted. But is it unwarranted to expect the historian to gaze into the countenance of things and see beauty even in the most profound distortion?' (*GS* III, p. 265).

Bibliography

Works by Walter Benjamin

Gesammelte Schriften, vols I–VII, ed. Rolf Tiedemann and Hermann Schweppenhäuser, with the collaboration of Theodor Adorno and Gershom Scholem. Frankfurt am Main: Suhrkamp Verlag, 1974 – ; Taschenbuch Ausgabe, 1991.

Berliner Kindheit um Neunzehnhundert, with an afterword by Theodor Adorno. Frankfurt am Main: Suhrkamp Verlag, 1950.

Briefe, ed. Gershom Scholem and Theodor Adorno. 2 vols. Frankfurt am Main: Suhrkamp Verlag, 1978.

Moskauer Tagebuch, ed. Gary Smith, with a foreword by Gershom Scholem. Frankfurt am Main: Suhrkamp Verlag, 1980.

Städtebilder, with an afterword by Peter Szondi. Frankfurt am Main: Suhrkamp Verlag, 1963.

Theodor W. Adorno – Walter Benjamin Briefwechsel 1928–40, ed. Henri Lonitz. Frankfurt am Main: Suhrkamp Verlag, 1994.

Walter Benjamin – Gershom Scholem Briefwechsel, ed. Gershom Scholem. Frankfurt am Main: Suhrkamp Verlag, 1980.

English Language Translations of Benjamin's Works

Aesthetics and Politics: Debates between Bloch, Lukács, Brecht, Benjamin, Adorno, tr. and ed. Ronald Taylor, with an afterword by Frederic Jameson. London: Verso, 1980.

'Central Park', tr. Lloyd Spencer, *New German Critique*, 34 (Winter 1985), pp. 28–58.

Charles Baudelaire: A Lyric Poet in the Era of High Capitalism, tr. Harry Zohn. London: Verso, 1983.

The Correspondence of Walter Benjamin, ed. and annotated by Gershom Scholem and Theodor Adorno, tr. Manfred Jacobson and Evelyn Jacobson, with a foreword by Gershom Scholem. Chicago and London: University of Chicago Press, 1994.

The Correspondence of Walter Benjamin and Gershom Scholem 1932–1940, ed. Gershom Scholem, tr. Gary Smith and André Lefèvre, with an introduction by Anson Rabinbach. Cambridge, Mass.: Harvard University Press, 1992.

Illuminations. ed. and with an introduction by Hannah Arendt, tr. Harry Zohn. London: Fontana, 1973.

Moscow Diary, ed. Gary Smith, tr. Richard Sieburth, with a preface by Gershom Scholem. Cambridge, Mass., and London: Harvard University Press, 1986.

'N. (Re The Theory of Knowledge, Theory of Progress)', tr. Leigh Hafrey and Richard Sieburth, in Gary Smith ed. *Benjamin: Philosophy, Aesthetics, History*, Chicago: University of Chicago Press, 1989, pp. 43–83.

One-Way Street and Other Writings, tr. Edmund Jephcott and Kingsley Shorter, with an introduction by Susan Sontag. London: Verso, 1985.

The Origin of German Tragic Drama, tr. John Osbourne, with an introduction by George Steiner. London: Verso, 1985.

Reflections: Aphorisms, Essays and Autobiographical Writings, ed. Peter Demetz, tr. Edmund Jephcott. New York: Harcourt, Brace, Jovanovitch, 1978.

Understanding Brecht, tr. Anna Bostock, with an introduction by Stanley Mitchell. London: Verso, 1983.

Secondary and Other Sources

Adorno, Theodor 1990: *Über Walter Benjamin*, ed. Rolf Tiedemann. Frankfurt am Main: Suhrkamp Verlag.

—— and Horkheimer, Max 1986: *Dialectic of Enlightenment*, 2nd edn. London: Verso.

Aragon, Louis 1987: *Paris Peasant*. London: Pan Books (Picador).

Barnes, Djuna (1936) 1985: *Nightwood*. London: Faber and Faber.

Barthes, Roland 1973: *Mythologies*, tr. Annette Lavers. London: Paladin.

Baudelaire, Charles 1965: *Art in Paris 1845–1862: Salons and Other Exhibitions*, ed. and tr. Jonathan Mayne. London: Phaidon Press.

—— 1975: *Selected Poems*, ed. and trans. Joanna Richardson. Harmondsworth: Penguin Books.

—— 1982: *Les Fleurs du mal*, tr. Richard Howard. London: Picador.

—— 1986: *The Painter of Modern Life and Other Essays*, ed. and tr. Jonathan Mayne. New York and London: Da Capo Press, in association with Phaidon Press, 1964.

Benjamin, Andrew and Osborne, Peter (eds) 1994: *Walter Benjamin's Philosophy: Destruction and Experience*. London: Routledge.

Berman, Marshall 1983: *All that is Solid Melts into Air: The Experience of Modernity*. London: Verso.

Betz, Albrecht 1984: Commodity and modernity in Heinle and Benjamin. *New German Critique*, 33 (Fall), 179–88.

Bollenbeck, Georg 1980: 'O, du armer Benjamin!' Einige Anmerkungen anlässlich einer missglückten Benjamin-Biographie. *Kürbiskern*, 1, 143–9.

Bolz, Norbert and van Reijen, Willem 1991: *Walter Benjamin*. Frankfurt am Main: Campus Verlag.

Bolz, Norbert and Witte, Bernd (eds) 1984: *Passagen. Walter Benjamins Urgeschichte des XIX Jahrhunderts*. Munich: Wilhelm Fink Verlag.

Breton, André 1960: *Nadja*, tr. Richard Howard. New York: Grove Press.

Brewster, Ben 1968: Walter Benjamin and the *Arcades Project*. *New Left Review*, 48 (Mar.–Apr.), 72–90.

Brodersen, Momme 1990: *Spinne im eigenen Netz. Walter Benjamin: Leben und Werk*. Bühl-Moos: Elster Verlag.

Bronner, Stephen and Kellner, Douglas (eds) 1989: *Critical Theory and Society: A Reader*. London: Routledge.

Bruck, Jan 1982: Beckett, Benjamin and the modern crisis in communication. *New German Critique*, 26, 159–71.

Buci-Glucksmann, Christine 1994: *Baroque Reason: The Aesthetics of Modernity*. London: Sage.

Buck-Morss, Susan 1977: *The Origin of Negative Dialectics: Theodor Adorno, Walter Benjamin and the Frankfurt Institute*. Hassocks, Sussex: Harvester Press.

—— 1983: Benjamin's *Passagenwerk*: redeeming mass culture for the revolution. *New German Critique*, 29 (Spring/Summer), 211–40.

—— 1986: The flâneur, the sandwichman and the whore: the politics of loitering. *New German Critique*, 39 (Fall), 99–140.

—— 1989: *The Dialectics of Seeing: Walter Benjamin and the Arcades Project*. Cambridge, Mass.: MIT Press.

Cohen, Margaret 1993: *Profane Illumination: Walter Benjamin and the Paris of Surrealist Revolution*. Berkeley, Los Angeles and London: University of California Press.

Doderer, Klaus (ed) 1988: *Walter Benjamin und die Kinderliteratur*. Weinheim and Munich: Juventa Verlag.

Döblin, Alfred 1978: *Berlin Alexanderplatz*. Harmondsworth: Penguin Books.

Dostoyevsky, Fyodor 1966: *The Gambler/Bobok/A Nasty Story*. Harmondsworth: Penguin Books.

Eagleton, Terry 1981: *Walter Benjamin: Or Towards a Revolutionary Criticism*. London: Verso.

Engels, Friedrich 1987: *The Condition of the Working Class in England*. Harmondsworth: Penguin Books.

Feuchtwanger, Lion 1937: *Moscow 1937: My Visit Described for My Friends*, tr. Irene Josephy. New York: Viking Press.

Foucault, Michel 1965: *Madness and Civilisation: A History of Insanity in the Age of Reason*, tr. Richard Howard. New York: Random House.

—— 1973: *The Birth of the Clinic: An Archaeology of Medical Perception*, tr. Alan Sheridan. London: Tavistock.

—— 1979: *Discipline and Punish: The Birth of the Prison*, tr. Alan Sheridan. London: Peregrine Books.

Frisby, David 1988: *Fragments of Modernity: Theories of Modernity in the Work of Simmel, Kracauer and Benjamin*. Cambridge, Mass.: MIT Press.

Fuld, Werner 1990: *Walter Benjamin: Eine Biographie*. Reinbeck bei Hamburg: Rowohlt Taschenbuch Verlag.

Gadamer, Hans-Georg 1975: *Truth and Method*. London: Sheed and Ward.

Gay, Peter 1984: *The Bourgeois Experience: Victoria to Freud*. Vol. 1: *Education of the Senses*. Oxford: Oxford University Press.

—— 1988: *Weimar Culture: The Outsider as Insider*. London: Peregrine Books.

Geist, Johann Friedrich 1985: *Arcades: The History of a Building Type*. Cambridge, Mass.: MIT Press.

Geuss, Raymond 1981: *The Idea of a Critical Theory: Habermas and the Frankfurt School*. Cambridge: Cambridge University Press.

Gilloch, Graeme 1992: The heroic pedestrian or the pedestrian hero? Walter Benjamin and the *flâneur*. *Telos*, 91 (Spring 1992), 108–16.

Goethe, Johann Wolfgang 1971: *Elective Affinities*, tr. R. J. Hollingdale. Harmondsworth: Penguin Books.

Habermas, Jürgen 1983: Walter Benjamin: consciousness-raising or rescuing critique. In *Philosophical-Political Profiles*, London: Heinemann Press, 129–64.

—— 1987: *The Philosophical Discourse of Modernity*. Cambridge: Polity Press.

Held, David 1980: *Introduction to Critical Theory*. London: Hutchinson Press.

Higonnet, Anne, Margaret and Patrice 1984: Façades: Walter Benjamin's Paris. *Critical Inquiry*, 10, 391–419.

Hoffman, Louise 1983: Walter Benjamin's infernal city. *Washington State University Research Studies*, 52, nos 3/4, 146–55.

Horkheimer, Max 1974a: *Critique of Instrumental Reason*. New York: Seabury Press.

—— 1974b: *Eclipse of Reason*. New York: Seabury Press.

Ivornel, Philippe 1986: Paris, capital of the Popular Front, or the posthumous life of the nineteenth century. *New German Critique*, 39 (Fall), 61–87.

Jäger, Lorenz and Regehly, Thomas (eds) 1992: *'Was nie geschrieben wurde, lesen'. Frankfurter Benjamin-Vortrage*. Bielefeld: Aisthesis Verlag.

Jameson, Frederic 1971: *Marxism and Form*. Princeton, N.J.: Princeton University Press.

Jay, Martin 1974: *The Dialectical Imagination: A History of the Frankfurt School and the Institute of Social Research 1923–1950*. London: Heinemann.

Jennings, Michael 1987: *Dialectical Images: Walter Benjamin's Theory of Literary Criticism*. Ithaca, N.Y.: Cornell University Press.

Konersmann, Ralf 1991: *Erstarrte Unruhe: Walter Benjamins Begriff der Geschichte*. Frankfurt am Main: Fischer Verlag.

Kracauer, Siegfried (1937) 1976: *Jacques Offenbach and das Paris seiner Zeit*. Published as vol. 8 of *Siegfried Kracauer: Schriften*. Frankfurt am Main: Suhrkamp Verlag.

—— 1987: *Strassen in Berlin und Anderswo*. Berlin: Das Arsenal.

Lindner, Burkhardt (ed.) 1978: *Walter Benjamin im Kontext*. Konigstein/Ts: Athenaeum Verlag.

—— 1986: The *Passagenwerk*, the *Berliner Kindheit*, and the archaeology of the 'recent past'. *New German Critique*, 39 (Fall), 25–48.

—— 1990: 'Medienbilder, Aura, Geschichtszeit': Nach Kracauer und Benjamin. *Neue Gesellschaft*, 9, 799–810.

Lukács, Georg 1974: *History and Class Consciousness*. London: Merlin Press.

Lunn, Eugene 1985: *Marxism and Modernism: An Historical Study of Lukács, Brecht, Benjamin and Adorno*. London: Verso.

Marcuse, Herbert 1964: *One-Dimensional Man*. London: Routledge and Kegan Paul.

Markner, Reinhard and Weber, Thomas (eds) 1993: *Literatur über Walter Benjamin: Kommentierte Bibliographie 1983–92*. Hamburg: Argument Verlag.

Marx, Karl 1976: *Capital, Volume One*, tr. Ben Fowkes. Harmondsworth: Penguin Books.

McCole, John 1985: Benjamin's *Passagenwerk*: a guide to the labyrinth. *Theory and Society*, 14, 497–509.

—— 1993: *Walter Benjamin and the Antinomies of Tradition*. Ithaca, N.Y.: Cornell University Press.

McLellan, David (ed.) 1977: *Karl Marx: Selected Writings*. Oxford: Oxford University Press.

Mehlman, Jeffrey 1993: *Walter Benjamin for Children: An Essay on his Radio Years*. Chicago and London: University of Chicago Press.

Menninghaus, Winfried 1980: *Walter Benjamins Theorie der Sprachmagie*. Frankfurt am Main: Suhrkamp Verlag.

—— 1986: *Schwellenkunde: Walter Benjamins Passage des Mythos*. Frankfurt am Main: Suhrkamp Verlag.

Missac, Pierre 1991: *Walter Benjamins Passage*. Frankfurt am Main: Suhrkamp Verlag.

Nägele, Rainer 1988: *Benjamin's Ground: New Readings of Walter Benjamin*. Detroit: Wayne State University Press.

—— 1991: *Theater, Theory and Speculation: Walter Benjamin and the Scenes of Modernity*. Baltimore and London: Johns Hopkins University Press.

Niethammer, Lutz 1992: *Posthistoire: Has History Come to an End?*, tr. Patrick Camiller. London: Verso.

Pensky, Max 1993: *Melancholy Dialectics: Walter Benjamin and the Play of Mourning*. Amherst: University of Massachusetts Press.

Proust, Marcel 1983: *Remembrance of Things Past*, vol. 1, tr. C. K. Scott Moncrieffe and Terence Kilmartin. Harmondsworth: Penguin Books.

Puttnies, Hans and Smith, Gary (eds) 1991: *Benjaminiana: Eine Biografische Recherche*. Giessen: Anabas Verlag.

Rabinbach, Anson 1979: Critique and commentary / alchemy and chemistry: some remarks on Walter Benjamin and this issue. *New German Critique*, 17 (Spring), 3–14.

Rajanti, Taina 1991: *The City as the Social Space of Modernity*. Research Report published by the Department of Sociology and Social Psychology, University of Tampere, Finland.

Roberts, Julian 1982: *Walter Benjamin*. London: Macmillan.

Rolleston, James 1989: The politics of quotation: Walter Benjamin's Arcades Project. *Publications of the Modern Language Association of America*, 104, no. 1, 13–25.

Saisselin, Rémy 1985: *Bricabracomania: The Bourgeois and the Bibelot*. London: Thames and Hudson.

Schiller, Dieter, Pech, Karlheinz et al. 1981: *Kunst und Literatur im Antifaschistischen Exil 1933–45*. Leipzig: Verlag Philipp Reclam.

Schiller-Lerg, Sabine 1984: *Walter Benjamin und der Rundfunk*. Munich: K. G. Verlag.

Scholem, Gershom 1969: *On the Kabbalah and its Symbolism*, tr. Ralph Manheim. New York: Schocken Books.

—— 1976: *On Jews and Judaism in Crisis: Selected Essays*, ed. Werner Dannhauser. New York: Schocken Books.

—— 1982: *Walter Benjamin: The Story of a Friendship*. London: Faber and Faber.

—— 1983: *Walter Benjamin und Sein Engel*. Frankfurt am Main: Suhrkamp Verlag.

Sennett, Richard 1986: *The Fall of Public Man*. London: Faber and Faber.

Simmel, Georg 1971: *On Individuality and Social Forms*, ed. Donald Levine, Chicago and London: University of Chicago Press.

Smith, Gary 1979: Walter Benjamin: a bibliography of secondary literature. *New German Critique*, 17 (Spring), 189–208.

—— (ed.) 1988: *On Walter Benjamin: Critical Essays and Recollections*. Cambridge, Mass.: MIT Press.

—— (ed.) 1989: *Benjamin: Philosophy, Aesthetics, History*. Chicago: University of Chicago Press.

Sontag, Susan 1978: The last intellectual. *New York Review of Books*, 25, no. 15, 75–82. Repr. with alterations as introduction to *One-Way Street and Other Writings*, London: Verso, 1985, 7–28.

Spencer, Lloyd 1985: Allegory in the world of the commodity and the importance of Central Park. *New German Critique*, 34 (Winter), 59–77.

Stüssi, Anna 1977: Erinnerung an die Zukunft: Walter Benjamins *Berliner Kindheit um Neunzehnhundert*. *Paelaestra*, 266.

Swift, Jonathan 1967: *Gulliver's Travels*. Harmondsworth: Penguin Books.
Tacussel, Patrick 1986: The city, the player: Walter Benjamin and the origins of figurative sociology. *Diogenes*, 134 (Summer), 45–59.
Tester, Keith (ed.) 1994: *The Flâneur*. London and New York: Routledge.
Tiedemann, Rolf 1973: *Studien zur Philosophie Walter Benjamins*. Frankfurt am Main: Suhrkamp Verlag.
—— 1983: *Dialektik im Stillstand: Versuche zum Spätwerk Walter Benjamins*. Frankfurt am Main: Suhrkamp Verlag.
Timms, Edward and Kelley, David (eds) 1985: *Unreal City: Urban Experience in Modern European Art and Literature*. Manchester: Manchester University Press.
Veblen, Thorstein 1992: *Theory of the Leisure Class*. New Brunswick, NJ, and London: Transaction Publishers.
Wagner, Gerhard 1990: Historisierung contra Fetishisierung – der technische Fortschritt in Walter Benjamins ästhetischer Reflexion. *Deutsche Zeitschrift für Philosophie*, 9, 859–65.
Wells, H. G. 1921: *Russia in the Shadows*. New York: G. H. Doran and Co.
Wilson, Elizabeth 1991: *The Sphinx in the City*. London: Virago.
Witte, Bernd 1986: Paris – Berlin – Paris: personal, literary and social experience in Walter Benjamin's late works. *New German Critique*, 39 (Fall), 49–60.
Wohlfarth, Irving 1979: Walter Benjamin's image of interpretation. *New German Critique*, 17 (Spring), 70–98.
—— 1986a: Et cetera? The historian as *chiffonnier*. *New German Critique*, 39 (Fall), 142–68.
—— 1986b: Re-fusing theology: some first responses to Walter Benjamin's 'Arcades Project'. *New German Critique*, 39 (Fall), 3–24.
Wolff, Janet 1990: *Feminine Sentences: Essays on Women and Culture*. Cambridge: Polity Press.
Wolin, Richard 1982: *Walter Benjamin: An Aesthetic of Redemption*. New York: Columbia University Press.
—— 1986: Experience and materialism in Benjamin's *Passagenwerk*. *Philosophical Forum*, 17, no. 3 (Spring), 201–16.
Zohn, Harry 1973: Presentation of Adorno – Benjamin. *New Left Review*, 81 (Sept. – Oct.), 46–81.
Zola, Emile 1962: *Thérèse Raquin*, tr. Leonard Tancock. Harmondsworth: Penguin Books.

Index